*Naturalistic Viewpoints
in Psychological Research*

CONTRIBUTORS

Roger G. Barker, Ph.D., Midwest Psychological Field Station and Department of Psychology, University of Kansas, Lawrence, Kansas

Paul V. Gump, Ph.D., Midwest Psychological Field Station and Department of Psychology, University of Kansas, Lawrence, Kansas

David Gutmann, Ph.D., Department of Psychology, University of Michigan, Ann Arbor, Michigan

J. Lee Kavanau, Ph.D., Department of Zoology, University of California at Los Angeles, Los Angeles, California

James G. Kelly, Ph.D., Department of Psychology, University of Michigan, Ann Arbor, Michigan

Emil W. Menzel, Jr., Ph.D., Delta Regional Primate Research Center (Tulane University), Covington, Louisiana

Harold L. Raush, Ph.D., Department of Psychology, University of Michigan, Ann Arbor, Michigan

Lee Sechrest, Ph.D., Department of Psychology, Northwestern University, Evanston, Illinois

Saul B. Sells, Ph.D., Institute of Behavioral Research, Texas Christian University, Fort Worth, Texas

Edwin P. Willems, Ph.D., Department of Psychology, University of Kansas, Lawrence, Kansas

Naturalistic Viewpoints in Psychological Research

EDITED BY

Edwin P. Willems / UNIVERSITY OF KANSAS

Harold L. Raush / UNIVERSITY OF MICHIGAN

Holt, Rinehart and Winston, Inc.

NEW YORK / CHICAGO / SAN FRANCISCO / ATLANTA
DALLAS / MONTREAL / TORONTO / LONDON / SYDNEY

Preface and Acknowledgments

WE CHOSE the word "viewpoints" for the title of this book in order to re-flect two major facets of its content. First, the book is not primarily a recipe for how to *do* naturalistic research, nor is it primarily a summary or review of naturalistic research. Rather, it is an interdependent set of statements and arguments, or points of view, *about* naturalistic research. What these labels mean and where the content of the book fits into the literature of psychology is spelled out in the first and last chapters. Second, this is a contributed volume, a cooperative effort, and it represents the viewpoints of ten different researchers. The contributors are the stars of the show and we want to thank them for their remarkable patience and dedication over the long months, which now make the volume possible. Moreover, we want to thank them for the times they rejected and the times they accepted our editorial suggestions—we learned much from both types of exchange.

Naturalistic Viewpoints in Psychological Research opens with an in-troduction that states the context, purpose, and hopes for the volume as a whole and sets the stage for the chapters that follow. Next comes the heart of the book, ten chapters by the contributors, and finally there is a summary that highlights issues and unresolved problems.

In Chapters 1 through 10, the contributors carry the burden of weighing, elaborating, filling in, and extending the issues, purposes, and arguments outlined in the introduction. The chapters vary in terms of their points of departure and the scope of the methodological arenas from which their arguments originate; on this criterion they fall into three clusters. The first three, by Saul B. Sells, Roger B. Barker, and Edwin P. Willems, argue from fairly general perspectives of ecological research and naturalistic methodology. In Chapters 4 through 7, Emil W. Menzel,

Jr., Harold L. Raush, Lee Sechrest, and David Gutmann start with more circumscribed, substantive areas of research. Finally, the vantage points of their own programs of research provide points of departure for James G. Kelly, Paul V. Gump, and J. Lee Kavanau in Chapters 8 through 10. It will become clear that this classification of chapters, while it offers one way to order the material, is a crude one. At times, the more specifically classified chapters allude to very general issues and the more generally classified chapters argue specific points of research procedure. The organization into parts is based simply upon similarities in points of departure.

At the beginning of each of the three parts, a commentary provides specific background, context, and introduction to the set of chapters it includes. The concluding essay presents a summary and a highlighting of issues and unresolved problems, again as viewed by the editors.

The original gleam for this project was in the eye of Harold L. Raush, who organized symposia by seven contributors on the topic of naturalistic research at the University of Michigan in May 1966, and at the meeting of the American Psychological Association in September 1966. A National Institute of Mental Health Training Grant (USPHS, MH05115–20) funded the symposium at the University of Michigan. With this start, three contributors were added and the main responsibility for editorial work on this volume was carried by Edwin P. Willems, supported in part by a grant in aid of research from Rice University.

We gratefully recognize the following agencies, institutions, publishers, and individuals who provided cooperation and support for various aspects of this project:

Presentations to the symposium at APA in September 1966, by David Gutmann, Harold L. Raush, Edwin P. Willems, Emil W. Menzel, Jr., Lee Sechrest, Roger G. Barker, and James G. Kelly were printed in *Human Development*, 1967, Vol. 10, No. 3–4. The publishers of *Human Development* gave permission for the adapting, extensive rewriting, and expanding of these seven papers for the present collection. They appear as Chapters 2, 3, 4, 5, 6, 7, and 8.

Chapter 1 (Sells) is adapted from the original paper in *Multivariate Behavioral Research*, 1966, Vol. 1, pp. 131–144, with permission of the publisher. Preparation of the chapter was supported by Office of Naval Research Contract No. Nonr 3436(00).

Chapter 2 (Barker) is based jointly on comments at the APA symposium mentioned above and a paper presented to the Southwestern Psychological Association, Houston, Texas, in April 1967. Preparation of the chapter was supported by Research Career Grant Award K6-MH-16, 682, the Public Health Service, National Institute of Mental Health, Department of Health, Education, and Welfare.

Research for Chapter 4 (Menzel) was supported by Grant MH–11, 425 from the National Institute of Mental Health, USPHS. The work in Japan was done in Katsuyama, Okayama Prefecture, while Dr. Menzel was attached to Osaka University. The original data on rhesus, which were collected in 1965 and 1966, are a contribution from the Ecology Section of the Laboratory of Perinatal Physiology, NINDB, NIH, PHS, USDHEW, San Juan, Puerto Rico. John Morrison and Donald Sade provided help, counsel, and advice in Cayo Santiago and Desechlo. William Mason and Hans Kummer gave advice on drafts of the manuscript. Support from NIH Grant FR00164 is also acknowledged.

Preparation of Chapter 5 (Raush) was supported by National Institute of Mental Health Grant MH–10,975, Communication Patterns.

Chapter 8 (Kelly) is based upon work supported by the College of Education, Ohio State University. Appreciation is extended to the Ohio State Test Development Center, the Ohio State Computer Center, and the Public Schools of Columbus, Ohio, for their support and cooperation. Randolph Harper, Michael Herzbrun, Suzanne Fry, Robert Lampl, and Pamela Grossman contributed to the collection and analysis of data. Michael Donavan contributed to the development of the Adaptation Scale, and Seymour Cabin, Sam Pisano, Julia Donnelly, and Wendell Scott assisted with the student interviews.

Preparation of Chapter 9 (Gump) was supported by Project No. 5–0334, Office of Education, Bureau of Research, U. S. Department of Health, Education, and Welfare. Beverly Ayers Nachamkin gave indispensable assistance in collection and analysis of data. Personnel of school systems in Lawrence, Oskaloosa, and Topeka, Kansas, generously shared ideas and facilities for the research.

Chapter 10 (Kavanau) is adapted from the original paper in *Science*, Vol. 155, pp. 1623–1639, March 31, 1967, © 1967 by the American Association for the Advancement of Science, with permission of the publisher. Work on the chapter was supported by NSF Grant GB3959. Appreciation is extended to the following persons who made helpful comments and suggestions concerning the various drafts of the manuscript: Drs. S. A. Barnett, D. H. Brant, J. T. Enright, R. H. Glaser, A. D. Grinnel, J. A. King, F. B. Turner, and B. W. Walker.

Quotations are made from the following sources, with permission of authors and publishers:

McGuire, W. J. Some impending reorientations in social psychology: Some thoughts provoked by Kenneth Ring. *Journal of Experimental Social Psychology*, 1967, **3**, 124–139.

Scott, W. A., & Wertheimer, M. *Introduction to psychological research.* New York: John Wiley & Sons, Inc., 1962.

Kavanau, J. L. Behavior: Confinement, adaptation, and compulsory regimes in laboratory studies. *Science*, 1964, **143**, 490 (January 31, 1964). Copyright 1964 by the American Association for the Advancement of Science.

Willems, E. P. Sense of obligation to high school activities as related to school size and marginality of student. *Child Development*, 1967, **38**, 1247–1260. (For the use of a figure in Chapter 3).

Finally, patient and invaluable counsel and help at various stages of this effort were given by Mrs. Gwen Willems, Drs. Trenton W. Wann and Shalom E. Vineberg, and the editorial staff of Holt, Rinehart and Winston, Inc.

EDWIN P. WILLEMS
HAROLD L. RAUSH

Lawrence, Kansas
November 1968

Contents

Introduction

EDWIN P. WILLEMS *and* HAROLD L. RAUSH

MOST OF US LAUGH at the proverbial inebriate who, upon losing his key at the doorsill, looks for it under the street lamp down the road because the light is better there. Similarly, most of us wonder at the investigator who, wanting to understand cue discrimination in primates, presses his search by studying the stickleback. Yet, while we recognize the disjunction between purposes and methods of search in these two cases, we too often either do not have or no not apply similar judgments of lack of congruency between research purposes and research methods in the mainstream of psychology.

Psychological research is a quest, and investigators of behavior are after something. The character of the faith of those persons whose interests and activities constitute that diverse and often diffuse aggregate, "psychological research," is that they are contributing to the understanding of behavior as we find it in common, everyday experience; it is this faith that often keeps the work going, no matter how esoteric and far afield it appears. Superimposed upon the activities of research is a prevailing concern about the best and most appropriate ways to conduct the activities. The following collection of essays, in attempting to resolve this problem, argues that at times naturalistic research is the best and most appropriate mode. At what times? How? In what specific ways is the argument valid? When should one choose naturalistic methods? The contributions to follow will carry the burden of exploring these and other related questions. However, to lay the groundwork for the volume and introduce its major purposes and areas of focus, we should begin a little farther back.

The Concerns of Methodology

In *Personal Knowledge* (1958), part of a remarkably insightful series of monographs on epistemology and the many-sided enterprise of research,

1

Michael Polanyi argues that when all our formal talk is said and done, "Scientists . . . spend their lives trying to guess right" (p. 143). Most of us are not accustomed to viewing research in the way that Polanyi suggests here. Although most investigators recognize that research involves much guesswork, most of us would hesitate to call our work a "guessing game," at least in its long-range perspective. We prefer to see ourselves as mapping nature *factually* and observing and explaining events *objectively*. That is, logic and objective observation are the earmarks we usually wish to ascribe to our efforts in research.

Polanyi would agree that logic and observation are indeed characteristics of the activity of research, but he would ask us to recognize that some crucial scientific processes never have been, and perhaps never will be, subject to canons of strict logical necessity. For example, neither (a) the relation between a scientific question and what one considers appropriate or adequate evidence, nor (b) the relation between a question and evidence, on the one hand, and what one considers an appropriate or adequate interpretation, on the other, are strictly impersonal, logical matters. In other words, what is logical to one man is illogical to another, what closes one man's curiosity piques another's, and what is true-blue observation to one person is hunch, inference, biased statement, or plain junk to another. Such disagreements and what they motivate in terms of exchange and activity provide much of the excitement, satisfaction, and even progress of research. More importantly, however, in view of the guesswork inherent in research and the disagreement originating from differences in personal tastes and working styles, scientists agree—and we emphasize *agree* in the sense of arriving at consensual agreement— upon various procedures and rules for minimizing personal bias and for optimizing reliability in the process of trying to guess right (Boring, 1952; Platt, 1962; Butterfield, 1952; Hildebrand, 1963).

In the behavioral disciplines, as in other areas of science, these agreed-upon guidelines and rules fall at numerous points along a spectrum ranging from great generality to extreme specificity. At the former pole is the philosophy of science, that is, consideration of the general functions, maxims, presuppositions, strengths, and limitations of science. At the latter pole are rules, prescriptions, and catalogs for the use of very specific techniques and methods of measurement and observation, such as interviews, questionnaires, phenomenological reports, standard adjustments, Q sorts, electronic monitoring, and so on.

Somewhere in the midrange between the general earmarks or the philosophy of science on the one hand, and the choice and application of particular techniques, measurements, and conditions of research on the other, is a wide band of concern that is commonly called *methodology*. Despite the fact that the boundaries of methodology are difficult to determine with precision, there are two basic questions that provide the springboards for most methodological discussion and represent its focal concerns. The first question, often called *the* methodological question, asks, "How do I obtain interpretable data?" or, "How do I obtain data for which the ambiguity of evaluation is reduced to the lowest possible degree?" It is this question that leads to the frequent and popular methodological discussion of the functions of control groups, the use of before-and-after designs. the nature of random sampling, and the strengths of blind and double-blind strategies, to name just a few issues. However, there is a second, perhaps prior and more fundamental, question that falls within methodology and places the first question in perspective.

This second question asks, "Given a purpose or set of purposes, a question or set of questions, what kinds of investigative exercises, operations, and strategies should I embark upon to fulfill the purposes and answer the questions?" Frequently, this question is much harder to answer than the first. However, it is also more important, because it probes directly into the issue of appropriateness, adequacy, or suitability of strategies of research, where appropriateness must be evaluated in part against what the investigator is looking for, that is, what his questions are.

The Present Volume

We are now in a position to describe the content of the present collection of essays and make some statements about what they are intended to accomplish. The collection as a whole is pitched at the level of methodology. Thus, although philosophical issues become implicated, and although there will be discussion of specific techniques, the collection is neither a philosophy of science nor a catalog of techniques. More importantly, however, of the two methodological questions, the volume falls under the rubric of the second more than the first. That is, we are concerned with the question of appropriateness or suitability of investigative strategies to investigative questions. More specifically still, the major purpose of the volume is to demonstrate and elaborate upon the following proposition: Naturalistic research, which means investigation of phenomena within and in relation to their naturally occurring contexts, is the only appropriate or suitable way to answer some investigative questions and fulfill certain investigative purposes.

In addition to the various individualized examples and arguments, three prominent, recurring themes or attempts to achieve this major purpose can be abstracted from the collection as a whole. First, there is the attempt to begin filling a gap in the methodological literature, a gap that exists where there should be detailed discussion of the functions, strengths, and weaknesses of naturalistic research. Second, there is a recurring attack against an attitude that is usually negative and condescending toward naturalistic research. Third, there is the attempt to consolidate an awakening (or reawakening?) interest in naturalistic research and to rally support for it.

FILLING A GAP

The attempt to begin filling a gap in the formal literature of methodology requires some background and clarification. If, for the moment, we assume two strongly polarized commitments, one favoring manipulational laboratory experiment and the other favoring naturalistic research, it is not hard to find succinct, reasonable assertions and statements of scientific faith supporting each. For example, consider the following assertions favoring the manipulational, experimental mode of research:

> There is no doubt, however, that in our discipline as in others, the laboratory experiment is a preferred mode for the observation of nature. It is so preferred because of the greater control it gives us over the inputs to the experimental subject. Unlike the usual situation in the field or in the "real world," when we observe the behavior of the subject of a psychological experiment we are in a position to attribute his behavior to the antecedent conditions we have ourselves arranged.
>
> In the paradigm psychological experiment, there is a subject whose behavior is to be observed and an experimenter whose functions include the control of inputs to the subject. (Rosenthal, 1967, p. 356)

> The primary contribution of the psychologist to behavioral science lies in the fact that he has adapted behavioral analysis to laboratory situations; indeed, it is almost the trade-mark of the psychologically oriented behavior scientist that he leaves the laboratory only for avocational purposes. . . . Geographically the psychologist seldom wanders far afield, and the tests that he devises are products of his laboratory researches and are designed for other laboratory investigations. (Harlow, 1958, p. 4)

It should be clear, then, that the ideal of science is the controlled experiment. Except, perhaps, in taxonomic research, research with the purpose of discovering, classifying, and measuring natural phenomena and the factors behind such phenomena, the controlled experiment is the desired model of science. (Kerlinger, 1964, p. 291)

On the other hand, consider the following pleas favoring a naturalistic mode of research:

The experimental method is necessarily an artificial one. Herein lies both its strength and weakness. Because of its artificiality, experimentation is able to establish causal relationships under highly controlled conditions, which makes it eminently suitable for testing theory. However, where an attempt is made to understand events in the natural world, which all theory must eventually do if it is to be more than an intellectual exercise, it is necessary to bridge the gap between the natural event and the experimental situation. It is here that experimentation in psychology has been at its weakest. Because an event can be produced in the laboratory does not mean that the event is so produced in the natural world. Because a child can be shown to learn by trial and error in the laboratory does not mean that this is the way he learns in everyday life. I can produce a light by pressing a button on a flashlight, but this does not prove the sun is a giant flashlight, which someone turns on and off on a twelve-hour schedule. Such thinking is obviously magical rather than scientific. Yet, I submit that many psychologists who are revered for their scientific purity, and who proudly hold up their hard heads, engage in just such magic when they develop universal theories of behavior from data gathered on interested rats running mazes and disinterested sophomores forgetting nonsense syllables. (Epstein, 1962, pp. 269–270)

. . . a science which does not include among its data, phenomena as they exist unarranged by the investigator and without input from the methods used to reveal, describe and enumerate them is only half a science. If biology were limited to processes *in vitro*, it would be a very defective biology. (Barker, 1964, pp. 5–6)

In this game of collecting assertions and beliefs, pro and con, we can also find such intermediate views as the following:

Neither commitment to a theoretical belief nor allegiance to a methodological principle should become so important to the psychologist that he blinds himself to the proper subject matter of psychology. It is the full understanding of this rich, complicated, and often baffling subject matter that is the ultimate goal of psychology. Every theoretical formulation and every method of research must be evaluated in terms of its contribution toward achieving this goal. (Cartwright, 1959, p. 11)

Although differences in theoretical orientation cannot easily be resolved, there need not be an unresolvable dichotomy between studying the development of the behavior of an organism in its natural environ-ment and the development of behavior of that organism in the laboratory. The tasks are different, but they complement, rather than negate, each other. Sometimes, to be sure, the laboratory study is designed to discover a *principle* of behavior rather than to chart a particular organism's behavior under a particular set of circumstances. Still, no contradiction exists once it is agreed that all types of study may contribute to the understanding of behavior. (Rheingold, 1967, p. 287)

Collecting and enumerating assertions does little beyond providing a warm glow to persons who have chosen sides, and the collector of such tidbits will find an occasional specimen in the present essays to add to his collection. However, two important issues run through the collecting game. The first, most subtle and troublesome, issue is focalized in the simple assertions about the desired model of science. Compromise views notwithstanding, there is a tendency to prescribe priorities among the models of research, and there emerges a tendency to define the exercise of research in terms of one set of techniques. Platt (1964) warns of this tendency:

Beware of the man of one method or one instrument, either experimental or theoretical. He tends to become method-oriented rather than problem-oriented. The method-oriented man is shackled; the problem-oriented man is at least reaching freely toward what is most important. (p. 351)

Maslow (1946) comments:

By means-centering, I refer to the tendency to consider that the essence of science lies in its instruments, techniques, procedures, apparatus and its methods rather than in its problems, questions, functions or goals. . . . Means-centering at the highest intellectual levels most usually takes the form of making synonyms of "science" and "scientific method." (p. 326) . . . Means-centered scientists tend, in spite of themselves, to fit their problems to their techniques rather than the contrary. (p. 327)

Whether we call the tendency "method-orientation" or "means-centering," there are two subtle but pervasive by-products of viewing any particular mode of research or set of techniques, a priori, as the desired model of science. One by-product is the tendency to try to fit every research problem, every hypothesis, every hunch about behavior, every question, to that mode. Second, and more important, if a question or hunch does not fit or lend itself to that mode, there is the tendency to view it as not amenable to scientific study. Whether such deductive, a priori judgments come from a committed stance within the laboratory experimental mode or the naturalistic mode is not the issue. The issue is that we believe such an imperialism of method puts the cart before the horse. Platt's "reaching" symbolism is pertinent here. If there is a model of research, it is a person "reaching," seeking answers to his questions. On this view, while specific techniques and modes of research are requisite for certain kinds of studies, the techniques and modes themselves do not constitute the model of research; they are simply tools.

The assertions favoring different research strategies also point to a second important issue. The quoted passages suggest strengths and weaknesses of two vaguely defined modes of research: manipulational-experimental and naturalistic. Further, the passages suggest that there are demonstrable reasons why an investigator should choose one mode over the other. The reasons for, as well as strengths of, the manipulational, experimental mode are covered in an abundant and detailed literature that forms part of the apperceptive mass of most investigators of behavior (for example, Bachrach, 1962; Campbell & Stanley, 1963; Hyman, 1964; Kerlinger, 1964; Lyons, 1965; Scott & Wertheimer, 1962; Sidowski, 1966; Underwood, 1957). This literature summates to a carefully articulated perspective, viewpoint, or rationale regarding the purposes, functions, checks, and balances of the manipulational, experimental mode of research. The literature treating the naturalistic mode of research is in no way comparable, either in quantity or definitude. More important, is it possible, or even worthwhile, to articulate a perspective regarding the reasons for, and strengths of, the naturalistic mode of research? The assumption underlying this volume is that such an effort is both possible *and* worthwhile. Granting that they are separate, provisional tries, the essays to follow will carry the burden of arguing that there are demonstrable questions and purposes in behavioral research that can be answered and realized only through naturalistic methods of research. Furthermore, the burden is carried by behavioral scientists who argue from within the boundaries of the behavioral sciences, rather than by analogy from other sciences. That is, the time has come when we can no longer be content with citing astronomy as a nonexperimental science to justify naturalistic research in psychology.

ATTACKING AN ATTITUDE

The reader, while perusing the essays in this volume, will quickly discern that cropping up here and there in the methodological discussion is an atmosphere of attack, sometimes couched in argumentative language. We freely admit that one of the burdens of the collection as a whole is to grind the proverbial axe. However, we should make clear just what the axe-grinding is about. The target of this attack is an attitude, an attitude that has been succinctly summarized by McGuire (1967) as follows:

> There may be a few centers where doctoral training also includes some hypothesis-testing research in natural settings, or at least survey research. It is my clinical judgment, however, that even in the latter departments, nonlaboratory experimentation is quickly perceived by the student as being taught as a secondary approach for second-class citizens when the royal road of manipulatory laboratory experimentation is somehow blocked. (p. 133)

That is, given our common disposition to defend a person's right to do the kind of research that he finds interesting and worthwhile, there is still the tendency, just as common, to view naturalistic research as a preliminary, early-stage, or even bird-watching, type of activity. As Lorenz (1963) says in a recent essay entitled *A Scientist's Credo:* "The term naturalistic has . . . assumed a definitely derogatory implication. All that I do is considered 'just naturalistic' and case histories are 'just anecdotal . . .' " (p. 7). In military terms, it is common to view naturalistic research as *reconnoitering*, as preliminary but secondary to the more important *campaign*, which belongs to a very different set of activities. Thus, we all know what is meant when phrases such as "just naturalistic research" or "only naturalistic observation" are used. A second means of supporting the major purpose of the volume is to repeatedly attack this prevalent attitude from a number of vantage points.

CONSOLIDATING INTEREST

Closely related to filling in and enriching the methodological literature is a third, more evocative aim: to consolidate what we judge to be a renewed interest in naturalistic research and to rally support for it. Whether the interest we are speaking of is an awakening one or a reawakening one is not crucial; the question would be of more concern to the historian of science than to us. Before the turn of the century, C. Lloyd Morgan, in explicit, self-conscious psychological research, used naturalistic observations to test the hypothesis that dogs used reasoning to open gate latches (Morgan, 1904). However, it would probably not be too controversial to assert that only quite recently would we witness a prediction such as the following one by McGuire (1967):

> Laboratory work has become the "OK" approach in the psychological establishment and new people in the area are flocking to it. . . . I would venture the opinion that this concentration of work has reached the point

of diminishing returns, and that inevitably the more adventurous people in the field are beginning to deviate into other approaches such as doing research in natural settings. Once these adventurous innovators . . . try out the natural environment for their research, I feel that . . . favorable forces . . . will yield them considerably more success than was offered by previous deviations into the natural environment as recently as 10 years ago. As the watchful waiters view the innovators' success from the acceptable premises of the laboratory, the premature elder statesmen and perspicacious Young Turks who are entrenched in the establishment will follow them into the natural environment and these stars will soon be followed by a partial redeployment into this new setting. (p. 132)

McGuire's prediction, especially the parts about "adventurous people" and "innovators," will be music to the ears of the devotee of naturalistic research. However, there are two problems with such a prophecy. First, it does not answer such questions as when, under what conditions, why, and for what investigative purposes one should choose naturalistic methods. Second, prophesying does not make it so. Thus, a third means of support to the major purpose of the volume is to repeatedly evoke sentiments and attitudes regarding the exercise of research that will help to bring McGuire's prophecy to fulfillment. If we add here the fact that most advocates and practitioners of psychological research have fairly strong feelings and commitments on the issues to be discussed, we have all the conditions and ingredients for the realization of our hopes: that dialogue, controversy, assimilation, discussion, evaluation, agreement, and disagreement with the stances taken will enrich the current picture of, and prospects for, research methodology.

REFERENCES

Bachrach, A. J. *Psychological research: An introduction.* New York: Random House, 1962.

Barker, R. G. Psychology's third estate. Paper read at meeting of the Greater Kansas City Psychological Association, Kansas City, Missouri, Spring (unpublished paper), 1964.

Boring, E. G. The validation of scientific belief. *Proceedings of the American Philosophical Society*, 1952, **96**, 535–539.

Butterfield, H. *History and human relations.* New York: Macmillan, 1952.

Campbell, D. T., & Stanley, J. C. *Experimental and quasi-experimental designs for research.* Chicago: Rand McNally, 1963.

Cartwright, D. Lewinian theory as a contemporary systematic framework. In S. Koch (Ed.), *Psychology: A study of a science.* Vol. II. New York: McGraw-Hill, 1959. Pp. 7–91.

Epstein, S. Comments on Dr. Bandura's paper. In M. R. Jones (Ed.), *Nebraska symposium on motivation.* Lincoln, Neb.: University of Nebraska Press, 1962. Pp. 269–272.

Harlow, H. F. Behavioral contributions to interdisciplinary research. In H. F. Harlow & C. N. Woolsey (Eds.), *Biological and biochemical bases of behavior.* Madison, Wis.: University of Wisconsin Press, 1958. Pp. 3–23.

Hildebrand, J. H. "To tell or hear some new thing." *American Scientist*, 1963, **51**, 2–11.

Hyman, R. *The nature of psychological inquiry.* Englewood Cliffs, N. J.: Prentice-Hall, 1964.

Kerlinger, F. N. *Foundations of behavioral research.* New York: Holt, Rinehart and Winston, 1964.

Lorenz, K. A scientist's credo. In H. S. Gaskill (Ed.), *Counterpoint: Libidinal object and subject.* New York: International Universities Press, 1963. Pp. 6–26.

Lyons, J. *A primer of experimental psychology.* New York: Harper & Row, 1965.

Maslow, A. H. Problem-centering vs. means-centering in science. *Philosophy of Science*, 1946, **13**, 326–331.

McGuire, W. J. Some impending reorientations in social psychology: Some thoughts provoked by Kenneth Ring. *Journal of Experimental Social Psychology*, 1967, **3**, 124–139.

Morgan, C. L. *An introduction to comparative psychology.* (2d. ed.) New York: Charles Scribner's Sons, 1904.

Platt, J. R. *The excitement of science.* Boston: Houghton Mifflin, 1962.

Platt, J. R. Strong inference. *Science*, 1964, **146**, 347–353.

Polanyi, M. *Personal knowledge.* Chicago: University of Chicago Press, 1958.

Rheingold, H. L. A comparative psychology of development. In H. W. Stevenson, E. H. Hess, & H. L. Rheingold (Eds.), *Early behavior: Comparative and development approaches.* New York: Wiley, 1967. Pp. 279–293.

Rosenthal, R. Covert communication in the psychological experiment. *Psychological Bulletin*, 1967, **67**, 356–367.

Scott, W. A., & Wertheimer, M. *Introduction to psychological research.* New York: Wiley, 1962.

Sidowski, J. B. (Ed.) *Experimental methods and instrumentation in psychology.* New York: McGraw-Hill, 1966.

Underwood, B. J. *Psychological research.* New York: Appleton-Century-Crofts, 1957.

Part I
ARGUMENTS FROM GENERAL NATURALISTIC PERSPECTIVES

COMMENTARY

IN REMARKABLY SIMILAR and yet subtly different ways, Saul Sells and Roger Barker have become identified with an ecological perspective in psychology and the study of complex behavioral phenomena in their naturally occurring contexts. Some of these similarities and differences emerge in the essays that follow. From their respective vantage points, Sells in Chapter 1 and Barker in Chapter 2 argue cogently and similarly that the behavioral disciplines in general and in psychology in particular need: (a) a deep-seated expansion and shift in point of view to include a truly ecological perspective; (b) investigation of the interdependence and complexity of naturally occurring phenomena; (c) a greatly expanded investigative *armament* of techniques for observation and analysis; (d) a greatly expanded *logistical* base of support, personnel, facilities, and time perspective; and (e) extensive archives of data on both behavior and environments. Furthermore, consistent with their ecological perspectives, both continually promote an expanded investigative focus on the patterned, nonpassive environment in which behavior occurs. In other words, Sells and Barker agree that *what* psychology studies, *how* psychologists study it, and how psychologists *view* what they study have been too limited. However, they differ in two major ways, namely, on the directions from which they arrive at the points of convergence and on the professional framework within which they feel their hopes can be realized. While Sells begins with an evolutionary-ecological view of behavioral science and seems to conclude that we can nudge psychology as we know it into the directions he finds desirable, Barker begins with the conceptual inability of psychology to cope with many pressing issues and concludes that an altogether new discipline, a new science, is the urgent need.

A point of agreement between the first two authors provides the background for Chapter 3, Willems' essay. This point of agreement is the prescription that the behavioral disciplines expand the use of naturalistic methods of research, in other words, methods to investigate phenomena within, and in all their complex relations to, their intact, natural contexts and habitats. With this prescription as his starting point, Willems offers a scheme for describing research activities that he feels allows him to define naturalistic research and subsume it under a common framework with other modes. Then, to supplement the assertion about the need for naturalistic research, Willems discusses a number of considerations or criteria that might enter into the methodological plan of a rationale for naturalistic methods.

Finally, there is at least one major theme that runs through all of the first three essays. Sells speaks of nonillusory conclusions from research, Barker speaks of the relevance of data to everyday human affairs, and Willems discusses the issue of generalization. All suggest the fundamental importance of naturalistic research in mapping and filling in the gaps in our understanding of behavior as we find it in common, everyday experience.

1

Ecology and the Science of Psychology

SAUL B. SELLS

IN THE HIERARCHY of the life sciences, psychology occupies a position between the biological disciplines, which focus on the structure, development, and functioning of organisms, and the social science disciplines, in which the significant unit of observation is a population group. Psychology, which is both biological and social, takes the molar behavior of the individual in his physical and social setting as its observational unit.

A major concern of the biological and social sciences has long been the nature of the interaction of organisms and populations with the embedding environment, which supports, influences, and determines limits of structure and function for the life that exists within it. The generic term for the scientific study of organism-environment interaction is *ecology*.

Traditionally, ecology has been recognized as a branch of biology, while the term *human ecology* has been used to designate the investigations, principally by sociologists and geographers, of the distributions of human population groups in relation to material resources, health, social, economic, and cultural patterns. These disciplines have produced significant bodies of knowledge and theory, and they have developed distinctive journals, literature, and learned societies.

No such formal development has yet occurred in psychology, although an ecologic emphasis has emerged in recent years and may well be gathering enough momentum to crystallize as a major trend in the next decade. If this should happen, however, the new trend will undoubtedly be a protest movement against strongly entrenched traditions, which may themselves have evolved as ecologic phenomena in the development of the science. Indeed, it might be argued that both the phenomena that psychology studies and the research techniques that it employs have evolutionary histories in the sense discussed in this paper.

The discussion will review some significant, converging developments contributing to the ecologic trend in psychology and also some issues and difficulties that must be faced and eventually resolved. This presentation is focused principally on implications of the ecologic emphasis on content and method in psychology.

Ecology and the Content of Psychology

PHYLOGENETIC PERSPECTIVE

One generalization in psychology that appears to be widely accepted is that the behavior of organisms is rooted in biological development. As a result, the behavior mechanisms that organisms have developed must be understood in a phylogenetic perspective. Even the psychologist who views practical human problems as predominant must acknowledge that a thorough science of psychology embraces the entire range of living species. Indeed, the interdependence of structure and function makes it imperative for the behavioral scientist to understand both the long- and short-term development of the biological structures and systems that determine and are determined by the molar behavior of the organism (Murphy, 1947, 1958).

One distinguished psychologist (Hebb, 1958) has stated a position related to this issue as follows:

> The most pressing problems of behavior are those of mental illness and social conflict. . . . The 'pure-science' approach, the development of theoretical understanding, complements the practical approach by providing the only guarantee of better methods in the future. Mental illness involves perception, memory, emotion, thinking; so does the attitude of hostility to other peoples. But we do not fully understand perception, memory, and so on; thus, anything that tells us more about these processes, whether it is the study of the eye-blink in a man or a study of the mating habits of the rat, is a potential addition to our understanding of mental illness or the causes of social conflict. (p. 18)

This argument also implies that the illumination of pressing human problems constitutes a raison d'être of experimental and comparative psychology. But this is not necessary. The phylogenetic perspective is intrinsic to the structure of the science of psychology. Homo sapiens, as well as every other species, is an emergent member of a complex, dynamic system of living organisms, which reflects systematic continuities, even in the face of observed discontinuities, and in which historical position and relationship provide significant insights concerning structure and function. In this system, studies of eye-blink phenomena and mating habits of any species have only the most limited meaning when pursued in isolation, as ends in themselves, but they have great potential value when they are related to a comprehensive network. Such a network can be regarded as analogous to a periodic table in the sense of being a definitive, systematic, and causally integrated account of developmental facts that is organized and oriented toward both phylogenetic and ontogenetic perspectives.

ADAPTATION

In order to organize the science of behavior phylogenetically, psychological inquiry must take account of the most pervasive characteristic of biological systems—the principle of *adaptation*. Essentially, this involves the self-regulating tendency of living organisms to maintain themselves by various means of accommodating or adjusting to changes in the environment. At different levels the principle of adaptation can be observed in the mechanisms of species change: in growth, tissue regeneration, regulation of biological functions, and in molar behavior processes, such as learning and motivation.

In an earlier paper (Sells, 1963a), these phenomena were treated operationally as interactions, which are systematic and adaptive rather than random encounters between inner and outer forces. Interactions are the subject, for example, of Dobzhansky's (1962) account of natural selection, Davis' (1961) description of cold acclimatization, Pribram's (1960) discussion of variable, tunable homeostats, and the more recent literature on the Law of Effect in learning (Kimble, 1961), all of which are straightforward, deterministic accounts of observed events.

Natural selection occurs when two or more classes of individuals, genotypically distinct in some characteristic, transmit their genes to succeeding generations at different rates and one is better able than the others to survive under prevailing environmental conditions. Purpose is unnecessary to the linkage of the events described. The record of survival and extinction of classes differentially adapted to environmental change, though incomplete and not without problems, supports this conclusion, and the evidence is considered tenable that cumulative change of a magnitude recognized as evolution of "higher" types occurs as progressive adaptive change. Thus, the evolutionary progression of Hominidae, Hominae, Homo, and Homo sapiens discloses the appearance of new patterns of behavior reflecting the sequential, cumulative effects of complex new organism-environment interactions continually enabled by the development of emergent structures. The occurrence of these causally linked events, in which complex consequents follow antecedent change, appears to be as lawful and untainted with hormic implications as any of the phenomena of gravity or thermodynamics.

THE FEEDBACK MODEL

Adaptive function of an organism also implies the existence of feedback mechanisms. The posture of the organism at any moment is in effect the expression of an intrinsic (and not necessarily consciously experienced) *hypothesis* concerning the nature of the environment. Every response is similarly an *interrogation* of the environment, and the resulting feedback provides information (also not necessarily conscious) that enables adaptive response. The existence of biological and neurophysiological feedback systems is a necessary assumption about adaptive organisms.

The specific nature of the biochemical and bioelectric feedback mechanisms involved in adaptive biologic function and behavior is not yet clear, but this is not essential to the present discussion. However, the argument developed here does depend on the assumptions that such mechanisms are essential components of adaptive organisms and that both biological functions and molar behavior are controlled by information-processing systems in which anticipation,[1] expectation, posture, or set is one fundamental characteristic, and adjustment, based on information-feedback, is another.[2]

[1] The adoption of computer terminology by psychologists has made it possible to discuss *anticipation* and *information* inherent in feedback mechanisms without resorting to anthropomorphic expressions. This is apparent in the substitution by Cofer and Appley (1964) of the *equilibration model* for the *need-reduction model* in their discussion of feedback systems relevant to motivation and in their proposed sensitization (SIM) and anticipation (AIM) mechanisms as proposed models for motivation theory. Other noteworthy developments incorporating or implying feedback concepts include Woodworth's comprehensive laws of homogeneity (1938), Hebb's concept of response equivalence (1949), the concept of reinforcement in learning, Piaget's concepts of accommodation and assimilation (Hunt, 1961), Helson's adaptation level theory (1964), the TOTE unit of Miller, Galanter, and Pribram (1960), the Sherifs' (1956) principles of stimulus structure and psychological selectivity in perception, and the information-processing model of motivation presented by Hunt (1963).

[2] This interdependence was perhaps most critically appreciated by Ashby (1962) who faced the problem of specification of environmental inputs in his computer model of a brain. Here the rigorous requirements for detailed information demonstrate the inadequacy of the often-cited global expression of interaction, $R = f (I \times E)$, in which R (behavior) is a function (f) of the interaction of organism (I) and environment (E). Not only must the nature of the function term be explicated, but the variables comprising the I and E sets must be specified and measured before such an equation can be realistically useful.

These characteristics of adaptive behavior emphasize the importance of the environment with which organisms interact in biological and behavioral development and function.

THE ECOLOGIC NICHE AS CONTEXT

The arguments advanced thus far are the basis for four postulates concerning the strategic role of the *ecologic niche* in the structure of behavior.

First, it is recognized that every species and class of living organisms has evolved by adaptation to a particular set of environmental conditions with reference to which its morphologic structures, physiologic systems, and behavior response repertoire are optimally suited. This environmental pattern is defined as the ecologic niche, and it represents the adaptive *match* between circumstances and species schema (Hunt, 1961).

Second, these very structures, physiological systems, and repertoires of responses, defined by the ecologic niche, are the characteristics that are strategically relevant to the periodic table of phylogenetically oriented data referred to above. Focusing on behavior, it may be said that the response repertoire represents the *natural* way in which a species "makes its living" in its natural environment.

Third, the differences between species in historical position, critical environment, and related response repertoires all limit the types of cross-species comparisons that may be meaningful and suggest types of comparative studies that may profitably illuminate behavior in phylogenetic perspective.

And finally, the understanding of behavior requires systematic study of the characteristics of the environmental pattern defining the ecologic niche of each species and the adaptations required by that environment, as well as of response processes.

These postulates are the basis for two contextual prescriptions concerning the content of psychology: (1) There is a need for a master plan, corresponding to the periodic table mentioned above, to place psychological research in phylogenetic perspective. Such a schematic analysis could serve as a systematic guide to the definition of empirical information required for a comprehensive science of psychology. Considering the aspirations of psychology as a systematic science, it is sobering to consider (a) how little we know of species outside of rats, chicks, monkeys, college students, military basic trainees, babies, and hospital patients, and (b) the limited and ecologically distorted strategies and conditions we typically use to study them. (2) For every species and class this schematic table should contain a detailed description and quantitative analysis of both the features of the environment defining the ecologic niche and the matching behavior response repertoire.

The conspicuous lack of such normative data is strongly voiced in the following remarks by Roger Barker (1965) in a recent address to the American Psychological Association:

> This state of affairs is most surprising in view of the situation in the old, prestigeful sciences which psychology so admires and emulates in other respects. In these sciences, the quest for the phenomena of science as they occur unaltered by the techniques of search and discovery is a central, continuing task; and the development of techniques for identifying entities and signaling processes without altering them (within organisms, within cells, within physical systems, and within machines) is among the sciences' most valued achievements. Handbooks and encyclopedias attest to the success of these efforts. I read, for example, that potassium (K) ranks seventh in order of abundance of elements, and constitutes about 2.59 percent of the igneous rocks of the earth's crust; that its components are widely distributed in the primary rocks, the oceans, the soil, plants, and animals; and that soluble potassium salts are present in all fertile soils. (Encyclopaedia Britannica, 1962). The fact that there is no equivalent information in the literature of scientific psychology (about playing, about laughing, about talking, about being valued and devalued, about conflict, about failure) confronts psychologists with a monumental incompleted task. (pp. 5–6)

The programmatic work of Kinsey and his associates on human sexual behavior (1948, 1953) and of Barker and the staff at the Midwest Psychological Field Station, University of Kansas, on recording units in the "stream of behavior" of children in several locales has demonstrated the importance of ecologic norms for understanding particular problems (1963). For example, Clifford Fawl (1963), a student of Barker's found that observational records of children's behavior in their natural surroundings, as contrasted with the psychological laboratory, indicated that *frustration* occurred rarely, and when it did occur, it did not have the behavioral consequences observed in the laboratory (Barker, 1965). Barker commented on this as follows: "It appears that the earlier experiments (by Lewin, Dembo, and Barker) simulated behavior very well as we defined and prescribed it for subjects (in accordance with our theories); but the experiments did not simulate frustration as life prescribes it for children" (p. 5).

We may wonder about other experimental treatments of segments of behavior and their relations to the occurrence of the designated behaviors in real-life situations.

Another example, from a paper by Gump and Kounin (1960), illustrates this point further. Gump and Sutton-Smith (1955) investigated the reactions of poorly skilled players when they were put in more or less difficult game positions or roles. For example, in games of tag, the *it* position is more demanding under some rules than others.

As they played the game experimentally, an *it* in the center of a rectangular playing field attempts to tag opponents who run to and from *safe* areas at each end of the rectangle. One variant of the game gives *high power* to the *it* position by permitting the child in that position to "call the turn" when runners may attempt to cross from one safe position to another. Another variant gives *low power* to the *it* by permitting players to run whenever they choose. In one phase of the experiment, slow runners were assigned to high-power *it* positions, and in another, to low-power *it* positions.

The hypotheses, that poorly skilled boys would be more successful in high-power than low-power *it* positions and that scapegoating of these inept boys would be less frequent in the high- than in the low-power positions, were unequivocally confirmed. However, Gump and Kounin also observed boys in natural, rather than experimental situations, in gyms, playgrounds, and camps, and obtained the following impressions:

> (a) Poorly skilled boys do not often get involved in games they cannot manage; (b) if they do get involved, they often manage to avoid difficult roles by not trying to win such a position or by quitting if they cannot avoid it; and (c) if they occupy the role and are having trouble, the game often gets so boring to opponents that these opponents let themselves be caught in order to put the game back on a more zestful level. (p. 148)

The experimental game, which was watched by adults, was artificial in that poor competitors were inappropriately placed in skilled positions and in these circumstances no opponent ever let himself be caught. It actually created a highly unusual and, to the children, desperate circumstance, in which interfering adults were intervening agents. Gump and Kounin concluded that "the experiment probably does suggest hypotheses as to why certain games and roles are avoided by inept children, and it shows the extent to which children can scapegoat when conditions are artificially favorable" (p. 148).

A third example may be found in the 1961 report of Keller and Marian Breland, which not only recognized the primary relevance of the ecologically matched behavior response repertoire, but presented evidence of the *prepotency* of such responses over others to which animals were conditioned in the laboratory.

The Brelands, who built a highly successful business on the operant conditioning of animals for commercial exhibits, encountered a number of "disconcerting failures" in which conditioned animals, after thousands of reinforcements of specific (ecologically artificial) learned responses, gradually drifted into behaviors entirely different from those which were conditioned.

The direction of this drift was toward what the authors called "instinctive behaviors having to do with the natural food-getting behaviors of the particular species." For example, "dancing chickens" drifted toward persistent scratching behavior, which is a prominent feature of the natural response repertoire of gallinaceous birds in their native habitat; chickens that were conditioned to peck a souvenir toy onto a chute drifted toward hammering them apart, thereby reverting to their natural habit of breaking open seed pods, killing insects, and the like; and the pig who was trained to pick up a coin and carry it to the bank, gradually began to drop it and "root it along the way," thus demonstrating the prepotency of a strongly established food-getting component of the natural repertoire of his species.

It is really providential that the early success of their enterprise resulted in the continuation of many of their "experiments" for a sufficiently long period (far beyond the duration of most laboratory experiments) in order that the so-called "instinctive drift" could occur. Their scientific insights may be regarded as a handsome repayment to academic science, whose impeccable empiricism they have extensively exploited.[3]

For the present discussion these studies symbolize a host of experimental analyses of behaviors that occur only in the artificial and unrealistic experimental situations contrived to fit the hypotheses of experimenters who are either ignorant of or indifferent to the conditions of occurrence of those behaviors in natural settings.

Although the position advocated here favors multivariate field observation and experiment over univariate laboratory experiment as the methods of choice in psychological research, the value of the laboratory as an adjunct to the field research station, to isolate, test, verify, and replicate particular aspects of phenomena observed in natural settings, should not be overlooked. Unfortunately, it has become an orthodoxy in many university circles that the laboratory is supreme, that investigation without experimental manipulation of treatments and testing of hypotheses is unworthy of the term *research*, and that laboratory environments are preferable to natural settings. But our position is that unless the laboratory is a valid simulation of the conditions of the natural setting with respect

---

[3] No disparagement of the experimental method *per se* was intended by the Brelands; nor by the present writer.

to the ecological criteria advanced in this paper, it may fail in its primary purpose of contributing to the understanding of behavior, even though it may well serve the economic goal of producing more graduates.[4]

Ecology and the Methods of Psychology

Acceptance of the ecologic principles discussed above has a number of profound implications for the scientific methods of psychology. In the first place, methods must be adapted to the circumstances of the real world in which behavior occurs naturally rather than for the convenience of the scientist. To this end, a new generation of field-oriented workers in psychology is needed.

However, this world of reality is complicated, often uncontrollable, and frequently intolerant of prying investigators. It operates according to rules of privacy and inviolacy and at a pace that often seems to defy investigative resourcefulness. These are problems that have beset many an unwary investigator and they have long been appreciated. They enable us to understand, if not approve, the advantages of the uncomplicated, traditional laboratory milieu.

What is the resolution of the dilemma? First, vastly greater communication and cooperation between psychology and both the biological and the social sciences are needed, for the methodology most appropriate to many of the fundamental psychological problems is necessarily interdisciplinary.

INTERDISCIPLINARY APPROACH

Source data on major parameters of both the physical and social environmental behavioral effects have been compiled and published by oceanographers, climatologists, limnologists, physicists, geologists, geographers, anthropologists, sociologists, and even psychologists, as well as workers in many other disciplines. The following examples are mentioned merely to illustrate the wide range of excellent material available: Tromp's (1963) comprehensive work on medical biometeorology, dealing with weather, climate, and the living organism; environmental and operational

---

[4] Many critics have recently drawn attention to the hollow, unproductive, artificial, and even pointless activities in many animal and so-called experimental laboratories, and urge attention to realistic human problems; see, for example, the papers by Bakan, N. Sanford, and Berg in the March 1965 issue of the *American Psychologist*.

data on the polar basin and the arctic region, in Sater's (1963) report for the Arctic Institute of North America; the effects of unusual environments encountered by men in military and space operations, studied by Burns, Chambers, and Hendler, psychologists (1963); extensive files on the detailed social, economic, political, legal, judicial, religious, health, familial, educational, scientific, military, and behavioral structure, folkways, and norms of the peoples of the world, coordinated by Murdock and others (Murdock, 1958); and definitive studies of human social structures, social systems, culture, and social change, in the two-volume work edited by Parsons, Shils, Naegele, and Pitts (1961).

Zoologists and other biologists have published extensive material on the behavior of animals in their native habitats. Recent books by Portmann (1961) and Etkin (1963) on social behavior and organization of vertebrates illustrate scientific contributions by these colleagues which are of value to psychologists.

Recently, the Federation of American Societies for Experimental Biology (Altman & Dittmer, 1964), under Air Force support, published a *Biology Data Book*, for which 470 botanists, zoologists, and medical scientists contributed and reviewed data. The *Data Book* presents authoritative information on the parameters of genetics, reproduction, growth and development, morphology, nutrition and digestion, metabolism, respiration and circulation, blood, biological regulators, environment and survival, and other factors for many species of plants, vertebrates, invertebrates, and man. While much of the detailed data is of primary interest to biologists, this publication contains much material of psychological interest, such as effects of temperature, shade, and light on growth and survival of many species, effects of exposure to ionizing radiation, estimates of the number of species of plants and animals and taxonomic classifications of living animal species.

The purpose of citing this vast and wide-ranging array of literature is to document the point that the task of compiling a schematic periodic table focused on the environmental niches and behavior repertoires of animal species will receive a large assist from the older sciences that long ago appreciated its importance. These disciplines have faced and in many cases overcome the difficulties of inaccessibility of phenomena, danger, discomfort, and privacy.

PSYCHOLOGICAL FIELD RESEARCH

A number of field studies, representing a wide range of behavior, support the belief that there are no insuperable obstacles to effective field observations and no lack of ingenuity among investigators convinced of the importance of the approach. The interview procedures of Kinsey and his co-workers (1948–1953) paved the way for others to penetrate the seeming iron curtain of mystery and repression surrounding human sexual behavior. The behavior protocols of Barker and his colleagues (1963) demonstrated that observational techniques need not be confined to the baby's crib or the conference table. Both of these pioneers produced data of acknowledged richness and importance to the structuring of scientific inquiry in psychology.

Zinner (1963) recorded observations of 56 specific behaviors[5] on 90 airmen, over a period of 25 days, with the help of 98 specially trained airman observers, in 30 different real-life situations in military basic training.[6]

In general agreement with a less ambitious observational study of one nine-year-old boy in two different situations of one day's duration each, by Gump, Schoggen, and Redl (1963), Zinner observed a number of dependencies between situations and specific behaviors, for example, situations that either facilitated or inhibited smoking or talking in varying degree. Factors extracted from his data were stable over subjects and occasions.

Observations of behavior in its natural setting, without interference or manipulation by the investigator, not only frees psychology from insurmountable limitations due to experimental exclusion of complicating, but ecologically highly relevant variables; it also reduces the equally inescapable difficulty of *iatrogenic* influences on results, that is, the built-in effects of the experimenter's hypotheses expressed in his particular designs and procedures (Kintz *et al.*, 1965). Even simple invertebrates such as planaria have demonstrated such experimenter effects, according to a report by Rosenthal and Halas (1962).

On the other hand, this enthusiasm must be tempered by concern with the real problems of effective field-oriented methods. There is no question that they will raise the cost of psychological research to an awesome degree, for they involve multivariate observation and analysis on a time scale far in excess of present practices and over numbers of subjects,

---

[5] . . . such as using left, right, or both hands, eating, hands in pockets, drinking, holding an object, nonpersonal rubbing of shoes, brass or windows, writing, urinating, leaning against something, smoking, talking to one person, saying Grace, smiling, and the like. . .

[6] . . . such as Wake up, from lights-on until the subject left the personal area, Personal area involving bunk and footlocker, Latrine, Marching to mess hall for breakfast, Table at breakfast, and so on from 4:45, in the morning until 5:00 in the afternoon. . .

situations, and replications that imply massive organizations for data collection, reduction, and analysis.

In addition there are technical difficulties. The two most important of these are: (1) the problem of recording observations appropriately and completely and of reducing observational protocols to reliable units for quantitative analysis, and (2) the problem of encoding the environment.

THE PROBLEM OF RECORDING BEHAVIOR

The first problem may look more difficult than it actually is. Zinner's observations were highly reliable. However, the behaviors he observed were selected to be objectively discrete and overt and his observers were carefully trained. Dickman (1963), a student of Barker's, on the other hand, found that naive beginning psychology students agreed poorly on the analysis into units of continuous samples of behavior presented in a motion picture. Still, improvement occurred with practice.

Dickman also pointed out that:

> . . . the "stream of behavior" attains orderliness in the eyes of other humans to the extent that goals and motives are imputed to the behavior. Independent observers of such a behavior continuum demonstrated significant agreement on general patterning and specifically on the points at which units began or ended. They agreed very poorly on identical incidence of units, yet they were able to agree on the general meaning of the sequence. (pp. 40–41)

He attributed this paradoxical result to differences in the inclusiveness of goal or behavior perspectives of the judges.

To some extent this problem is reminiscent of the experience of McClelland and his associates (Atkinson, 1958) in their efforts to obtain reliable scoring methods for TAT protocols. However, Barker (1963) has suggested that increased familiarity with observational methods will lead to improvement of these methods.

THE PROBLEM OF ENCODING THE ENVIRONMENT

The problem of encoding the environment is the big hurdle. However, one program of research on this problem (Sells, 1963a, 1963b) makes it look more viable in the frame of reference of field study than from the perspective of the laboratory. The isolation of laboratory performance from the context of a stream of behavior, which Barker has emphasized, prompts one to think of the environment in discrete, molecular terms, while the real-life setting suggests the patterned regularity and coherent structure of the familiar physical and social environment. The physical world consists not of discrete bits of light, heat, moisture, and the like, but of patterned events, with system qualities, in which day-night cycles, months, and seasons have associated with them characteristic temperatures, light, climatic variations, activity patterns, modes of dress, and the like. Similarly, the social world consists of patterned events with system qualities embracing multiple discrete stimuli which typically (except in unusual, extreme conditions) influence behavior, not in isolation, but by virtue of what Sherif and Sherif (1956) have called their *membership character* derived from the qualities of the respective systems. In this frame of reference a given unit may belong to more than one system and function differently in each.

The important work of Hadden and Borgatta (1965) on the factor structures of census characteristics in American cities paves the way to a systematic accounting of fundamental variables in the ecology of urban environments. A number of studies (Findikyan & Sells, 1964, 1965; Sells & Findikyan, 1965; Friedlander, 1965; Pace & Stern, 1958; Stern, 1956; Thistlethwaite, 1959a, 1959b; Astin & Holland, 1961; Astin, 1962, 1963) have demonstrated the value of multivariate analysis of variables used to measure aspects of the social environment. Such studies are particularly important, for example, in identifying characteristics of organizations, of social climates, of work situations, and of other subsystems of the social environment that may be useful for measurement purposes. The key purpose of the multivariate position is that of accounting for simultaneous and joint effects of multiple events whose independence cannot be assumed. This purpose and what it assumes are as applicable to the basic psychological processes of learning, perception, and motivation as they are to more complex behavior, such as school and job performance, personal adjustment, and group behavior. Behavior in its everyday setting is sequential, and temporal factors are always important. Furthermore, such behavior is hierarchical and it always occurs in a physical and social context which exercises both direct and indirect, subtle and obvious influences whose contributions need to be evaluated if thoroughgoing and valid explanation is to be achieved. More of the rationale for such multivariate analysis is provided elsewhere (Sells, 1963b, 1966).

Dependencies between characteristics of situations and behaviors encourage further exploration of environmental determiners of behavior. Until we can assign to environmental variables the proportions of variance in behavior for which they account, our understanding of behavior will be incomplete. When this is accomplished, the goals of an ecologic approach to the science of psychology will have been achieved.

REFERENCES

Altman, P. L., & Dittmer, D. S. *Biology data book.* Wright-Patterson Air Force Base, Ohio; Biophysics Laboratory, Aerospace Medical Research Laboratories, USAF. Report No. AMRL-TR-64-100, October, 1964.

Ashby, W. R. Simulation of a brain. In H. Borko (Ed.), *Computer applications in the behavioral sciences.* Englewood Cliffs, N. J.: Prentice-Hall, 1962. Pp. 452–467.

Astin, A. W. An empirical characterization of higher educational institutions. *Journal of Educational Psychology,* 1962, **53,** 224–235.

Astin, A. W. Further validation of the environmental assessment technique. *Journal of Educational Psychology,* 1963, **54,** 217–226.

Astin, A. W., & Holland, J. L. The environmental assessment technique: A way to measure college environments. *Journal of Educational Psychology,* 1961, **52,** 308–316.

Atkinson, J. W. (Ed.) *Motives in fantasy, action, and society: A method of assessment and study.* Princeton, N. J.: Van Nostrand, 1958.

Bakan, D. The mystery-mastery complex in contemporary psychology. *American Psychologist,* 1965, **20,** 186–191.

Barker, R. G. (Ed.) *The stream of behavior.* New York: Appleton-Century-Crofts, 1963.

Barker, R. G. Explorations in ecological psychology. *American Psychologist,* 1965, **20,** 1–14.

Berg, I. A. Cultural trends and the task of psychology. *American Psychologist,* 1965, **20,** 203–207.

Breland, K., & Breland, M. The misbehavior of organisms. *American Psychologist,* 1961, **16,** 681–684.

Burns, N. M., Chambers, R. M., & Hendler, E. *Unusual environments and human behavior.* New York: Free Press, 1963.

Cofer, C. H., & Appley, M. H. *Motivation: Theory and research.* New York: Wiley, 1964.

Davis, T. R. A. Chamber acclimatization in man. Report on Studies of Physiological Effects of Cold on Man. *Army Medical Research Laboratory,* Report No. 475, 1961.

Dickman, H. R. The perception of behavioral units. In R. G. Barker (Ed.), *The stream of behavior.* New York: Appleton-Century-Crofts, 1963. Pp. 23–41.

Dobzhansky, T. *Mankind evolving.* New Haven, Conn.: Yale University Press, 1962.

Etkin, W. (Ed.) *Social behavior and organization among vertebrates.* Chicago: University of Chicago Press, 1963.

Fawl, C. L. Disturbances experienced by children in their natural habitats. In R. G. Barker (Ed.), *The stream of behavior.* New York: Appleton-Century-Crofts, 1963. Pp. 99–126.

Findikyan, N., & Sells, S. B. *The dimensional structure of campus student organizations.* Texas Christian University, Institute of Behavioral Research, June, 1964. Technical Report No. 5, Contract No. Nonr 3436(00).

Findikyan, N., & Sells, S. B. *The similarity of campus student organizations assessed through a hierarchical grouping procedure.* Texas Christian University, Institute of Behavioral Research, March, 1965. Technical Report No. 6, Contract No. Nonr 3436(00).

Friedlander, F. *Behavioral dimensions of traditioned work groups.* U. S. Naval Ordnance Test Station, China Lake, California, 1965. Unpublished Manuscript.

Gump, P. V., & Kounin, J. S. Issues raised by ecological and "classical" research efforts. *Merrill-Palmer Quarterly*, 1960, **6,** 145–152.

Gump, P. V., Schoggen, P., & Redl, F. The behavior of the same child in different milieus. In R. G. Barker (Ed.), *The stream of behavior.* New York: Appleton-Century-Crofts, 1963. Pp. 169–202.

Gump, P. V., & Sutton-Smith, B. The "it" role in children's games. *The Group*, 1955, **17,** 3–8.

Hadden, J. K. & Borgatta, E. F. *American cities: Their social characteristics.* Chicago: Rand McNally, 1965.

Hebb, D. O. *The organization of behavior.* New York: Wiley, 1949.

Hebb, D. O. *A textbook of psychology.* Philadelphia: Saunders, 1958.

Helson, H. *Adaptation-level theory.* New York: Harper and Row, 1964.

Hunt, J. McV. *Intelligence and experience.* New York: Ronald, 1961.

Hunt, J. McV. Motivation inherent in information processing and action. In O. J. Harvey (Ed.), *Motivation and social interaction.* New York: Ronald, 1963. Pp. 35–94.

Kimble, G. A. *Hilgard and Marquis' conditioning and learning.* New York: Appleton-Century-Crofts, 1961.

Kinsey, A. C., Pomeroy, W. B., & Martin, C. E. *Sexual behavior in the human male.* Philadelphia: Saunders, 1948.

Kinsey, A. C., Pomeroy, W. B., Martin, E. C., & Gebhard, F. H. *Sexual behavior in the human female.* Philadelphia: Saunders, 1953.

Kintz, B. L., Delprato, D. J., Mettee, D. R., Persons, C. E., & Schappe, R. H. The experimenter effect. *Psychological Bulletin*, 1965, **63,** 223–232.

Miller, G. A., Galanter, E., & Pribram, K. H. *Plans and the structure of behavior.* New York: Holt, Rinehart and Winston, 1960.

Murdock, G. P. *Outline of world cultures.* New Haven, Conn.: Human Relations Area Files Press, 1958.

Murphy, G. *Personality: A biosocial approach.* New York: Harper and Row, 1947.

Murphy, G. *Human potentialities.* New York: Basic Books, 1958.

Pace, C. R., & Stern, G. G. An approach to the measurement of psychological characteristics of college environments. *Journal of Educational Psychology*, 1958, **49,** 269–277.

Parsons, T., Shils, E., Naegele, K. D., & Pitts, J. R. *Theories of society. Foundations of modern sociological theory.* 2 Vols. Glencoe, Ill.: Free Press, 1961.

Portmann, A. *Animals as social beings.* New York: Viking, 1961.

Pribram, K. H. A review of theory of physiological psychology. *Annual Review of Psychology,* 1960, **11,** 1–40.

Rosenthal, R., & Halas, E. S. Experimenter effect in the study of invertebrate behavior. *Psychological Reports,* 1962, **11,** 251–256.

Sanford, N. Will psychologists study human problems? *American Psychologist,* 1965, **20,** 192–202.

Sater, J. E. *The arctic basin.* Centerville, Md.: Tidewater Publishing Corp., 1963.

Sells, S. B. An interactionist looks at the environment. *American Psychologist,* 1963, **18,** 696–702. (a)

Sells, S. B. (Ed.) *Stimulus determinants of behavior.* New York: Ronald, 1963. (b)

Sells, S. B. Multivariate technology in industrial and military personnel psychology. In R. B. Cattell (Ed.), *Handbook of multivariate experimental psychology.* Chicago: Rand McNally, 1966. Pp. 841–855.

Sells, S. B. & Findikyan, N. *Dimensions of organizational structure. A factor-analytic reevaluation of the Hemphill Group Dimensions Description Questionnaire.* Texas Christian University, Institute of Behavioral Research, November, 1965, Contract No. Nonr 3436(00).

Sherif, M., & Sherif, C. W. *An outline of social psychology.* New York: Harper and Row, 1956.

Stern, G. C. *Activities Index, Form 156.* Syracuse, N. Y.: Syracuse University, Psychological Research Center, 1956.

Thistlethwaite, D. L. College environment and the development of talent. *Science,* 1959, **130,** 71–76. (a)

Thistlethwaite, D. L. College press and student achievement. *Journal of Educational Psychology,* 1959, **50,** 183–191. (b)

Tromp, S. W. *Medical biometeorology.* New York: Elsevier Publishing Co., 1963.

Woodworth, R. S. *Experimental psychology.* New York: Holt, Rinehart and Winston, 1938.

Zinner, L. The consistency of human behavior in various situations. A methodological application of functional ecological psychology. Unpublished doctoral dissertation, University of Houston, 1963.

2
Wanted: An Eco-Behavioral Science

ROGER G. BARKER

WHAT ARE THE CONSEQUENCES for human behavior of such environmental conditions as poverty, controlled climate in working and living areas, congested cities, transient populations, high population density, computer technology, ghettos, large schools, "bedroom" communities? Such questions about the effects of the environment upon human behavior and development are being asked with increasing urgency, and the behavioral sciences, for the most part, do not have answers to them. Nonetheless, behavior scientists often respond hopefully with the promise that, given enough time and resources, answers will be provided by the old and well-established methods, concepts, and theories of the psychological sciences, which in the past have answered so many other questions about human behavior in the areas of perception, learning, intellectual processes, motivation, and so on. The new and urgent questions have instigated discussions and plans for a new psychological speciality called naturalistic or field psychology which would parallel experimental and clinical psychology.

The view I shall present here is that, on the contrary, the present methods, concepts, and theories of the psychological sciences *cannot* answer the new questions, and that a new science is required to deal with them, a science that requires facilities that are not now available.

Limits of the Science of Psychology

Scientific psychology knows nothing, and can know nothing, about the real-life settings in which people live in ghettos and suburbs, in large and small schools, in regions of poverty and affluence. One might think that in the course of its necessary concern with stimuli, psychology would have become informed about the human environment. But this is not the case. Psychology has necessarily attended to those elements of the environment that are useful in probing its focal phenomena, namely, the behavior-relevant circuitry within the skins of its subjects, within psychology's black box. Psychology knows much about the physical properties and dimensions of the environmental probes it uses—of distal objects of perception, for example, and of energy changes at receptor surfaces. But the problem is that, in the course of its investigations, it has excised these environmental elements from the contexts in which they normally occur: mealtimes, offices, airplanes, arithmetic classes, streets and sidewalks.

In view of psychology's concern with such dismantled fragments of the environment, it is not surprising that general conceptions of the environment occupy a minor place in the science, and that these conceptions provide a distorted view of intact settings in which behavior occurs. The most common notion, which can hardly be called a theory, is that the non-behavioral, ecological environment of man is an unstructured, probabilistic, and largely passive arena within which man behaves according to the programming he carries about inside him. Brunswik (1955), for example, speaks of "the behaving organism living in a semi-chaotic environmental medium" (p. 686); Leeper (1963) of "the kaleidoscopically changing stimulation" organisms receive (p. 388); and Lewin (1951) writes that ". . . psychology should be interested . . . in those areas of the physical and social world which are not part of the life space . . . (but this) has to be based partly on statistical considerations about nonpsychological (events)" (pp. 58–59).[1] Although these assertions are true within the limited environmental perspective of the science of psychology, they are not true within a wider perspective. It is the universal testimony of the physical and biological sciences that the ecological environment circumjacent to men is organized and patterned in such stable, improbable ways that it is, in fact, one task of these sciences to explore, describe, and account for the patternings.

Psychology has fallen into a self-validating roundabout here. Its prevailing methods of research shatter whatever pattern and organization may exist within the natural environment, and the conclusion is reached on the basis of the resulting evidence that the environment is not a source of the order and organization observed in behavior. This leads to further study of the mysterious mechanism of the black box that appears to bring order out of chaos; and this is done via ever more theory-determined, and less setting-determined environmental variables. It is my impression that psychology fell into this error when it became, so early in its history and for whatever reason, a science of the laboratory and the clinic, installing

---

[1] Parentheses indicate my additions.

psychologists as environment surrogates, and thereafter neglecting the psychologist-free environment. For over a century now, psychology has largely directed inputs to its subjects in accordance with theoretical games evolved from input-output relations previously observed in laboratories and clinics, and it has inevitably become more and more removed from settings that are not arranged by scientists and more and more impressed with the black box as the determinant of behavior.

Here is an example of what we have come to. The problem of Citizen X is presented in a current work. Citizen X is active all day; immensely active; but, although constantly task involved, he is never ego involved. The following characterization is given of the days of Citizen X:

> He moves and has his being in the great activity wheel of New York City . . . he spends his hours . . . in the badlands of the Bronx. He wakens to grab the morning's milk left at the door by an agent of a vast Dairy and Distributing system whose corporate manoeuvers, so vital to his health, never consciously concern him. After paying hasty respects to his landlady, he dashes into the transportation system whose mechanical and civic mysteries he does not comprehend. At the factory he becomes a cog for the day in a set of systems far beyond his ken . . . though he doesn't know it, his furious activity at his machine is regulated by the "law of supply and demand." . . . A union official collects dues; just why he doesn't know. At noontime that corporate monstrosity, Horn and Hardart, swallows him up, much as he swallows one of its automatic pies. After more activity in the afternoon, he seeks out a standardized daydream produced in Hollywood. . . . (adapted from Allport, 1964, p. 284)

In this account, it would appear that we are at last getting down to psychologist-free situations within an urban environment, to their nature and their consequences for behavior and personality. The author reports that Citizen X is confronted by the vast, anonymous dairy; that he is incorporated into the incomprehensible subway; that he is driven and regulated by the overwhelming factory; that he is swallowed by the mechanical cafeteria; and that he relaxes in a readymade movie daydream. Citizen X, according to the author, is mightily busy, but he is not really involved, and in this respect he is representative of an important segment of our population. Allport confronts us with an important social question, namely: "What precisely is wrong with Citizen X?" He does not ask, "What is the nature of the city at its interface with Citizen X?" or, "What occurs between the interior programming of Citizen X (his motives and cognitions) and the city settings he inhabits to generate the grabbing, hasty, dashing, uncomprehending, furious, standardized, uninvolved behavior he displays?" The author is correct: what goes on within the black box is the only question psychology can answer, even though it is not the question society is asking. So far is the science of psychology removed from real-life settings.

But, it would seem that the black box is a legitimate focus for psychology. It makes psychology a prospectively unified science, explicated by a single set of interrelated concepts; and it makes it a practically important science, for the answers to many human problems (though not the problem of cities as human habitats) are to be found in the internal programming people carry from setting to setting. It is a wonder that psychology has ever been *expected* to have relevance to situations at large where such nonpsychological variables as poverty and wealth, segregation and nonsegregation, overpopulation and underpopulation prevail. Our only error, as psychologists, has been to ignore the limits of our competence, or allow others to ignore those limits.

Behavior and Environment: Separated and Interdependent

Psychological phenomena and the environments in which they occur are interrelated; they are interdependent. They are interdependent in the way a part of a system and a whole system are interdependent. The electrical generator of an engine and the functioning engine, or the bats and balls and a game of baseball are examples. Predictions from electrical generators to engines, and vice versa, and from bats and balls to ball games and vice versa, require complete accounts of the superordinate phenomenon (of the engine, the ball game) and of the place of the part system within the whole. This is true, also, for naturally occurring situations and behavior. Just as the theory of electrical generators cannot account for the behavior of internal combustion engines, nor engines explain generators, so, in a similar way, is psychology unable to explain the functioning of taverns, school classes, or other real-life settings, and theories of settings unable to account for all of the behavior of the inhabitants. Generators and the environing engines within which they function, and people and the settings which constitute their environments are different phenomena, and require for their explanation different concepts and theories.

The distinction between the phenomena to which the urgent questions about poverty, technology, population, and so on refer and the phenomena with which psychological science deals is not a tactical distinction; it is a basic one. These are conceptually incommensurate phenomena. We shall see, too, that they require different methodologies for their investigation.

Nature of the Environment

When we do look at the environment of behavior as a phenomenon worthy of investigation for itself, and not merely as an instrument for unraveling the behavior-relevant programming within persons, we find that it is *not* a passive, probabilistic arena of objects and events. This discovery was forced upon us in the research with which I have been associated.[2] We made long records of children's behavior throughout whole, ordinary days by means of a traditional person-centered approach, and we were surprised to find that some attributes of behavior varied less across children within settings than within the days of children across settings (Barker & Wright, 1955). We found that we could predict many aspects of children's behavior more adequately from knowledge of the behavior characteristics of the drugstores, arithmetic classes, and basketball games that they inhabited than from knowledge of the behavior tendencies of the particular children. Since then, systematic studies have confirmed this general observation (Raush *et al.*, 1959, 1960; Ashton, 1964). Indeed, the conformity of people to the patterns of real-life settings is so great that deviations therefrom are often newsworthy, or considered indicative of serious abnormality requiring social or medical attention. Such deviancies within the settings of the town of Midwest, which we have studied over a period of almost 20 years, are an infinitesimal proportion of the opportunities for deviancy.

A simple hypothesis to account for the conformity of persons to the patterns of the settings in which their behavior occurs is that there are, after all, *some* interior motivational and cognitive constancies across persons which interact with a limited and fixed array of environmental input from a setting, producing a limited range of behavior across inhabitants within settings. However, work by Willems (1964) and by Gump (1964) show that this is not the case for a wide variety of settings. Their findings show that the everyday situations within which people live (restaurants, basketball games, band concerts) do not provide inhabitants with a limited and fixed array of environmental inputs, but with inputs that vary widely in accordance with the differing motives and cognitions of the inhabitants. Furthermore, the inputs vary in such a way that the characteristic behavior patterns of the settings are generated and maintained *in spite of* the great variety of interior conditions inhabitants bring to settings. According to these findings, the environments in which people live are homeostatic systems which maintain their characteristic patterns

---

[2] See Barker (1963a, 1963b, 1965), Barker and Gump (1964), Barker and Wright (1955), and Ragle, Barker, and Johnson (1967).

within preset limits by means of control mechanisms. This, after all, is not surprising; we all experience it. On the turnpike, when our speed deviates to the slow side, we receive recurring physical and social inputs to speed up; and if we do not do so sufficiently, we are eventually ejected from the turnpike (by a rear end crash or by a traffic officer); when our speed deviates to the fast side, we receive recurring physical and social inputs to slow down; and again, if we do not do so sufficiently, we are finally ejected by a head-on crash, by missing a curve, or by a traffic officer. It is important to note that the turnpike is not concerned with the sources of the deviancy of its vehicular components. Slowness because of an overloaded and underpowered car is just as unacceptable to a turnpike as slowness because of an overly cautious driver.

Our data show that people and other entities are components of the environmental units they inhabit in the same way that a generator is a component of an engine and a bat of a ball game. Real-life settings are *eco-behavioral* entities,[3] and the concepts and principles which explicate them are utterly alien to those that explicate their component parts, such as the behavior of individual persons.

Here is one instance of many environmental differences that two towns—Midwest, Kansas and Yoredale, Yorkshire—provide their inhabitants (Barker & Barker, 1963; Schoggen, Barker & Barker, 1963; Barker & Barker, 1961; Barker, 1960; Barker, Barker, & Ragle, 1967). Some settings require child components; they coerce and incorporate children into their ongoing programs. This is true of 10 percent of Midwest's settings and of 18 percent of Yoredale's settings. Other settings do not tolerate child components; they have child-proof boundaries and they eject any children who manage to enter. This is true of 8 percent of the settings of Midwest and of 31 percent of the settings of Yoredale. This environmental difference between the towns makes a great difference in the behavior and experiences of the children of Midwest and Yoredale, and a complete analysis of the psychology of all inhabitants of the towns would not account for it. Forces for and against children are properties of a town's settings (its school classes, its pubs, its courts, its Golden Age Club), and not of its individual citizens. Transposing the children of Midwest to Yoredale, and vice versa, would immediately transform their behavior in respect to the parts of the towns they would enter and avoid, despite their unchanged motives and cognitions. The forces of a community's settings vis-à-vis children are examples of the power of environmental units over behavior, of their superordinate position with

---

[3] Eco-behavioral as in *ecological* and *behavioral*.

respect to their human components, and of the need for an eco-behavioral science independent of psychology.

Facilities for an Eco-Behavioral Science

The eco-behavioral science that will answer the pressing questions society faces today requires, above all, concepts and theories appropriate to the phenomena involved. But these will not arise *de novo*; they will be grounded upon empirical data concerning the patterns of events within the psychologist-free settings where people live their lives. Special facilities are required in order to obtain these data.

THE NEED FOR ARCHIVES

By definition, phenomena cannot be induced to occur by an investigator if his purpose is to study them under natural, that is, scientist-free, conditions. Since many important phenomena occur infrequently under these conditions, it may require long periods of observation and be expensive to secure adequate instances of them. This is a fact that confronts every science in connection with its ecological investigations. The yield of data is low, for example, in studies of earthquakes, migrating birds, and bank failures. It is taxing and expensive to wait for earthquakes and bank failures and to search for banded birds. Nevertheless, geologists, biologists, and economists continue to investigate these phenomena, and it is worthwhile asking how they do it.

For one thing, these scientists do not consider infrequent occurrence as unfortunate, as dross; they accept it for what it is, namely, one attribute of a phenomenon that must be recorded accurately along with its other attributes, and one that must be taken into account by theory. For seismological theory, it is probably as important to know the nature and distribution of the earthquakes of the Middle West of the U. S. as of the more frequent earthquakes of the West Coast. Here, then, is a central operational difference between experimental and ecological science: experiments alter phenomena of infrequent occurrence and make them frequent; in this state they can be studied efficiently. In ecological investigations, where phenomena are studied *in situ,* nature is the only inducer and the investigator can be only a transducer; so far as frequent instances are concerned, efficiency is impossible to plan and program. More basic, however, for ecological research is the necessity of recording instances *in situ*. This requires both temporally and geographically contextual data that are difficult and expensive to obtain.

One way other sciences facilitate the study of ecological phenomena is by accumulating, preserving, and making generally accessible a pool of data relating to the phenomena. Archives and museums of primary data are standard research facilities of sciences with productive ecological programs. Through this arrangement, a lone seismographer, ornithologist, or student of banking has access to many data which he is free to study and analyze in his own way according to his own theories. This has not been possible for psychologists; the science has been almost devoid of data archives. But even more basic is the fact that psychology has had no methods for securing archival data. It has been almost exclusively an experimental science, and the data of experiments have little value for archives. The inputs and constraints imposed by experiments are usually so uniquely tied to the intentions of the investigator, to his hypothesis for example, that a new investigator has little freedom to ask new questions of the data. About all that one can do with the data of others' experiments is to try to replicate them. Although it is an essential task, replication is nonetheless, a merely technical one. Of course, the attributes of experimental data which limit their archival value are not defects. Quite the contrary, in fact; to the degree that experiments arrange inputs and channel outputs to answer specific questions they are good experiments. Good experimental data are problem centered and theory guided, and their significance is usually limited by the particular problem or theory that prompted and guided their generation.

The converse is true for ecological studies. Here, the task of the investigator and his apparatus is to translate phenomena and their descriptions without alteration into the language of data. In their most adequate form, ecological data are phenomena centered and they are atheoretical. It has been a heresy in some quarters to speak of atheoretical data. Experience has taught us, however, that even within a purely psychological context, atheoretical data can be obtained and are of value. About fifteen years ago, 18 full-day records of children's behavior and situation were collected at the Midwest Psychological Field Station. Although we had plans, guided by theories, for *analyzing* these records, the plans and theories did not guide the *making* of the records. Our only intention was to translate the stream of behavior into a verbal record with as much completeness as possible. We made our own use of the records, and made them available to others (Barker, 1963a, 1963b; Schoggen, Barker, & Barker, 1963; Barker, Wright, Barker, & Schoggen, 1961). Over the years, ten other studies leading to theses or to publications have been based almost wholly upon these records, and other studies are in progress. In addition, the records have been used for pilot studies and as a source of illustrative material by a number of scholars, and they have provided data for more than a hundred undergraduate projects ranging from studies of children's attitudes toward foods to tests of Freudian theories of mother-son and father-daughter relations. Most of the subsequent studies have been made by investigators who had no part in assembling the records; they concern problems that were far from the minds of the data collectors; and they involve a multitude of theories and analytical procedures. There is no reason to think that these specimens of individual behavior will not continue to be of use in connection with problems not yet conceived. This experience has taught us that data that are dross for one investigator are gold for another.

Thus an eco-behavioral science must have data archives. The psychologists involved in this development will have much to learn about collecting, preserving, and retrieving ecological data. Undoubtedly, there are many such data suitable for archives mouldering unknown and unused in files and storerooms; on the other hand, the new audio-visual recording techniques threaten to overwhelm a data depository with useless material. The problem of standards for atheoretical, phenomena centered data is a difficult and important one; it deserves the best efforts of psychologists and eco-behavioral scientists.[4]

THE NEED FOR FIELD STATIONS

Ecological scientists are not a source of input to or constraint upon the phenomena they study; they do not instigate the occurrence of the phenomena with which they deal. They must, therefore, set up shop in regions where their phenomena are rich and accessible; and their shops must be manned and equipped appropriately. Field stations and observatories are regular features of the establishments of other sciences. An eco-behavioral science must also have its Woods Holes and Mount Wilsons. In our experience, ecological data are, in general, more difficult to procure than experimental data. Special facilities are required; and the locating, equipping, and manning of a field station is as specialized and as expensive as establishing a clinic or an experimental laboratory.

Two different problems are involved in the collection of ecological data. One concerns specific data-generating procedures, for example, observing and making records, taking photographs, making recordings, using documents and records. The other problem relates to general policies and

---

[4] McGuire (1967a, 1967b) has recently taken a similar stance on the importance of data archives, and has discussed archives already available and investigative means for expanding them and improving their quality.

programs to be followed in establishing and operating a facility for gathering nonexperimental, eco-behavioral data. I shall consider the last problem, although I can do little more than list some of the factors we have found to be of importance.

A field station should be within a bounded community or institution; it should have a locale which constitutes the universe of phenomena studied at the station. This locale should have identifying features in terms of common parameters of its larger geo-cultural context; it should be within a particular suburb, central city, rural community, ghetto, industrial plant, school, and so forth. There should be no constraints placed within the locale by the investigators. The locale should be of appropriate size, that is, comprehendable from the level of individuals to the most inclusive level; in the beginning it is essential to avoid very large systems. A field station must have a longer life expectancy than the psychological and eco-behavioral phenomena it investigates, and many of these phenomena have long temporal durations, for instance, technological change. Furthermore, the collection of data relevant to stable conditions is often a long-time process. A field station is *not* a project; it is a program.

The relation of the station and its staff to the locale it investigates is of utmost importance. There must be access without interference, acceptance without reaction. The ecologist-citizen relation is not a physician-patient, experimenter-subject, or counselor-client relation. It is a new relation yet to be defined, but some aspects of it are clear. The ecologist-citizen relation is a privileged relation based on trust. Not all problems studied and techniques used must be reported, although, to meet the requirements of acceptable research, they must be reportable. The field station must operate within the mores and tolerances of the community; this is a part of the essential policy of a field station of respecting and not altering its phenomena. As a consequence, some studies and techniques are not admissible. The ecologist-citizen relation imposes personnel requirements upon a field station. It must have expert staff members whose jobs include maintaining communication between station and community, defining the functions of the field station, and especially, differentiating the field station from common conceptions of clinics and laboratories. The station must have local staff members for field work; this provides some protection against misunderstandings. Local residence is essential for many staff members, and they must participate in community affairs. Publications must be in objective, conceptual terms, and they must be nonevaluative. Station-community trust and mutual acceptance are the first requirements, and these must be maintained and renewed by continual effort. Although I have only highlighted certain guidelines here, their importance can be documented by both the successes and failures of field station efforts.

Some may think these requirements very restricting. Our experience in Kansas and Yorkshire is that they impose fewer limitations than skeptics suspect. This is the case, in part, because a field station has sources of support in the locale also. Citizens are seriously concerned with the problems on which eco-behavioral field stations work, and the field station brings some demonstrable aspects of status and substance to the community. One conclusion seems obvious. A university campus is usually about as suitable a place for a psychological field station as it is for a biological field station or an astronomical observatory, unless, of course, the school, itself, is the station's target locale.

METHODS OF DATA ANALYSIS

One of the purposes of experimental techniques is to arrange the data that issue from data-generating systems so they will fit prevailing machines, formulae, and concepts. So, we have forced-choice tests, five-point scales, normalized distributions, equated control groups, and so on. These are not sins. They facilitate the purposes of experiments: to solve problems and test hypotheses which the investigators bring to the data. But, if one's intention is to explore behavior and its naturally occurring environment, it is the phenomena that must dictate the choices, the scales, and the distributions. It is our experience that psychological measurement experts do not know statistical and analytical techniques for dealing with natural phenomena, even where the techniques are available from other sciences. We need mathematical innovators and we need textbooks and handbooks of data-reduction methods culled from quantitative botany, demography, geography, physiology, and economics. When those who work on eco-behavioral problems do not have the analytical tools they need, they inevitably cast data in the molds of experimental psychology, molds that often destroy the very nature of the phenomena they are investigating.

Here, then, are three facility-operations problems that arise directly from the fundamental nature of eco-behavioral research: (a) an archival problem, (b) a field station problem, and (c) an analytical problem. These problems are great, but the possibility of arriving at scientifically meaningful and socially useful results are also great, and they justify the commitment of intellect, effort, and money to the task.

REFERENCES

Allport, G. W. *Pattern and growth in personality.* New York: Holt, Rinehart and Winston, 1964.

Ashton, M. An ecological study of the stream of behavior. Unpublished master's thesis, University of Kansas, 1964.

Barker, R. G. Ecology and motivation. In M. R. Jones (Ed.), *Nebraska symposium on motivation*. Lincoln: University of Nebraska Press, 1960. Pp. 1–49.

Barker, R. G. On the nature of the environment. *Journal of Social Issues,* 1963, **19,** No. 4, 17–38. (a)

Barker, R. G. (Ed.) *The stream of behavior.* New York: Appleton-Century-Crofts, 1963. (b)

Barker, R. G. Explorations in ecological psychology. *American Psychologist,* 1965, **20,** 1–14.

Barker, R. G., & Barker, L. S. Behavior units for the comparative study of cultures. In B. Kaplan (Ed.), *Studying personality cross-culturally.* New York: Harper & Row, 1961. Pp. 457–476.

Barker, R. G., & Barker, L. S. Sixty-five and over. In R. H. Williams, C. Tibbitts, & W. Donahue (Eds.), *Processes of aging.* Englewood Cliffs, N.J.: Prentice-Hall, 1963. Pp. 246–271.

Barker, R. G., Barker, L. S., & Ragle, D. M. The churches of Midwest, Kansas and Yoredale, Yorkshire: Their contributions to the environments of the towns. In W. Gore & L. Hodapp (Eds.), *Change in the small community.* New York: Friendship Press, 1967. Pp. 155–189.

Barker, R. G., & Gump, P. V. *Big school, small school.* Stanford, Calif.: Stanford University Press, 1964.

Barker, R. G., & Wright, H. F. *Midwest and its children.* New York: Harper & Row, 1955.

Barker, R. G., Wright, H. F., Barker, L. S., & Schoggen, M. *Specimen records of American and English children.* Lawrence, Kan.: University of Kansas Press, 1961.

Brunswik, E. The conceptual framework of psychology. *International encyclopedia of unified science.* Vol. 1, Part 2. Chicago: University of Chicago Press, 1955. Pp. 656–750.

Gump, P. V. Environmental guidance of the classroom behavioral system. In B. J. Biddle & W. J. Ellena (Eds.), *Contemporary research on teacher effectiveness.* New York: Holt, Rinehart and Winston, 1964. Pp. 165–195.

Leeper, R. W. Learning and the fields of perception, motivation, and personality. In S. Koch (Ed.), *Psychology: A study of a science.* Vol. 5. New York: McGraw-Hill, 1963. Pp. 365–487.

Lewin, K. *Field theory in social science.* New York: Harper & Row, 1951.

McGuire, W. J. Some impending reorientations in social psychology: Some thoughts provoked by Kenneth Ring. *Journal of Experimental Social Psychology,* 1967, **3,** 124–139.

McGuire, W. J. Theory-oriented research in natural settings: The best of both worlds for social psychology. Paper read at a symposium, Department of Psychology, Pennsylvania State University, University Park, Pennsylvania, May, 1967.

Ragle, D. M., Barker, R. G., & Johnson, A. Measuring extension's impact. *Journal of Cooperative Extension,* 1967, **5,** No. 3, 178–186.

Raush, H. L., Dittmann, A. T., & Taylor, T. J. Person, setting and change in social interaction. *Human Relations*, 1959, **12**, 361–378.

Raush, H. L., Dittmann, A. T., & Taylor, T. J. Person, setting and change in social interaction: II. A normal control study. *Human Relations*, 1960, **13**, 305–332.

Schoggen, M., Barker, L. S., & Barker, R. G. Structure of the behavior of American and English children. In R. G. Barker (Ed.), *The stream of behavior*. New York: Appleton-Century-Crofts, 1963. Pp. 160–168.

Willems, E. P. Forces toward participation in behavior settings. In R. G. Barker & P. V. Gump, *Big school, small school*. Stanford, Calif.: Stanford University Press, 1964. Pp. 115–135.

3

Planning a Rationale for Naturalistic Research

EDWIN P. WILLEMS

> Let us note that "methodological" and "logical" are not synonyms. Good methodological practice is not always a logical matter. It is, in truth, usually an empirical matter. Effective methodology is largely determined by what works. Often it is the case that if we were wise enough, or clairvoyant enough, to determine good methodology a priori, we would have no need for the methodology; we could intuit the knowledge that the method is to subserve. (Spiker, 1966, p. 49)

THIS SHORT PASSAGE by Spiker mentions two fundamental methodological propositions: One, which will not be elaborated upon here, suggests that specific methods and techniques of research *serve* investigators. That is, specific methods and techniques are tools, or means, in the research enterprise, and their appropriateness and meaning are determined in part by the questions, purposes, and problems that guide the enterprise. The second proposition, that good methodological practice is usually an empirical matter and "is largely determined by what works," provides a more direct point of departure and will be a continual guideline for this essay.

Discussions of the relative merits and usefulness of naturalistic research methods, as against explicitly arranged, controlled, manipulated laboratory methods, have a peculiar tendency to deteriorate into polemics and petulant, empty argumentation, a tendency that sometimes spills over into the published literature. It is common to hear words like "rigor" vs. "sloppiness," "control of variance" vs. "meaningfulness," "sterile" vs. "true-to-life," "rich" vs. "nitpicking," and "scientific" vs. "anecdotal." These words themselves point to some of the reasons for the controversies, but there are at least two additional reasons that are not so commonly recognized. The first of these reasons is sometimes called the "tool illusion"

(Baker, 1963, p. 164); it is what Professor Egon Guba once called the "law of the hammer." The law says: If you give a child a hammer, things to be pounded become the most important things around. In the society of research investigators, the analogue to this law points to the fact that we often not only allow our favorite methods and techniques to dictate the choice and merits of our own research problems, but we often let our own favorite methods dictate and evaluate the merits of someone else's research problem. Believing in the inherent, a priori correctness and scientific efficacy of certain methods, we prescribe and proscribe, praise and blame.

A second reason for much of the empty disputation about methods is the ambiguity of the word, "natural." Too often we hear the word "natural" used in the sense of "real" and "true," as against "unreal" and "untrue," or even "unnatural." Is the finding from a naturalistic study more "real" or more "true" than the finding from a laboratory experiment? It is this question that stimulates much of the heat of methodological argument. This author, for one, cannot answer it on an a priori basis. However, as I shall try to show later, there can be specifiable differences in the empirical findings from the two modes of research, and these differences suggest some important scientific issues.

This essay begins with the assumption that naturalistic research uniquely serves certain scientific purposes, and the essay is motivated by the belief that the reasons for choosing naturalistic methods, or the rationale for naturalistic methods, can be planned and stated in non-speculative, nonpolemical methodological terms, that is, in terms of "what works" for specific investigative purposes. The major part of the essay will attempt to state, by capitalizing heavily on published research, some of the components of such a rationale. However, before proceeding to that discussion, it is important to clarify what is meant by "naturalistic research." Thus, the next section will present a framework for describing research activities in such a way that the naturalistic mode of research can be viewed in relation to other modes.

A Characterization of Research Activities

One immediate problem in discussing naturalistic research is to sharpen the meaning of the adjective, "naturalistic," so that it denotes something relevant to the process of empirical investigation. It is common to define naturalistic research as research on natural phenomena. Not only does this definition stumble on a circularity, but, as Raush suggests (Chapter 5 of this volume), it is fruitless to try to locate the criteria of naturalness in the events and phenomena that one is studying. Frequency of occurrence is one such phenomenon-based criterion that leads nowhere. For example, tonsillectomies might occur more frequently than paralysis-inducing accidents, but would not necessarily be judged more natural. Degree of human artifice is a second phenomenon-based criterion that breaks down. For example, a visit to a dentist involves a high degree of human instigation and arrangement, but probably would not be judged less natural than a tornado, at least for purposes of research. Finally, the degree to which a situation or event is true to human nature might be invoked. However, this criterion begs the question of what is true to human nature.

One of the issues running through the search for phenomenon-based criteria of naturalness is that for some people, that which is natural is good and that which is artificial is bad. I submit that in behavioral research, naturalness or naturalism, if we can speak of it at all, is a function of *what the investigator does.* That is, when discussing behavioral research, we should disavow the value judgments and their accompanying search for phenomenon-based criteria of naturalness and rather focus *descriptively* upon the conduct of research itself. On this view, phenomena that are highly unusual, occur very infrequently, and involve a high degree of human artifice and arrangement can be the targets of naturalistic investigation. In other words, I would argue (a) that it is possible to differentiate research activities in terms of the part the investigator plays, or where he places himself, in the process of research, and (b) since we can then speak jointly of what an investigator does and what he finds, this differentiation is more useful than focusing only on the phenomena he studies.

A number of writers on methodology have discussed and categorized the strategies of research (for example, Scott & Wertheimer, 1962; Underwood, 1957; Shontz, 1965; Kerlinger, 1964; Barker, 1964a, 1965; Gump & Kounin, 1959–1960; Willems, 1965; Campbell & Stanley, 1963; Sears, 1957; Webb, Campbell, Schwartz, & Sechrest, 1966). From this literature we can abstract the suggestion that the set of activities an investigator actually engages in while conducting his research falls somewhere in a two-dimensional descriptive space. The first dimension, which is most frequently thought of in differentiating research activities, describes *the degree of the investigator's influence upon, or manipulation of, the antecedent conditions of the behavior studied,* on the assumption that the degree of such influence or manipulation may vary from high to low, or from much to none. The second dimension, which is less commonly considered than the first, describes *the degree to which units are imposed by the investigator upon the behavior studied.*

Figure 3–1 displays these descriptive dimensions in orthogonal relation. Entries on the body of the figure denote sectors that will be used below for illustrative purposes. The figure represents a descriptive view of research activities in the following way. Assuming that the target of an investigation is some behavioral phenomenon, it is possible to describe two separate, though often interdependent, ways in which the investigator may function in the process of obtaining behavioral data: (a) by influencing or arranging the antecedent conditions of the behavior, and (b) by imposing restrictions or limitations on the range or spectrum of response, that is, the behavior itself. Furthermore, as described by Figure 3–1, each of these functions can vary on a continuum.

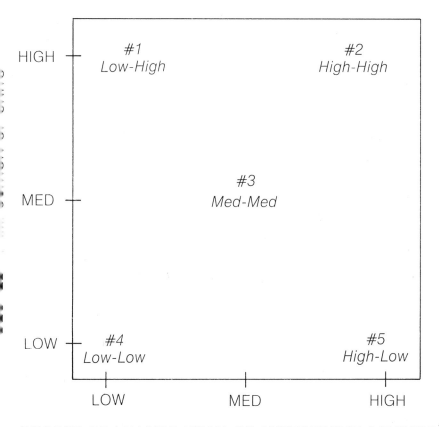

FIGURE 3.1. *A space for describing research activities.*

How the two-dimensional space describes research activities can be shown by a concrete example. Several years ago, we conducted a study of the reasons for, or pulls toward, attending school activities reported by high school students (Willems, 1964; Willems & Willems, 1965). We selected five specific nonclass activities in several schools and tried three techniques for gathering data. In the first technique, we asked the students, in standardized individual interviews, "What, if any, were for you real reasons for or pulls toward attending this activity?" and recorded their responses. In the second technique, we presented students with decks of cards, each of which contained a predetermined reason for attending, and asked the students to sort out those that were, for them, reasons for attending each of the five activities. In the third technique, the predetermined items were printed on checklists, and students were asked to check those that were, for them, reasons for attending. Each of these three techniques yielded data on the number of reasons for attending five selected activities. When we correlated the number of such responses to the number of activities the students had actually attended, the interview data yielded the highest correlations, the card sort data the next highest, and the checklist data the lowest. In terms of the descriptive space, we had not manipulated the antecedent conditions of attendance at school activities and reasons for attending ("Low" on the abscissa), but we had varied the imposition upon, or restriction of, response units (ranging on the ordinate). The interview method, the technique with the least restriction of response alternatives, yielded data with the highest predictive validity. Thus, we had a behavioral, empirical, and relatively nonpolemical basis for choosing among techniques, and we ended up using one that tended toward the Low-Low sector of the descriptive space.

Does this descriptive space actually describe anything? To answer this question, I shall try to place five published studies in the five areas denoted on Figure 3–1. A study by Bechtel (1967) can be placed at #1 (Low-High). Bechtel developed an electronic apparatus called a *hodometer* to record the use of space in an art gallery. The hodometer is composed of mats, each one-foot square and sensitive to pressure. The mats, each with a micro switch connected to a counter, are laid on the floor and covered by a carpet, thereby offering an unobtrusive tabulation of the occupancy of space in the room. The important point for present purposes is that under conditions where he did not manipulate or arrange the room environment, as in his study of an art gallery, Bechtel's program rates low on manipulation of antecedent conditions and high on imposition of units, in other words, the number of micro switch contacts per room area. Second, a recent study of the effect of perceptual set on figural aftereffects (Willems,

1967a) can be rated at #2 (High-High). The main independent variables were induced and constrained by sequences of prearranged stimuli (antecedent conditions) and responses were restricted to perception of vertical bars on a standard test figure. Third, position #3 (Med-Med) on the figure is more difficult to fill because of possible disagreements over what constitutes a middle range on each dimension. However, a study by Verplanck (1955) provides a first approximation. Verplanck arranged for his research assistants to engage persons in conversation during the course of their everyday affairs, and to give positive and negative reinforcement or no response to statements of opinion. This procedure seems to represent a middle range of manipulation of antecedent conditions of the verbalizations and a middle range of imposition of units upon the verbalizations. Sector #3 probably describes what are commonly called field experiments, of which there are many possible candidates, for example, Lefkowitz, Blake, and Mouton, 1955; Bryan and Test, 1967. Fourth, position #4 (Low-Low) is less difficult to fill. Purcell and Brady's (1966) use of unobtrusive electronic monitoring equipment to record the intact verbal behavior of children in their everyday routines falls into sector #4. Many examples of what is commonly called naturalistic observation would fall here. Finally, Barker, Dembo, and Lewin's (1943) study of frustration and regression can be seen to exemplify sector #5 (High-Low) on the figure. Here, the investigators carefully sequentialized and manipulated the antecedents of play and goal blockage, but obtained rich, open-ended, descriptive records of behavior from which to infer frustration and constructiveness of play.

Other published investigations and a host of hypothetical ones could be described in terms of Figure 3–1. However, there are other important implications of viewing research activities in general, and naturalism in particular, in terms of what the investigator does. First, as traditionally conceived, the laboratory experiment is a strategy through which an investigator *produces* phenomena and makes them occur at his behest, at will. In contrast, naturalistic study, as traditionally conceived, is a strategy by which an investigator records, or commits to researchable form, phenomena that he does not produce or bring about. In terms of the two-dimensional space, I submit that in the controversies over the merits of manipulated laboratory research and naturalistic research, what is usually called laboratory experimentation falls in the High-High sector, and what is usually called naturalistic research falls in the Low-Low sector. That is, the controversies usually focus on the most extreme cases, and upon cases that represent only a small portion of the possibilities.

Second, and perhaps more important, the descriptive space avoids arbitrary dichotomies, and suggests that the manner in which the investigator functions in the process of generating data—and therefore what is often called the degree of "naturalness"—falls on continua whose various points are so difficult to differentiate that they cannot be defended with finality and rigor. McGuire (1967), in the process of describing some emerging trends in social psychology, reminds us that "experiment," in its etymologically correct usage, means "to test, to try" (p. 128), pointing up the arbitrary nature of most attempts to encapsulate research strategies. I take it that what we commonly call naturalistic observation, field experiment, and laboratory experiment, would fall on the main diagonal from Low-Low through Med-Med to High-High on Figure 3–1, respectively, and that the degree of "quasiness" in Campbell and Stanley's treatment of experimental and quasi-experimental design refers to a similar dimension (1963, p. 64). However, if the figure is a tenable means for characterizing research activities, then it is clear that the main diagonal describes only a small proportion of the possible set of research activities, that is, our usual categories correlate manipulation and imposition of units too highly and exclude a great number of possibilities. Perhaps, our usual ways of viewing the alternatives of naturalistic research and other modes are far too restricted.

Naturalistic Research: Why and When?

With the two-dimensional characterization of research in mind, the remainder of this essay deals with the question, "So what?" As has been suggested in the introduction of this volume, the rationale and defense of manipulational, laboratory research strategies has an abundant literature, while the explicit rationalization of naturalistic research activities is spotty and incomplete. What are some of the issues, concerns, or components that should go into planning a rationale that would lead an investigator to choose methods tending toward low manipulation and low impositions of units? I shall discuss one finite, beginning set of such issues, a set which is neither necessarily independent nor exhaustive. For convenience, I shall use the term "naturalistic" to refer to studies and methods that tend toward the low end on either or both of the two dimensions.

EVERYDAY BEHAVIORAL ACHIEVEMENT

One legitimate scientific question which leads to a choice among alternative methods is "What kinds of actual everyday behavioral achievements do persons make?" For example, explicitly controlled laboratory experimentation has made great strides in untangling the theoretical issues involved in the perception of size and distance (see Epstein, Park, & Casey, 1961). However, Brunswik pointed out (Brunswik, 1955; Postman & Tolman, 1959) that if one asks to what extent persons actually achieve veridical perception of size in their everyday lives, something else than laboratory experimentation is called for. For Brunswik, this question of everyday functional achievement dictated a choice of methods by which he asked a subject, during her daily rounds of activity, to periodically judge the linear dimensions of objects at which she happened to be looking. The subject achieved a correlation of .99 between the physical size of objects and her estimates of size.

In a second example, Imai and Garner (1965) studied perceptual classification of stimuli that could be classified in various ways. When they dictated, or controlled, the attribute by which subjects were to classify, they obtained clear, lawful data on the extent to which the subjects did what they were told to do. However, only when Imai and Garner allowed subjects relatively free rein in classifying did they discover what strategies the subjects themselves chose in achieving perceptual classification.

Jay (1965), in her extensive summary of field studies of monkeys and apes, points out that while many investigations demonstrate the importance of learning, perception, affection, curiosity, and so on, the adaptive functions of and everyday achievement within each of these aspects of behavior become ". . . clear only in a free-ranging social situation where the advantages of being an intelligent, perceptive, affectionate, curious animal can be seen as they cannot be in a laboratory or cage." (p. 526)

These examples illustrate a principle that might be included in a rationale for naturalistic methods: If the research question is what kinds of behavioral achievements persons or animals make when left to their own resources, the methods used should involve at least low manipulation and perhaps low imposition of units.

DISTRIBUTION OF PSYCHOLOGY'S PHENOMENA IN NATURE

Closely related to the study of everyday functional achievements is another concern of any science: the distribution of its phenomena in nature. To the zoologist, the chemist, the archeologist, and the geologist, this arm of science is a familiar one. However, apart from some sociological data, census tract data, mortality tables, some educational records, selective service summaries, and the norms of a restricted set of psychological tests, little is known about the distribution of psychology's phenomena outside of the experimental laboratory. Barker (1964b) says:

> Every beginning textbook tells the student that failure and frustration are important behavior phenomena, and that rewards and punishments are important attributes of man's environment. But where is the information on the forms, abundance, and the distribution of these important phenomena outside the very limited, specially contrived situation of psychological laboratories and clinics? As a psychologist, what answer should I give a layman seeking information from me, as a scientific expert, on the occurrence among men of frustration, for example? To what handbook of data should I refer him? (p. 2)

We know little about the distribution of humor, sadness, problem solving, disappointment, frustration, dependency training, cooperation, commitment, initiation of social contacts, cue learning, and interval judgments, to name just a few possibilities. While the documentation of such phenomena is a time-consuming problem, it is an empirical one, as Allport's (1934) success at documenting degree of conformity in a wide array of everyday circumstances would suggest.

An example from a classic psychological area is pertinent here. In their study of frustration and regression, Barker, Dembo, and Lewin (1943) brought children who ranged in age from two to five years to the laboratory and allowed them to play with a set of attractive toys. Later, in the same room, the children were again allowed to play, but certain attractive toys were now inaccessible to them because a wire screen barrier had been dropped across the room. Under these conditions, frustration of such magnitude was induced that the children regressed, that is, the constructiveness of their play decreased markedly, and they reverted to modes of play typical of much younger children. One might well ask, however, how are frustration and regression distributed in the everyday lives of children?

Written narrative accounts describing continuous, day-long observations of at least 18 children in their everyday surroundings and routines are available at the Midwest Psychological Field Station of the University of Kansas. These *specimen records* (Barker, 1963, 1964a; Barker & Wright, 1955; Barker, Wright, Barker, & Schoggen, 1961; Schoggen, 1964; Wright, 1967) describe the complete days of the children, that is, their behaviors, conversations, interactions, and locations. Fawl (1963) used 16 of these records, representing 16 days, or over 200 hours of observation of children, and analyzed them for the occurrence of goal blockage, frustration, and accompanying negative effect. Fawl was surprised to find relatively few occurrences of blocked goals, and when they did occur, to find that they usually failed to produce an apparent disturbance on the part of the child. Disturbance, when it did occur, was mild in intensity. In other words, in over 200 hours of the everyday lives of children, there was a surprisingly infrequent occurrence of a phenomenon that has an important place in some theories of child development and personality. Methods involving no manipulation of antecedent conditions and a content coding of behavior units inherent in a narrative record told Fawl something about the distribution of one of psychology's phenomena in nature.

Dyck (1963), also using the specimen records, found that when social contacts occurred between parents and the children, parents initiated 34 percent of them, and that when such contacts occurred between teachers and the same children, teachers initiated 73 percent of them. A controlled laboratory experiment, by definition and purpose, says little or nothing about such everyday distributions.

BEHAVORIAL REPERTOIRES

A third issue, although it is closely related to the first two, requires separate mention because it is so often overlooked entirely, and because the importance of naturalistic research methods in its fulfillment is so often overlooked. To Kessen (1967), the issue is the fundamental importance of a complete and careful description of infant behavior in general as a context for understanding any particular aspect of infant behavior. To Rheingold (1967), it is to become thoroughly acquainted with the "natural" (p. 288) behavior of the organism one wishes to study, where such thorough acquaintance is an explicitly stated aim of research. To Breland and Breland (1966), it is the importance of knowing the animal one is studying, as well as knowing the many things occurring in the animal's world that have never been observed in the psychological laboratory (p. 113). To Sells (Chapter 1 of this volume), it is the importance of documenting the behavioral repertoire of the organism under study, whether human or infrahuman, and the placing of the repertoire into phylogenetic perspective, or in a classificatory "periodic table" of behavior. The issue can be stated as follows: (a) It is at all times scientifically worthwhile, and sometimes scientifically crucial, to have a description of the behavioral repertoire of the species, or particular age range in a species, that one is studying. (b) Observation of the species in its natural habitat is important in developing this acquaintance. Such observation, called an *ethogram* (Hess, 1962, p. 160) when it covers the life cycle of the species, is one earmark of ethology. As Hess points out, since captive animals and laboratory studies often produce "abnormal stereotyped behavior" (p. 160), naturalistic research provides the crucial data. For a discussion of how important the information on behavioral repertoires and ecology can be, see Klinghammer's (1967) analysis of early experience and mating behavior in altricial birds.

THE PROBLEM OF YIELD

A fourth issue for inclusion in a rationale for naturalistic methods is closely related to the everyday distribution of phenomena, but is important because it is often turned into a criticism of naturalistic research. The criticism often runs something like this: After all, as scientists, we are seeking general laws of behavior. We must assure ourselves of adequate empirical yield from our studies in terms of frequency and intensity of occurrence. Many, if not all, naturalistic studies, when compared to laboratory experiments, involve a disproportionate amount of time and effort relative to data yield. Therefore, the optimal set of methods fall in the area of laboratory experiments, where phenomena can be arranged and produced.

A demonstration of just this problem is a study reported by Gump and Kounin (1959–1960). These investigators had made extensive studies of classroom settings, seeking what effects disciplinary or control techniques had upon children other than the target child, and they wished to extend the study to other contexts, in this case a public camp. They chose two camp settings for study: a cabin clean-up period and a rest period. One observer took a specimen record of the behavior of adult cabin leaders, and others took specimen records of individual campers. Over a six-week period, involving six observers, about 46 hours of camper behavior were recorded. The total yield of responses by nontarget children was about one incident for every 18 pages of verbal record. Such a low frequency is an interesting finding in itself, but it fits the criticism of economy of effort and yield. How shall such a criticism be answered? In a rationale for naturalistic methods, the answer should be an empirical one, if possible, and the answer is that the economy-of-yield argument is not unidirectional; it does not apply uniquely to naturalistic studies.

A concrete example was reported by Kounin (1961) where the purpose was to study the effects of various types of control techniques by teachers upon students who ranged from low to high on commitment to the task. After carefully training their experimental teachers, the investigators arranged for a sample of adolescents to come to the university campus during the summer, for pay, to serve as experimental students.

However, the investigators were completely unable to induce low commitment under this experimental arrangement; the yield for that cell of their design was zero. In intact, naturally-occurring classrooms, they were able to find students low in commitment. The problem of ratio of effort to yield is not unique to naturalistic studies.

ARTIFICIALITY: TYING AND UNTYING OF VARIABLES

One more question in this highly interrelated set of issues is the one of artificiality of findings and conditions of investigation. One of the favorite arguments against manipulational laboratory research by the proponents of naturalistic research is that the conditions of investigation, and therefore the findings, are artificial in the typical laboratory study. The problem with this accusation is that it is just as value laden and difficult to document as accusations of "unnatural" and "unreal." What are the specifiable *criteria* of artificiality? Perhaps more important, when would one choose to engage in research that rates high or low on so-called artificiality? Egon Brunswik dwelt at length on this problem and stated it in terms of "tying and untying of variables" in his critiques of manipulational laboratory research (Brunswik, 1955; Postman & Tolman, 1959). In Brunswik's terms, artificial tying occurs when variables are allowed or made to vary together in ways that persons never confront in their everyday lives, whereas artificial untying occurs when natural covariations of variables are eliminated through experimental control. Several areas of research illustrate these points and indicate a fifth consideration in a rationale for naturalistic methods.

In one study (Gump & Kounin, 1959–1960), the investigators wanted again to test the effects of various kinds of control techniques by teachers upon nontarget students, this time in college classes. They arranged for student accomplices to come late to classes, and they trained teachers to sometimes try supportive, friendly reactions and sometimes threatening, punitive ones on the late arrivals. They found that punitive, as compared to supportive, reactions resulted in lowered ratings of the teachers' competence, likeability, and fairness by nontarget students. However, on later questionnaires, the investigators found that most of the students were surprised that one of their college teachers would take time out to correct a student for coming late to class. In their efforts to produce an experiment, they had taken a phenomenon out of its everyday context and combined several factors in ways that were not customary for those students.

Klinghammer (1967), discussing early experience, imprinting, and mate selection in altricial birds, points out that the theoretical controversy over what is a *substitute* imprinting object and what is a *primary* imprinting object has resulted from experimental procedures that provide animals with "additional experiences" (p. 39), or tied variables, that they never confront in a natural, or nonexperimental, situation. According to Kling-hammer, exposure to a potential mate from the birds' own species *and* exposure to an object outside the birds' species "is bound to have a disruptive effect on behavior." (p. 39)

Hovland's (1959) discussion of conflicting data from experimental and nonexperimental studies of attitude change and social influence can be seen as a detailed, analytical catalog of tied and untied variables. He begins by describing the kinds of discrepancies observed from the two types of studies and then lists some of the empirical factors that account for them. One example he cites is that in experimental studies influence attempts are tied to full exposure, or enforced exposure, while in naturalistic situations persons expose themselves to communications. (p. 9)

Another illuminating example is the study by Gump and Sutton-Smith (1955), who investigated the performances of poorly skilled boys when they were placed in more and less difficult roles in games. (This study is reviewed in detail by Sells in Chapter 1 of this volume.) All of these examples illustrate tying and untying of variables as a basis for choice among methods, but they also point to another issue, namely, the interplay, or interdependence, of manipulational research and naturalistic research. Manipulated experimentation has explored the range and extent of object substitution in imprinting in a way that naturalistic research cannot. It was only against the background of laboratory experiments that Hovland could catalog the methodological problems involved in research on attitude change. In Gump and Sutton-Smith's studies, the naturalistic methods documented what boys actually do in games, while the experiment, by forcing poorly skilled boys into difficult roles, suggested *why* they do what they do in games. That is, their manipulational research suggested that experiences of failure and negative social feedback upon performance are factors that keep poorly skilled boys out of the difficult roles. This reciprocity and interdependence of research strategies needs continuous re-emphasis. Neither strategy, manipulational nor naturalistic, is a weak derivative, poor second cousin, or second-rate supplement of the other. For example, field workers have observed hundreds of hours devoted to social play among monkeys and apes in the wild, thus documenting the occurrence and range of play in nature. However, it was Harlow's *experiments* that showed just how essential social play is to the development of behavior (see Mason, 1965). McGuire (1967) predicts a "shift from the laboratory to the natural environment as the setting for social psychological research in the coming years" (p. 132). However, he also predicts that this "redeployment . . . will be partial" (p. 132), and argues that the interdependence and reciprocity of strategies is too important to be lost.

REPLICABILITY

Leaving behind the rather interrelated issues of everyday behavioral achievement, the distribution of phenomena in nature, behavioral repertoires, economy and yield, and tying and untying of variables, several important issues remain to be considered in a rationale for naturalistic methods. One such issue is replicability. Naturalistic research is often criticized on the grounds that it is not replicable, and it often seems to be assumed that behavior represents a class of such unstable and complicated phenomena that unless it is constrained by experimental controls, it is not amenable to scientific study. Fortunately, replicability is not a matter for pure speculation to decide; it can be decided empirically, case by case, replication by replication.

Although relatively few studies of any methodological type are explicitly replicated, I can report on the replication of a study using methods that can be rated low on manipulation of antecedent conditions and somewhat less than high on imposition of units (Willems, 1967b). Under investigation was the relation of high school size and marginality of students to *sense of obligation*, that is, the personal, subjective disposition "I ought to . . ." or "I must . . ." with reference to participating in and helping with school activities. In 1961, and again in 1965, using a profile including IQ, grades, father's occupation, and father's and mother's education, I selected *marginal* (poorly suited) and *regular* (better suited) students in small and large schools. The differences in school size were kept similar in the two studies, but the sample sizes were 40 in 1961 and 80 in 1965. In both studies, subjects were asked, with reference to five selected non-class activities, "What, if any, were for you real reasons for or pulls toward attending?", and their verbatim responses were later coded as to sense of obligation. Figure 3–2 displays the results for numbers of responses indicating sense of obligation. With different samples, different sample sizes, four years apart, the results were similar, both in terms of overall pattern and absolute values on the response scales. Furthermore, in 1961 five out of ten large school marginal students reported no codable instance of sense of obligation at all, and in 1965 eight out of twenty reported none. In other words, the replication of findings was strong.

The major points here are (a) replication of specific *techniques* is possible for any public, scientific method, whether manipulational or

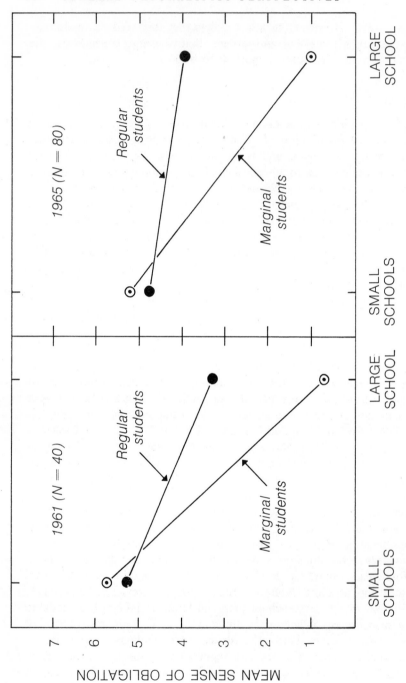

FIGURE 3.2. *Average numbers of responses indicating sense of obligation reported by regular and marginal students in small and large schools, four years apart.*

naturalistic, and (b) replicability of *findings* is a matter to be decided on the basis of the data, rather than on a speculative, a priori basis.

CONTROL GROUPS

Replicability seems to be an empirical matter, to be decided case by case for any class of methods, but naturalistic strategies are also frequently criticized on the grounds that too seldom do they, or too seldom can they, employ proper control groups. A good example of this problem is the long controversy over the effectiveness of psychotherapy, involving Eysenck (1952), Luborsky (1954), Rosenzweig (1954), DeCharms, Levy, and Wertheimer (1954), Kiesler (1966), and others. Kerlinger (1964) states the problem well when he suggests that the lack of explicit control over variables, the complexity of relations among variables, and absence of random assignment of subjects to research conditions in naturalistic studies often provide ". . . a loophole for other variables to crawl through" (p. 363). The problems here are classic ones in the literature on methodology, and they have received careful treatment by writers such as Underwood (1957) and Campbell and Stanley (1963). The effects of passage of time, effects of variables correlated with presumed independent variables, and the equivalence of comparison groups before the occurrence of some incident whose effects are being measured are but three considerations. Appropriate control groups are serious problems for naturalistic research, but the problems should be empirically solvable through a combination of ingenuity of investigators and an understanding of the function of control groups.

If a control group is a group of subjects either assigned to conditions or selected so as to yield data that will allow a choice among interpretations, the criticism can be put into perspective. One answer for naturalistic research is to select naturally occurring, intact samples of subjects in appropriate ways, a strategy so common that I will not elaborate upon it here. However, one other possible strategy is less commonly used, at least explicitly, and does merit some mention. This strategy involves what Shontz (1965) has called "implicit comparison groups" (p. 169). Here, the investigator capitalizes upon previous studies of his own, studies by others, or even stable generalizations in the related literature to serve the function of the control group. One example will demonstrate how this might be done.

In the studies of sense of obligation, I sought differences in school size of some magnitude, and in each case the large school was located in an urban area while the small schools were located in small, rural towns.

Thus, rural-urban differences provided many possible confounding variables to undermine the tenability of a school size hypothesis. In this case, a study by Campbell (1964) came to the rescue. Campbell asked students on questionnaires about reasons for attending school activities, and focused on what he called "personal responsibility" (p. 144), a concept very similar to sense of obligation. Campbell compared numbers of responses indicating personal responsibility reported by students in (a) a small, locally-circumscribed high school, (b) a relatively large, locally-circumscribed high school, and (c) a relatively large consolidated high school. The crucial factor in Campbell's study was that all three schools were located in small rural towns. He found reliable differences between students in the small local school and both of the large schools, suggesting strong support for the school size hypothesis, and weighing against rural-urban differences as an explanation.

The important point here is that the function and exploitation of control groups cannot be used as a speculative, a priori argument against naturalistic research. Again, the considerations should be what is done and what is found.

ETHICAL CONSIDERATIONS

Research that is low in manipulation of conditions may also provide some avenues out of some of the recent controversy over the ethics of research. McGuire (1967), in his recent paper on trends in social psychology, raises this possibility, and argues as follows (p. 131). There are at least three ethically sensitive areas of research in social psychology. First, and perhaps most serious, is the common use of noxious experimental conditions, which include painful or even dangerous physiological treatments, anxiety arousal, and other potentially harmful psychological manipulations. Second, there is the frequent use of deception, or, scientifically justified lies, and the possible deterioration of trust and interpersonal relations that emerge as a result of deception, no matter how thorough the experimental debriefing. Perhaps even more distressing is recent evidence that debriefing may not be nearly as effective as investigators have assumed (Walster, Berscheid, Abrahams, & Aronson, 1967). Third, there is the problem of invasion of the subject's privacy. As McGuire points out, the last problem will hardly be solved, and may even be aggravated, by naturalistic research and unobtrusive observations. "However, the first two problems can be largely circumvented when the social psychology theorist develops the will and the skill to test his hypotheses in a real world that he never made, and takes experimental advantage of natural manipulations that he can neither produce nor control" (p. 131). Furthermore, it is possible that the more directly obvious social relevance that often accompanies naturalistic research will provide greater justification for the inevitable invasions of privacy. This is not to suggest that the ethical problems of naturalistic research are simpler; in fact, the opposite may be the case. The point is rather that naturalistic research may solve *some* ethical quandaries.

RESEARCHABILITY OF CERTAIN PHENOMENA

One issue that does not require much elaboration, but which should contribute to a rationale for naturalistic methods, is the fairly obvious fact that many phenomena and their correlates would not enter the scientific domain at all without naturalistic methods. For ethical reasons and sometimes because of their intrinsic nature, the correlates and effects of natural disasters, physical disabilities, child rearing regimens, deaths, accidents, and other classes of events are, after certain points, researchable only through naturalistic methods. And yet, if reliable data can be obtained, such phenomena should enter the behavioral sciences.

I should point out that researchability may clearly be a reason for using laboratory methods, or experimental methods, as well. I have been investigating figural aftereffects (Willems, 1967a), and at present I see no way to study them with other than strong manipulational methods, nor do I see any reason why I should try.

DISCREPANT FINDINGS AND GENERALIZATION

Much of what I have said about the study of everyday behavioral achievement, the distribution of phenomena in nature, behavioral repertoires, tying and untying of variables, and yield is relevant to what is perhaps the most important scientific issue that a rationale for naturalistic methods should take into account. This is the problem of generalizing findings and laws from research to everyday circumstances, and it has an empirical root in the problem of discrepant findings. It is one thing to have a particular investigative purpose lead to a choice of naturalistic or manipulational methods, but it is somehow another matter when two different approaches are used to study what is assumed to be the same phenomenon and discrepant findings are the outcome. Such discrepancies point to an important scientific function for naturalistic methods, as several examples will suggest.

Adriaan Kortlandt (1962), in a summary of his observations of chimpanzees in the wild, offers a number of comparisons between what one would conclude about the behavior of chimps from studies of captive animals and from naturalistic studies. First, according to Kortlandt, one would conclude from captive chimps that infants are spoiled and frequently disobey parental calls. In the wild, on the other hand, even with all their freedom, infant chimps do not appear spoiled, and they always obey their mothers at the first hint. Second, whereas one would conclude from studies of captives that chimps appear increasingly "dull and vacant" (p. 131) with passing years, older chimps in the wild, if anything, become more lively, alert, and curious. Third, from studies of captive chimps, one would generalize that they live in harem groups of size five to fifteen. Kortlandt saw no such grouping in the wild. Fourth, one would probably conclude from captive chimps that they are essentially arboreal, whereas "in the wild they behave like such basically terrestrial animals as baboons" (p. 133). Finally, compared to captive animals, behavior of young chimps in the wild is markedly retarded, developing human-like characteristics much later than captives. Despite the fact that Kortlandt's captive baselines are from chimps in zoos and not in experimental laboratories, the point still emerges that the investigator of chimp behavior would be in error on at least five counts if he generalized from captive chimps to the wild state.

S. L. Washburn reports that baboons have been studied frequently in captivity, as in zoos and primate laboratories (1963). It is common to find that when two or more baboons are confined together, one emerges as the leader. This observation is not surprising, but *how* leaders emerge in confinement is important. Washburn reports that under these conditions, the leaders emerge and maintain their leadership through physical intimidation and comparative brute power. Washburn goes on to report the results of observations of baboons in their natural habitats, and one set of findings is of special interest. Leaders also emerge in the wild, but they appear not to emerge by physical intimidation and brute power. Instead, such attributes as superior cunning, sexual expertise, and attractiveness seem to be the route to leadership among baboons in the wild.

The work of Beecher on pain-relieving drugs also suggests that when the investigator's concern is to generalize to real life phenomena, naturalistic methods must enter his program of research (1956, 1959a, 1959b, 1960). Beecher's findings suggest that many controlled laboratory experiments on pain and pain-relieving drugs contribute little to the understanding of pain and analgesia as they occur in the world outside the laboratory. Compounds that seem to relieve pain under controlled laboratory conditions often fail to do so in the wards of hospitals, while substances which, by laboratory experiment, would seem to be ineffective are frequently highly effective in the clinical situation. In other words, on the matter of pain relief, there is explicit need for naturalistic research to optimize generalization and to check laboratory findings.

In an investigation of decision-making procedures in groups, Hall and Williams (1966) combined variations in manipulation of antecedent conditions in a single study. They were investigating the effect of group conflict upon processes and outcomes in making group decisions, and they compared the performances of 20 established, intact groups of management trainees to 20 ad hoc groups, groups with no history as groups outside the laboratory. Hall and Williams explicitly set out to assess the generalizability of findings from ad hoc laboratory groups to established groups, and their finding was that such generalization is precarious business. The ad hoc groups differed from the established groups in their processes of making decisions, the nature of their decisions per se, and especially in the way they dealt with conflict. In other words, apart from common sense and speculation, there are now data to suggest that on several dimensions, generalization from ad hoc experimental assemblies to established groups would be in error.

When an attempt is made to generalize from a manipulational study to an everyday phenomenon or a phenomenon that one has not produced, it is necessary to assume that the manipulated circumstances comprise a *model* of the everyday phenomenon, or that they *represent* it. The possible array of factors that limit the fit of the model or disrupt representativeness is too extensive to treat exhaustively here, but I should say a word about the work of Rosenthal (for example, 1966) on unintended effects in behavioral research, which has had such a disquieting impact on the atmosphere of research. One directly relevant aspect of Rosenthal's work focuses on the volunteer subject, the correlates of volunteering, and their implications for the generality of research findings (1965). Based upon his own work and a review of related literature, Rosenthal can state with some confidence that such characteristics of volunteers as abilities, interests, motives, age, and sex, can interact with experimental conditions to such an extent that generality is sharply limited. Of course, when naturalistic studies involve voluntary participation by subjects, as in surveys and interviews, the confounding due to correlates of volunteering may be operating, too. However, one reason why McGuire (1967) predicts a growing commitment to naturalistic research in social psychology is the problem of subject representativeness and generalization in manipulational research (pp. 130–131).

As can be readily seen, I have chosen examples that display discrepancies between the findings from manipulational and naturalistic studies of what are assumed to be the same phenomena. In the process, I have not done justice to the many happy instances of good agreement. I could cite other examples of the problem of discrepant findings and generalization (Kavanau, 1964; Chapter 10 of this volume; Hovland, 1959; Breland & Breland, 1966), but the issues seem fairly clear. I should emphasize that the findings for Washburn's confined baboons, Beecher's laboratory subjects, Hall and Williams' ad hoc groups, and the captive chimps to which Kortlandt refers were accurate and reliable *for those subjects and those conditions.* That is, the reliability of those data is not under question here. However, it is also clear that the investigators would have been in error if they had made straightforward generalizations to everyday occurrences on the basis of those subjects alone. Bauer (1964), in a review of issues in research on social communication and social influence, does not hesitate to conclude flatly ". . . that the characteristic behavior of the audience in the natural habitat is such as to bring about crucial modifications of the results seen in the laboratory" (p. 321). It is seductively easy to be content with results obtained in manipulated laboratory experiments and to assume that caution is the only requirement for generalizing. All of the examples I have cited indicate that caution is not the only requirement, and that naturalistic methods perform a unique function in the problem of generalization. Again, this is an empirical matter rather than a speculative one.

Of course, pointing to discrepancies in findings, stating the problem of generalizing, and asserting that naturalistic methods perform a unique function represent only a beginning and tell investigators little about how to view the functions of manipulational and naturalistic research, when to use methods falling into either strategy, or how to dovetail their functions in the problem of generalizing. One very readable and informative treatment of the matter of dovetailing is offered by Breland and Breland (1966), especially in their conception of the laboratory as a surrogate of an organism's ecological niche (pp. 62–69). The Brelands propose a number of guidelines and implications for generalizing in the study of animal behavior, and they conclude (a) that it is no longer feasible for psychologists to generate complete theories, taxonomies, and generalizations from the strictures of the laboratory, and (b) that one of the most pressing current needs is to relate what organisms do in the laboratory to what they do in the wild (p. 114).

In this same vein, Scott and Wertheimer (1962) conclude:

> When it comes to generalizing research findings to the normal, everyday behavior of the organism, naturalistic observation would appear to enjoy a clear lead over the other methodologies—assuming, of course, that

it is based on an adequate sampling of the behaviors under study. Not only can the investigator be sure that the relationships he has observed occur in the subject's natural habitat, but through time-sampling of behavior he can determine the relative frequencies with which the events appear. This can provide an index of the "importance" of a functional relationship to the organism in its natural ecology. In laboratory studies, on the other hand, the particular functional relationship observed may be in large part a product of the special, artificial conditions of the experiment. Such a restriction in generality is likely to be particularly serious in those "hold constant" experiments in which control of extraneous variables artificially places them at levels that would hardly be encountered in the subject's normal activity. A given experiment may show conclusively a relationship between the independent and dependent variables, which, however, is demonstrated only under such peculiar circumstances that the result is uninteresting, except as a curiosity. (pp. 95–96)

Relevant to the problem of generalization, as well as to the issue of artificiality and tying of variables discussed earlier, is Pugh's (1966) discussion of strategies for studying human behavior in organizations (see especially pp. 235–236). Pugh says:

One may ask why it is considered less artificial to study men getting paid for standing on the assembly line at a motor factory screwing on car-door handles than to study men getting paid for taking part in a laboratory ergograph experiment. The answer is that it is not so much the actual laboratory task itself that is artificial . . . as the social situation in which it is performed. The social role of mass production operator is far removed from that of laboratory subject. The enormous disparity in the duration of role occupancy is sufficient to ensure differences in sanctions and motivations, with consequent divergence in performance. (p. 236)

Pugh is pointing to two descriptive properties of laboratory studies that limit generalization to everyday phenomena. First, he mentions the global social situation in which the experimental task is performed. Pugh's use of words here reminds one of the more extensive treatment by Orne (1962), who showed that persons do unique things in the social situation of the experimental laboratory. Second, Pugh mentions the difference in time perspective, or "duration of role occupancy" between lab and everyday circumstance, and how it might affect the results of research. Kounin's (1961) failure to induce low commitment mentioned earlier might be an example of the effects of differing time perspective.

Finally, Hovland (1959), in his discussion of manipulational and naturalistic strategies for studying social influence, concludes: "I should like to stress in summary the mutual importance of the two approaches to the problem of communication effectiveness. Neither is a royal road to wisdom, but each represents an important emphasis" (p. 17). As I tried to indicate in the section on artificiality and tying of variables, we often can, and often should, press our explorations into phenomena by changing, interrupting, or producing them at our behest. However, my argument here is that any program of research that includes generalization as one of its aims should purposefully include data yielded by methods that tend toward low manipulation and low imposition of units, in other words, naturalistic methods. Stated in a slightly different way, the argument goes as follows: (a) Appropriate generalization to everyday events is a problem of ecological validity. Ecological validity is not used here in Brunswik's technical sense, but in the more intuitive sense of correspondence between our generalizing statements and what occurs in the organism's natural habitat. (b) Achievement of ecological validity requires, at least in part, an ecological or contextual perspective in research. (c) It is widely accepted that an ecological perspective requires naturalistic methods. (d) Therefore, naturalistic methods are important in any program of generalizing. Much work remains to be done in explicating the factors and guidelines for such a program beyond the bare hints offered by the Brelands, Scott and Wertheimer, Pugh, Orne, and the present essay.

Conclusion

In summary, the burden of this essay has been to communicate the following messages:

(1) It would be desirable to remove the evaluations of manipulational, experimental research and naturalistic research from the realm of speculation and polemics. Two reasons for the polemical nature of the controversies are (a) over commitment to, and judgmental use of, one strategy or another, and (b) the troublesome word, "natural."

(2) For purposes of behavioral research, we can view degree of naturalism in terms of the activities of the investigator. One way to describe research activities is to place them on two orthogonal, descriptive dimensions: (a) degree of investigator influence upon, or manipulation of, the antecedents of the behavior studied, and (b) degree of imposition of units upon the behavior. On this view, manipulational and naturalistic research strategies are not pure, dichotomous cases, but meld into each other on continua.

(3) Viewing naturalistic research as tending toward low manipulation

and low imposition of units, there are considerations, issues, and purposes such as the following that might well lead investigators to choose naturalistic methods for their research: (a) the study of everyday behavioral achievement, (b) documentation of the distributions of behavioral phenomena in nature, (c) descriptive and taxonomic study of behavioral repertoires, (d) expenditure of effort relative to empirical yield, (e) artificiality and tying of variables, (f) replication in proper perspective, (g) control groups in proper perspective, (h) ethical considerations in research, (i) researchability of certain phenomena, and (j) discrepant findings and generalization.

In the passage quoted at the beginning of this essay, Spiker suggests that methods and strategies for generating and collecting data are tools; they serve investigators in the quest for understanding. The actual execution of research is always a curious and complex product of the purposes and questions of an investigator, together with his choice of methods to achieve his purposes and answer his questions (Taylor *et al.*, 1959). Therefore, the evaluation of research and the selection of methods should, at least in part, take into account those purposes and questions, which at times and in the best scientific interest, will lead an investigator to choose methods that tend toward naturalistic ones.

REFERENCES

Allport, F. H. The J-curve hypothesis of conforming behavior. *Journal of Social Psychology*, 1934, **5,** 141–183.

Baker, R. A. A final word from the editor. In R. A. Baker (Ed.), *Psychology in the wry.* New York: Van Nostrand, 1963. Pp. 163–167.

Barker, R. G. (Ed.) *The stream of behavior.* New York: Appleton-Century-Crofts, 1963.

Barker, R. G. Observation of behavior: Ecological approaches. *Journal of Mt. Sinai Hospital,* 1964, **31,** 268–284. (a)

Barker, R. G. Psychology's third estate. Paper read at meeting of Greater Kansas City Psychological Association, Kansas City, Missouri, (unpublished mimeo), 1964. (b)

Barker, R. G. Explorations in ecological psychology. *American Psychologist,* 1965, **20,** 1–14.

Barker, R. G., Dembo, T., & Lewin, K. Frustration and regression. In R. G. Barker, J. S. Kounin, & H. F. Wright (Eds.), *Child behavior and development.* New York: McGraw-Hill, 1943. Pp. 441–458.

Barker, R. G., & Wright, H. F. *Midwest and its children.* New York: Harper & Row, 1955.

Barker, R. G., Wright, H. F., Barker, L. S., & Schoggen, M. *Specimen records of American and English children.* Lawrence, Kan.: University of Kansas Press, 1961.

Bauer, R. A. The obstinate audience: The influence process from the point of view of social communication. *American Psychologist,* 1964, **19,** 319–328.

Bechtel, R. B. Hodometer research in architecture. *Milieu,* 1967, **1,** (2), 1–9.

Beecher, H. K. Relationship of significance of wound to pain experienced. *Journal of the American Medical Association,* 1956, **161,** 1609–1613.

Beecher, H. K. Generalization from pain of various types and origins. *Science,* 1959, **130,** 267–268. (a)

Beecher, H. K. *Measurement of subjective responses.* New York: Oxford, 1959. (b)

Beecher, H. K. Increased stress and effectiveness of placebos and "active" drugs. *Science,* 1960, **132,** 91–92.

Breland, K., & Breland, M. *Animal behavior.* New York: Macmillan, 1966.

Brunswick, E. Representative design and probabilistic theory in a functional psychology. *Psychological Review,* 1955, **62,** 193–217.

Bryan, J. H., & Test, M. A. Models and helping: Naturalistic studies in aiding behavior. *Journal of Personality and Social Psychology,* 1967, **6,** 400–407.

Campbell, D. T., & Stanley, J. C. *Experimental and quasi-experimental designs for research.* Chicago: Rand McNally, 1963.

Campbell, W. J. Some effects of high school consolidation. In R. G. Barker & P. V. Gump, *Big school, small school.* Stanford, Calif.: Stanford University Press, 1964. Pp. 139–153.

DeCharms, R., Levy, J., & Wertheimer, M. A note on attempted evaluations of psychotherapy. *Journal of Clinical Psychology,* 1954, **10,** 233–235.

Dyck, A. J. The social contacts of some Midwest children with their parents and teachers. In R. G. Barker (Ed.), *The stream of behavior.* New York: Appleton-Century-Crofts, 1963. Pp. 78–98.

Epstein, W., Park, J., & Casey, A. The current status of the size-distance hypotheses. *Psychological Bulletin,* 1961, **58,** 491–514.

Eysenck, H. J. The effects of psychotherapy: An evaluation. *Journal of Consulting Psychology,* 1952, **16,** 319–323.

Fawl, C. L. Disturbances experienced by children in their natural habitats. In R. G. Barker (Ed.), *The stream of behavior.* New York: Appleton-Century-Crofts, 1963. Pp. 99–126.

Gump, P. V., & Kounin, J. S. Issues raised by ecological and "classical" research efforts. *Merrill-Palmer Quarterly,* 1959–1960, **6,** 145–152.

Gump, P. V., & Sutton-Smith, B. The "it" role in children's games. *The Group,* 1955, **17,** 3–8.

Hall, J., & Williams, M. S. A comparison of decision-making performances in established and ad hoc groups. *Journal of Personality and Social Psychology,* 1966, **3,** 214–222.

Hess, E. H. Ethology: An approach toward the complete analysis of behavior. In R. Brown, E. Galanter, E. H. Hess, & G. Mandler, *New directions in psychology.* New York: Holt, Rinehart and Winston, 1962. Pp. 157–266.

Hovland, C. I. Reconciling conflicting results derived from experimental and survey studies of attitude change. *American Psychologist*, 1959, **14**, 8–17.

Imai, S., & Garner, W. R. Discriminability and preference for attributes in free and constrained classification. *Journal of Experimental Psychology*, 1965, **69**, 596–608.

Jay, P. Field studies. In A. M. Schrier, H. F. Harlow, & F. Stollnitz (Eds.), *Behavior of nonhuman primates*. Vol. 2. New York: Academic Press, 1965. Pp. 525–591.

Kavanau, J. L. Behavior: Confinement, adaptation, and compulsory regimes in laboratory studies. *Science*, 1964, **143**, 490.

Kerlinger, F. N. *Foundations of behavioral research*. New York: Holt, Rinehart and Winston, 1964.

Kessen, W. Sucking and looking: Two organized congenital patterns of behavior in the human newborn. In H. W. Stevenson, E. H. Hess, & H. L. Rheingold (Eds.), *Early behavior: Comparative and developmental approaches*. New York: Wiley, 1967. Pp. 147–179.

Kiesler, D. J. Some myths of psychotherapy research and the search for a paradigm. *Psychological Bulletin*, 1966, **65**, 110–136.

Klinghammer, E. Factors influencing choice of mate in altricial birds. In H. W. Stevenson, E. H. Hess, & H. L. Rheingold (Eds.), *Early behavior: Comparative and developmental approaches*. New York: Wiley, 1967. Pp. 5–42.

Kortlandt, A. Chimpanzees in the wild. *Scientific American*, 1962, **206**, (5), 128–138.

Kounin, J. S. Dimensions of adult-child relationships in the classroom. Paper read at Topology Meeting, New York, August, 1961.

Lefkowitz, M., Blake, R., & Mouton, J. Status factors in pedestrian violation of traffic signals. *Journal of Abnormal and Social Psychology*, 1955, **51**, 704–706.

Luborsky, L. A. A note on Eysenck's article "The effects of psychotherapy: An evaluation." *British Journal of Psychology*, 1954, **45**, 129–131.

Mason, W. A. The social development of monkeys and apes. In I. DeVore (Ed.), *Primate behavior: Field studies of monkeys and apes*. New York: Holt, Rinehart and Winston, 1965. Pp. 514–543.

McGuire, W. J. Some impending reorientations in social psychology: Some thoughts provoked by Kenneth Ring. *Journal of Experimental Social Psychology*, 1967, **3**, 124–139.

Orne, M. T. On the social psychology of the psychological experiment: With particular reference to demand characteristics and their implications. *American Psychologist*, 1962, **17**, 776–783.

Postman, L., & Tolman, E. C. Brunswik's probabilistic functionalism. In S. Koch (Ed.), *Psychology: A study of a science*. Vol. 1. New York: McGraw-Hill, 1959. Pp. 502–564.

Pugh, D. S. Modern organizational theory: A psychological and sociological study. *Psychological Bulletin*, 1966, **66**, 235–251.

Purcell, K., & Brady, K. Adaptation to the invasion of privacy: Monitoring behavior with a miniature radio transmitter. *Merrill-Palmer Quarterly,* 1966, **12,** 242–254.

Rheingold, H. L. A comparative psychology of development. In H. W. Stevenson, E. H. Hess, & H. L. Rheingold (Eds.), *Early behavior: Comparative and developmental approaches.* New York: Wiley, 1967. Pp. 279–293.

Rosenthal, R. The volunteer subject. *Human Relations,* 1965, **18,** 389–406.

Rosenthal, R. *Experimenter effects in behavioral research.* New York: Appleton-Century-Crofts, 1966.

Rosenzweig, S. A transvaluation of psychotherapy: A reply to Hans Eysenck. *Journal of Abnormal and Social Psychology,* 1954, **49,** 298–304.

Schoggen, P. Mechanical aids for making specimen records of behavior. *Child Development,* 1964, **35,** 985–988.

Scott, W. A., & Wertheimer, M. *Introduction to psychological research.* New York: Wiley, 1962.

Sears, P. S. Problems in the investigation of achievement and self-esteem motivation. In M. R. Jones (Ed.), *Nebraska symposium on motivation.* Lincoln, Neb.: University of Nebraska Press, 1957. Pp. 265–339.

Shontz, F. C. *Research methods in personality.* New York: Appleton-Century-Crofts, 1965.

Spiker, C. C. The concept of development: Relevant and irrelevant issues. In H. W. Stevenson (Ed.), Concept of development. *Monographs of the Society for Research in Child Development,* 1966, **31,** No. 5 (Whole No. 107), 40–54.

Taylor, D. W. *et al.* Education for research in psychology. *American Psychologist,* 1959, **14,** 167–179.

Underwood, B. J. *Psychological research.* New York: Appleton-Century-Crofts, 1957.

Verplanck, W. The control of content of conversation: Reinforcement of statements of opinion. *Journal of Abnormal and Social Psychology,* 1955, **51,** 668–676.

Walster, E., Berscheid, E., Abrahams, D., & Aronson, V. Effectiveness of debriefing following deception experiments. *Journal of Personality and Social Psychology,* 1967, **6,** 371–380.

Washburn, S. L. Phi Beta Kappa Lecture. University of Kansas, 1963.

Webb, E. J., Campbell, D. T., Schwartz, R. D., & Sechrest, L. *Unobtrusive measures: Nonreactive research in the social sciences.* Chicago: Rand McNally, 1966.

Willems, E. P. Forces toward participation in behavior settings. In R. G. Barker & P. V. Gump, *Big school, small school.* Stanford, Calif.: Stanford University Press, 1964. Pp. 115–135.

Willems, E. P. An ecological orientation in psychology. *Merrill-Palmer Quarterly,* 1965, **11,** 317–343.

Willems, E. P. Nonstimulus and nonretinal mechanisms in figural aftereffects. *Journal of Experimental Psychology,* 1967, **74,** 452–454. (a)

Willems, E. P. Sense of obligation to high school activities as related to school

size and marginality of student. *Child Development*, 1967, **38,** 1246–
1260. (b)

Willems, E. P., & Willems, G. J. Comparative validity of data yielded by
three methods. *Merrill-Palmer Quarterly*, 1965, **11,** 65–71.

Wright, H. F. *Recording and analyzing child behavior.* New York: Harper &
Row, 1967.

Part II
ARGUMENTS FROM FOUR SUBSTANTIVE AREAS

COMMENTARY

AGAINST THE BACKGROUND of the three general essays, Chapters 4 through 7 discuss naturalistic viewpoints within more circumscribed areas: the study of subhuman primates, clinical psychology, research on attitudes and opinions, and the cross-cultural study of personality. As was the case with the first three essays, the next four represent the stances of particular individuals, but each author raises the kinds of general questions that the methodology of naturalistic research should take into account.

On the basis of their work with over 8000 animals, more than 60 species, and covering about 18 years, Breland and Breland (1966) say flatly, ". . . you cannot understand the behavior of the animal in the laboratory unless you understand his behavior in the wild." (p. 20) This proposition takes on specific, documented meaning in the hands of Emil W. Menzel, Jr., in Chapter 4. Menzel's target is research on subhuman primates, but within the framework of a retrospective account of his own research, he probes at the very foundations of methodology, processes of inference, levels of analysis, generalization, and the interplay of methods in the quest for understanding behavior. Observations of intact, investigator-free situations are not Menzel's only concern, but by working with the simple dictum, "Manipulate only as much as is necessary to answer your questions clearly," he offers data and impressions that add new perspective to such common concepts as stimulus, response, function, constancy, object, space, distance, location, molar vs. molecular, and unit of behavior, and bring new slants to such common questions as, "Why is the animal where he is, and why is he doing what he is doing?"

In Chapter 5, Harold L. Raush focuses upon the actual *clinical* work of the psychologist and develops a characterization of the clinician as a scientific naturalist. In the process of arriving at this characterization,

Raush debates and evaluates some common stereotypes concerning pure and applied science and the dichotomy between clinical practice and research. More importantly, he dips deeply into questions of representativeness, artificiality, intervention, interference, sampling, and control of variance, all of which cluster around the adjective, "naturalistic." From this treatment, he develops a view of methodological naturalism that emphasizes representativeness of and constraint upon the repertoires of input to and output from the target of research. Into this framework Raush then maps clinical psychology as *method* and indicates what clinical psychology, viewed as a naturalistic method, suggests in terms of questions and assumptions of research, and in terms of needed but sparsely available techniques.

Lee Sechrest, in Chapter 6, discusses implications for the study of attitudes and opinions, implications that follow from the point of view developed in *Unobtrusive Measures* (Webb *et al.*, 1966). Beginning with a definition of attitude, Sechrest turns what is commonly viewed as a weakness of attitude research, that is, low correlations among measures, into a promising methodological program of which naturalistic research is an important part. This program calls for multiple methods to triangulate upon, or home in upon, the concept of attitude. Sechrest's prescription is similar to Cronbach and Meehl's program of construct validation in the testing area (1955) and similar to Garner, Hake, and Eriksen's program of converging operations for the study of perception (1956). Against this conceptual and methodological background, Sechrest discusses the nature of, opportunities for, and some specific examples of "nonreactive" or naturalistic research on opinions and attitudes, as well as how such methods might function in a program of multiple methods.

With David Gutmann's essay (Chapter 7), both the target and grounds of discussion shift away from the naturalness of environmental conditions and their relations to overt processes of behavior. Gutmann's focus is *psychological naturalism*, that is, open-ended exploration into covert psychic processes, subjective states, and cultural themes in personality, where the categories and contents of exploration are determined to a minimal degree by prior theory. For Gutmann, the cross-cultural study of personality, when approached with such a minimal commitment to prior theoretical categories, is a paradigm case of psychological naturalism because it forces both the investigator and respondent into what he calls a *data-generating* mode rather than a *data-accumulating* mode. The invited, reciprocal interview is Gutmann's naturalistic technique for what he terms "making explicit data out of implicit order," and his discussion reminds one of Polanyi's distinction between "subsidiary" and "focal" awareness in science (1958, pp. 55–65). Furthermore, Gutmann's reference to the importance of ecology in the understanding of psychological structure is reminiscent of Griffith's (1961) suggestion that ecology might be important in understanding responses to standard personality measures. Gutmann's essay, which closes this set of four, presents a view of naturalism that differs in important ways from some of the views presented earlier.

REFERENCES

Breland, K., & Breland, M. *Animal behavior*. New York: Macmillan, 1966.

Cronbach, L. J., & Meehl, P. E. Construct validity in psychological tests. *Psychological Bulletin*, 1955, **52**, 281–302.

Garner, W. R., Hake, H. W., & Eriksen, C. W. Operationism and the concept of perception. *Psychological Review*, 1956, **63**, 149–159.

Griffith, R. M. Rorschach water percepts: A study in conflicting results. *American Psychologist*, 1961, **16**, 307–311.

Polanyi, M. *Personal knowledge*. Chicago: University of Chicago Press, 1958.

Webb, E., Campbell, D. T., Schwartz, R. D., & Sechrest, L. *Unobstrusive measures*. Chicago: Rand McNally, 1966.

4

Naturalistic and Experimental Approaches to Primate Behavior

EMIL W. MENZEL, JR.

A FEW YEARS AGO, a team of field workers (DeVore, 1965) and a team of laboratory experimentalists (Schrier, Harlow, & Stollnitz, 1965) examined closely the same phenomena in the same organisms, specifically, the behavior of certain primates. Both of these teams proceeded with the purpose of providing a broad perspective on what science knows today in the area of primate behavior, what problems remain unsolved, and what methods are at hand for solving these problems. Taken separately, the two works were scholarly, sound, and deservedly successful. Taken together, they remind one of the fable of the blind men examining different portions of an elephant. In the words of one reviewer (Altmann, 1965), it is difficult to conceive of two more different pictures of primate behavior than those seen in these books. Even the primates themselves look different, and there is little apparent overlap in the research questions, techniques, or theories.

While it might thus *seem* that naturalistic and experimental research have nothing to do with each other, this is true only from the narrow standpoint of specialists. Along with researchers such as Hinde (1958) and Schneirla (1950) and philosophers such as Polanyi (1958), I am, in fact, convinced that naturalistic and experimental studies can be compatible with each other; that their respective methods can be applied to any situation (instead of being linked to a given situation such as laboratory or field); that both types of information are necessary to a meaningful general science of primate behavior; that any sharp division between naturalistic and experimental methodology is not only undesirable but impossible; and that, finally, disputes as to which method or situation is intrinsically best are nonsensical.

The purpose of the present paper is to show, through a review of my own research experience in laboratory and in field work, why I believe this is so. There are several reasons for choosing a case history approach instead of attempting a polite, impersonal and scholarly review of method in the abstract. First, there is no such thing as *the* experimental method or *the* naturalistic method. What individuals do in studying given problems is the only guide we have. While my single case might be lacking in representativeness and in finesse, it reflects the biases I would otherwise present by other devices. Second, with few exceptions, individual primate researchers have worked either in the laboratory or in the field and not in both. It is probably for this reason, rather than from anything more fundamental, that little attempt has been made to pursue the same research questions in the two situations, or to develop a common vocabulary, a common set of techniques, or even mutual tolerance. Finally, Mason (in press) has recently tried, through a general review of the primate literature, to show why today's naturalists and experimentalists do what they do, why they differ, and what they have in common, and the present paper is designed to supplement rather than replicate such a general review.

The first chapter gives an account of what the words "naturalist" and "experimentalist" signify to me today. The next four describe in a series of stages how my attitudes, questions, methodological biases, sampling procedures, experimental techniques, and types of data progressively (*and jointly*) changed, especially since I left my original territory, the laboratory, to pursue a problem wherever it led. Chapter 5 illustrates how naturalistic and experimental approaches to certain problems of primate behavior eventually interlock one with the other. Unfortunately, this sort of approach does not permit me to go into detail on problems of response taxonomy or social behavior, even though certain work on these topics, especially the Japanese investigations of social organization, is probably the most important aspect of recent research on primate behavior. I shall concentrate on stimulus problems (especially the concepts of *space* and *object*) which should be of interest to both field workers and to laboratory men.

Concerning Naturalists and Experimentalists

I should start by stating that I was originally trained as an experimental psychologist. However, the more I have considered the matter, the more I would like to be a naturalist first and an experimenter second. In its literal dictionary definition, naturalistic research pertains to, or closely reproduces, nature and is natural or realistic; and I have always hoped that as a scientist I have been dealing with real problems that have something to do with real organisms. In this sense I would be delighted to be called a pure naturalist.

Of course, it is sheer metaphysical conceit to claim that we ever do achieve a strictly naturalistic picture of behavior. To do so would require access to phenomena "as they are." The best we can do is to try for samples of events that are representative and valid, and hope that our analysis of what happened is reasonably accurate. Until chimpanzees write books, the human element in animal psychology is inescapable. I see neither halos nor horns on either a *real experiment* or on *accurate observations*. Any method is a special case of human experience, and it cannot surpass the limitations of its human interpreters.

The naturalist, it seems to me, is a romantic who protests the inevitable. He starts from what he thinks is the most representative sample of events, and tries his best to describe and explain what is there. By this criterion he says: "Look at your animals and they will tell you what the important problems are." Unfortunately, judging from the literature, monkeys can lie just as badly as investigators do.

The experimentalist, on the other hand, is a scholastic. His delight is to find statements by an authority, make them operationally explicit, and then verify or discard them. Rather than look for natural units of behavior, or even devise apparatus as a simplified version of what he sees outside the laboratory, he attempts by procrustean force to define behavior logically in terms of the apparatus into which he puts an animal. To play this game properly, one must of course use a Standardized Test—preferably one that bears an imprimatur such as Skinner Box, Miller-Mowrer Box, or Maier's Test of Reasoning. In the hope that I can make field work scientifically respectable, I have considered patenting the tree as the Menzel Jumping Stand, the river as the Tulane Obstruction Apparatus, and the jungle as the Delta Primate Center General Test Apparatus. These situations have already had several million years of standardization as reliable and valid tests of primate behavior, and who could challenge such a psychological tradition?

Actually, of course, field situations need no such justification. Animals are there for good biological reasons. The occurrence of freeranging primates in a specific habitat in the Congo is no more accidental than the occurrence of the same species in an American laboratory, and the former is of greater scientific information value, for it can tell us an enormous amount about the subject organism, whereas the presence of animals in the laboratory is by itself of interest mainly to an historian of experimental psychology.

Until we have discovered all that is involved in the existing animal-environment complex, it is impossible to determine to what extent we are breaking down this complex by bringing the animal to the laboratory. Insofar as a species is not restricted by ecological barriers, it has either placed itself where we find it, or is there because an unbroken chain of ancestors, possibly for millenia, were in related situations. These facts (or rather, the necessity for understanding what such facts entail) make the field a prime test situation for anyone who takes biology and evolution seriously. Laboratory tests can be justified to the extent that they provide models of events that are found more generally and help us to discover what in one way or another has been there all along; but attempts to invent new organisms, environments, or behaviors for their own sake would border on travesty. It is not our artifacts and inventions but nature's products that are the subject matter of animal psychology.

All these arguments notwithstanding, there is still no logical basis for the current attitude in psychology and among some primate field workers that naturalistic and experimental research are in opposition to each other. This can hardly be so, because naturalistic research is the more generic. Naturalistic research is any form of research that aims at discovery and verification through observation, and this includes as specialized cases all techniques, apparatus, and procedures of experimentation. The major unique aspects of an experiment are the greater reliance upon devices such as microscopes and EEG to extend our powers of observation, the greater effort to simplify the task of recording by restricting the subject's movements or predefining the units of response, and the relative emphasis placed upon getting the independent variables under the observer's direct control. No scientist would deny that it is at times an advantage to strip a situation down to its essentials—as we try to do in experiments—to better get at reality. The naturalist (or the good experimentalist) insists, however, that we take care not to confuse our stripped-down models with the universe. It is precisely when we go on to say what the essentials are that we invariably display tunnel vision.

While it is clearly possible to observe and do naturalistic research without performing formal experiments, it is difficult, if not impossible, to determine where real experimentation—as a laboratory man defines it—begins, or where it leaves off and becomes something different (Schneirla, 1950). This is like looking for the pure cortex divorced of all contamination from the rest of the brain from whence it evolved. General observation is a necessary preliminary and counterpart to, and means of relating together the more specialized observations that we call experiments. Whether we like it or not, laboratory lore and woodsman's lore are the paleocortex of research. Without them a more cerebral science will not emerge. The problem is to make laboratory lore, woodsman's lore, and common sense explicit, and to take them past the point of banality and make them something better.

We are entirely too situation oriented, technique oriented, and tradition oriented in defining what we mean by science. Whether we work in the laboratory or in the field is ultimately of little importance, and the selection of variables and techniques of measurement is similarly a secondary issue. The critical issue is what sort of questions we want answered. Once this matter has been settled, the only precision worth bothering about is that of accurate perspective; and at least for me, as much perspective can be gained by chasing after monkeys in the woods with a notebook as by counting how often they salivate or press a lever. The more I see of primate behavior, both in the laboratory and in the field, the more I feel that psychology is doing everything it can to complicate and obscure its real problems in a welter of tests, techniques, specialized jargons, statistical machinations, and a priori assumptions as to what is important in behavior. The real problems of psychology are animals and people as such, and the phenomena of their behavior as such. Dogs salivate when they see food, monkeys love their mothers, chimpanzees would rather get a piece of banana than an electric shock, people are smarter than rats, children spend less time in eating than in playing, and children are often more infantile than adults. These are silly ways to state things, but the phenomena behind the statements are what experimental psychology has been built upon all along. Why should we be afraid of trying to state the obvious more fully and precisely, and place it into the perspective of daily activity, ontogenetic development, and the adaptation of the species to its characteristic ecology? Any specific bit of behavior will make sense only to the extent that some such perspective is achieved.

Here the field worker and the laboratory man, insofar as they are scientific organizers of data rather than catalogers or technicians, tend to adopt different but compatible methods of achieving perspective. The methods are analogous to *zooming in* and *zooming out* with a lens. To the extent that they are reproduced objectively, wide-angle, telephoto, and microscopic views must be *simultaneously* valid, and zooming from different directions merely focusses attention on different facets of the same phenomenon. We must try to achieve both generality and detail, and, if possible, do this under a single set of principles. A molecule might at a different lens setting become a mole, or vice versa, without affecting the inherent structure of an adequate theory (Allport, 1955). There are no grounds, logical or otherwise, for calling any view "simple." We can start anywhere and zoom in to infinite detail, or zoom out to infinite scope.

The field worker starts with the broad view of geography, ecology, range, habitat, and so on, successively narrowing his field of attention while trying to keep new details within the context of previous wider-angle surveys. When he is considering temporal variables, he starts out with the wide-angle view of evolution across millenia, before he zooms in and restricts his discussion to what happens to an organism after birth, or within the confines of a single trial in a learning test. Although he is not necessarily opposed to reductionism, he insists that we should first know what is there to be reduced. He tries to reduce "from above" (see Brunswik, 1955), and trusts that he will recognize small details when he gets to them.

The laboratory worker, on the other hand, has a strong predilection for starting with a small field of view, and zooming out. "Psychology from the ground up" is his slogan, and the ground is apt to be anywhere. Thus, for example, Pavlov chose salivation and Tolman chose a turn in a maze; and from such events, which they used as representative samples or models of behavior, they tried to construct a picture of the total behavior of man. Comparative psychologists have tried to work up to an even broader-angle view of organic and psychological evolution. They have alternatively tried mazes, delayed response, tool-using tests, learning sets, and an infinite variety of other apparatus (including the field), feeling certain that The Test lies just around the corner. This procedure of zooming out is not so ridiculous as it might sound. By way of analogy it might be pointed out that until recently most of the earth's geography was mapped on the basis of small scale, ground-level surveys; and surveys from airplanes and satellites have neither greatly altered our maps nor eliminated the need for further small scale research. No doubt, science would have proceeded more rapidly in this particular instance if grand aerial surveys had been available earlier; but fortunately, scientists were less intent on sticking to a single method than in tackling their problems in the most straightforward fashion possible.

In practice, each method, zooming in and zooming out, patently has its advantages and its limitations. Perhaps, however, the faults and the glories reside not so much in methods as in the men who apply the methods and must record what they see through their lenses. Pavlov observing dogs in a harness probably had a more balanced picture of primate behavior than most people in the field today, and Darwin in the field with a notebook had a more accurate picture of primate behavior than most laboratory men with an EEG and a computer. Unfortunately, few of us are Pavlovs or Darwins. And not even they knew how to zoom without often losing the objective or going out of focus. To make up for my own deficiencies here, it has become necessary to shift back and forth between laboratory and field, between observation and manipulation, between wide-angle and microscopic views of behavior. Whether or not my case is potentially representative, the reader may judge from what follows.

Problems in the Laboratory

Let me explain why I first went to the field. The first six years of my professional career were spent at the Yerkes Laboratories in Orange Park, Florida. My interests originally were in the effects of experience upon behavior. In collaboration with others, I studied how various rearing conditions affected the physical health, postural organization, learning, tool using, social behavior and emotional reactivity of infant chimpanzees, and I also studied isolation-reared infants in some detail to see how they changed after they came out of isolation and were given cumulative exposure to many novel objects and situations (Davenport, Menzel, & Rogers, 1961; Mason, Davenport, Menzel, in press; Menzel, 1964). From an analysis of infant development, I hoped to "zoom out" to explain some of the complexities of adult behavior.

As the infant research progressed, I became more and more dissatisfied with our conventional cataloging of drives, capacities, and processes, and our so-called operational tests of such things. Few infants respected the labels that are customarily applied to tests. They would play with a fear stimulus, avoid a food, socialize with an inanimate object and treat each other as ragmops; and rarely would a majority of the chimpanzees do the same thing at the same time with the same object. My faith in the procrustean method was shattered by the subjects. The logic of testing somehow had to be changed so that chimpanzee tests were redefined in terms of those forms of logic and illogic that chimpanzee behavior actually follows.

Once I got used to this mode of thinking, it soon seemed that common patterns of responsiveness and common stimulus determinants underlay virtually all test performances in the infant—so much so that *responsiveness to objects* appeared to be practically the only major phenomenon to be accounted for. More specific questions about behavior seemed to be relevant only after the animal had expanded and differentiated his repertoire. What patterns of reaction does a given species show, and what is the most meaningful way to describe these reactions? What is a novel object, or a social being, or a reinforcer, or a tool for the animal, and how do objects acquire their functions? Questions of this sort—which come closer to ethology than to American comparative psychology—came to plague me, although I did not phrase them in such general terms as I would now. I became interested not only in experiential factors and in the description of response patterns but also in characteristics such as stimulus size, complexity, movement, and distance. The isolation-raised chimpanzee provided answers of sorts; but the isolation-raised chimpanzee in a small cage with a laboratory-made test stimulus, although it is fascinating enough and complex enough to occupy ten laboratories for many years to come, did not impress me as a representative sample of primate ecosystems in general. I need not add that the data thus far available indicate a substantial difference between isolates and wild-born animals.

The issue of adequate stimulus and response sampling will come up again later, but the problem of "subject representativeness" must be stated more sharply here. Actually, group differences are of indirect importance to psychology. Group differences are of interest only insofar as they answer more general questions regarding why chimpanzees and people do what they do. To answer questions from the developmental standpoint, we must of course determine how our species starts out, for instance, as neonates or isolates, and how it progresses. We must, in short, zoom out. But we must also have some notion as to what alternative end points the developing infant might reach, and what alternative directions might be taken to reach them. The more precise and exhaustive our general information, the better we will understand any given experimental condition, for single experiments and observations, to make sense, must be compared with broader norms. This process of comparing and checking results is the general and original meaning of the word "control" (Boring, 1954), and as we found out quite pointedly in our infant research, adequate control is not achieved merely by physically manipulating and restricting one's conditions, and in being able to specify what objects each group has had. Had it not been for the addition of a wild-born comparison group to our project, which involved several highly restricted laboratory groups, we would in fact have been incapable of properly assessing the differences among the latter. All laboratory-raised groups differed much more from the wild-born group than from each other, and certain anomalies common to all laboratory groups might thus have been mistaken as "normal."

After this lesson, I was willing to concede that captive wild-born primates might in themselves differ from wild ones (see Hediger, 1955) and that even a gross description of wild animals could be better than none. If nothing else, the study of animals in their native habitats might alert us to aspects of our problems that were being ruled out of existence by the narrowness of our theoretical perspective and our selection of subjects and environmental variables. Whether all laboratory primates are "abnormal" and only wild ones are "normal" (K. Hall, in press) is beside the point. It is not representative or normal research *animals* or *situations*, but an accurate and generally valid set of scientific questions and answers about animal behavior, that ultimately matters. I would still recommend the isolation-raised animal and the laboratory neonate just as highly as the feral group for this purpose, as in fact many naturalists do.

At any rate, when an opportunity came to work in Japan for a year, I jumped at the chance. By working with wild monkeys and studying some of the same problems and using techniques similar to those I had already used in the laboratory, I hoped to test how accurate my views on "primate behavior" were.

Field Experiments

MARK 1

Imagine now, if you will, an enormous lens mounted above the earth, zooming in on an experimental psychologist (Menzel, 1966) who in turn is trying to zoom out from laboratory problems to behavior in the wild. First we see Asia with monkeys all over the place; then Japan, with several thousand native macaques in their characteristic arrays and ranges; then, closing in on a single aggregate of 150 monkeys in a ravine, we see the entire group, a few family groups, then subgroups only, and a single pair of monkeys; and finally, we stare with the psychologist, who has not had the advantage of an aerial perspective, point blank into the face of a single individual as he sits, nods, yawns, and shows no sign of caring anything about mother love, dominance, sex, curiosity, or principles of behavior.

At this point the psychologist is both chagrined and confused. There are subjects all around, but since he has no apparatus and has not found a procedure that the monkeys will tolerate, there are few results as he is prepared to see them. He still believes that to see order you must Control, that is, physically manipulate, your Conditions and use Important Psychological Variables. After numerous pilot studies, or hunches that failed and deserve to be buried, the course of action is finally clear. As Figure 4–1 shows, the psychologist paints a series of concentric circles on the ground and thus creates a standardized test situation. In the center

FIGURE 4.1. *An experimentalist's model of the universe. Note the kettle of soybeans and the big scarecrow in the center. To achieve a naturalist's view, erase the circles, take away the objects, and wait to see what happens when monkeys happen to sit at varying distances from food.*

of an experimental universe there must of course be a positive reinforcer (here a kettle of food) and a negative reinforcer (here a novel representational stimulus object, or scarecrow doll). The psychologist systematically varies the size of the scarecrow, he systematically varies the distance between scarecrow and kettle, and he repeats his test often enough to achieve appropriate balancing of stimulus orders and adequate replication. He records by time-sampling photography. As the psychologist sees several thousand of these photographs (which are a pale representation of what happened, but still far from being data as such), the results are highly reliable, the curves (see Figure 4–2) are as smooth as most he has seen in the laboratory, the data are significant beyond the .01 level, and the paper is publishable.

There is only one rub: What was going on out there, and what, exactly, were the results of the experiment? It seems quite true that, as common sense might suggest, the monkeys did not like the scarecrows. Using our laboratory vocabulary, we can go farther and say a fair amount about social interactions over food and strange objects, approach and avoidance, conflict behavior, the relationship between stimulus intensity and approach distance, and so on. In fact, I was at first highly pleased to see how well the microcosmic models of behavior that I had constructed

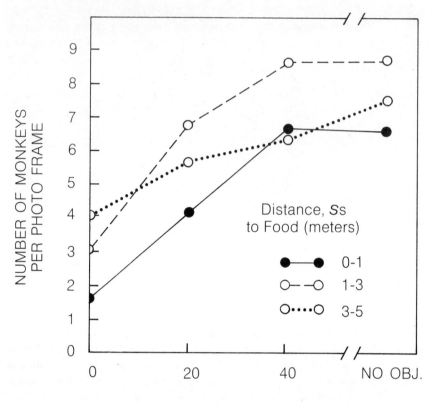

FIGURE 4.2. *An experimentalist's professed view of reality: approach-avoidance behavior of a Japanese monkey group, as a function of the distance between a positive reinforcer and a negative reinforcer. (Similar data were obtained when the size of the scarecrow was varied.)*

on the basis of work with isolation-raised infants, shored up by ideas from men such as Schneirla (1959), Hebb (1958), and Miller (1959), were able to supply the conceptual tools to zoom out and predict a significant portion of the tremendous complexity of an entire group of freeranging monkeys.

The source of my later unrest was clearly not in the failure of our experimental rationale, but rather in the nature of the success. At best we account for a mere fraction of the variance of behavior in any test. We can specify in partial fashion what our antecedent conditions are and establish reliable consequents. But between these terms there are always more gaps than closures. The experiment had answered some of the questions I had posed, and suggested more questions that could have been examined in the same setting, but were they really the most pertinent sorts of questions we could ask about wild monkeys? I did not know, because I was still ignoring what went on outside the predefined test situation; and from talking with other field workers I was gradually becoming aware of how poor this made my observation, even of the "facts" disclosed by the photographs.

Had one the insight and the technical capability, this situation was probably rich enough, naturalistically speaking, to allow us to study 90 percent of the behavioral repertoire of macaques, and yet my account said relatively little about broad aspects of adaptation. The view I took of the behavioral setting was still narrow, both ecologically and conceptually. Had I had a naturalist's orientation, I would also have realized that I could zoom in from above, as a field worker might (Carpenter, 1965; DeVore, 1965; Imanishi & Altmann, 1965) instead of only zooming out and thus losing perspective at many points. The study would have been far more accurate if I had asked, even with very crude measures: Where in the rest of the world do these same animals go? How are they identified as a group and what holds them together? How, when, and why do they leave this place and come back together to the tiny plot of ground on which I do my testing? My choice of a 10-meter circle rather than a one-meter area (such as is used in the laboratory) or a 100-meter area, or indeed the whole countryside was merely arbitrary. In any case, the nature of the beast would have remained similar, if not identical. For, in a fundamental sense, my previous laboratory data, present photographs, and the field worker's maps of geography, range and ecology, yielded data on identical problems: Where is the animal at particular points of time? How did he get there? Why is he there rather than elsewhere? Where will he be next and what will he do?

Are not the psychologist's data of threatening, fleeing, and picking up food, all aspects of approach and avoidance (Miller, 1959; Nissen, 1950; Schneirla, 1959)? And are not these supposedly generic concepts in turn aspects of distance from an object (Carpenter, 1964; Hediger, 1955), which in turn is merely a specialized instance of behavior in space from which one could have selected an infinite number of reference objects other than food or scarecrow, or latitude and longitude, for measuring behavior? In this sense, our selection and manipulation of single objects inevitably tend to blind us. We confuse the focus of our attention with reality; we confuse our view with the animal's view. There are not only times in which neither approach nor avoidance occur, but there are also many times in which the object with respect to which measurements should be made is unknown, and the terms approach-avoidance or behavioral distance thus lose their focal point and their meaning. The monkeys' world was far broader than the one I constructed for them, and it was organized hierarchically in far greater detail than the photographs showed, and it was especially as I realized this fact that the data made sense. Whatever insight I achieved came not so much from manipulating conditions experimentally, or from measuring the location of monkeys to the nearest meter, or from getting large samples of data, as from pondering: What has this situation sampled of the universe of ecology and behavior in freeranging monkeys? To what extent is the sample representative?

MARK 2

Of course, I did not know the answers to these questions. To know what one is controlling in an experiment, or what is natural or representative about a situation, one must have a broader and clearer idea of the universe than is provided by one observation or experiment. Neither the naturalist nor the experimentalist has any clairvoyance here. Both are caught in the dilemma of having to rely simultaneously on samples of information to judge the universe, and a half-intuitive idea of the universe to judge the samples (see Brunswick, 1955; Postman, 1955; Polanyi, 1958). However, there is a big difference in the sorts of samples they go after, and the way in which they go after them. Being in the domain of the naturalist at this stage of research, I decided to test his outlook. This meant that I had to cultivate enough naïveté, tolerance of ambiguity, and reliance on intuition to meet the problems at hand, namely monkeys. I had to use a whole body of experimental and observational skills, and simply trust that the neocortex would also come to my aid, and help to correct later for lack of precision and possible errors of interpretation (see Skinner, 1956, for parallel attitudes in an avowed experimentalist).

The next several steps I took led me increasingly farther from direct manipulative controls and fixed locations. In a series of observations and simple experiments on Cayo Santiago, Puerto Rico, I tried to take the work to where the monkeys were, rather than bring the monkeys to where I was. Instead of trying to physically control as much as possible, I tried the naturalist's alternative: Manipulate only as much as is necessary to answer your questions clearly, and otherwise leave things alone, for there is order even in what seems to you to be the worst confusion, and you might well introduce worse confusion if you use your hands before you use your eyes. For practical reasons, it became necessary to abandon neat metric layouts on the ground. Quantification and time-sampling photography were of limited use. The monkeys seemed to go exactly where photography was most difficult. Moreover, stimulus units and response units were soon seen to come in all different sizes and shapes, and the use of a fixed focal length of lens and a fixed interval of time sampling simply did not provide the flexibility that was required to identify and record the stimulus and the response. Food was seldom used as a focal variable. On many occasions, I still placed a toy or other object out for the monkeys, and it served as a reference variable for my descriptions, but more and more the task became: What reference points do the monkeys use? I already knew how I or a physicist might classify objects and situations, but how do monkeys seem to classify them; in other words, to what do they respond, and how do they respond?[1]

As a start, I tried to determine the extent to which monkeys respond differentially to familiar objects and to novel ones, and to thus assess in

[1] Psychophysics comprises only a slight variation on these questions. The psychophysicist examines the correlation between the subject's behavior toward an object and his own classifications of the stimulus, and from this infers what is an effective stimulus for the animal. Three things distinguish the psychophysicist from the naturalist, but none of the differences are absolute: (a) The psychophysicist—except when he, too, deals with social perception, for example—classifies objects in terms a physicist would use (grams, centimeters, seconds) instead of employing a layman's descriptive terms (trees, bananas, dolls) or functional terms (food, sex object, fear object). The naturalist is either more flexible or less discriminating. (b) The psychophysicist is seldom concerned with response taxonomy, which is of central importance to naturalists. He is principally concerned with the taxonomy of effective stimuli, or the mapping of a stimulus domain. Understandably, he is more apt to use single response measures, or even an arbitrary response unit (for example, lever pressing) as an index of stimulus discriminability. (c) Analogously, the objects that the psychophysicist studies are seldom the complex, naturally-occurring ones (bananas, trees, other animals) that are of interest to the naturalist. Indeed, some psychophysicists avoid the study of complex responses and complex objects for the same reason that the naturalist selects them: because they are of known functional significance. Occasionally, we find bizarre statements from experimentalists, to the effect that a true psychophysics requires the use of "precise, pure, and simple stimuli" (whatever these might be); in other words, bananas and trees are out. But so long as bananas are objects and psychophysics purports to deal with objects in general, why indeed would a psychophysics of bananas or any other object *not* be legitimate? No data whatsoever are required to show that techniques for correlating "a response" with "an object variable" are potentially applicable to *this* response or *that* object.

The distinctions between naturalistic and classical psychological approaches to psychophysical questions are of considerable practical importance, but they are not, I submit, fundamental from the standpoint of logic.

rough fashion how well they know their natural habitat. Rather than fabricate the objects, as would have been customary in the laboratory, I used what was already available in the field as a "standard of familiarity" (see Menzel, Davenport, and Rogers, 1961). Thus, I made a collection of 20 pairs of identical objects, which ranged from one-inch hermit crabs to ten-foot tree limbs, and included such things as coconut shells, vines, sea-washed bottles, and rocks. One object in each pair was altered, usually by spraying it with paint. Insofar as possible, I tried to balance out factors such as visual complexity. Then, the objects were placed out simultaneously along a trail, or near wherever I had found the objects, and I waited for the monkeys. Periodically, the positions of the objects were rotated to control for biases. The test was repeated on 26 different occasions, over a period of about two weeks, using a variety of locations on the 40-acre island. A written note was made on all animals that responded to either object, or passed by within a previously designated area. Insofar as I was able to identify individuals within a single test, no animal was scored twice. Similar controls were used in subsequent experiments.

Only about one-third of the monkeys who came by responded in any detectable fashion to the objects, and under these circumstances, active avoidance was not seen. Nearly all animals who did respond were juveniles or females (see Menzel, 1966, on age and sex differences). Of the 133 animals who approached, 93 percent went to the novel object, or first approached it and then went on their way or responded to the unaltered object. Prolonged staring, smelling, and tapping were the most common reactions. Thus, there was a clear differential response across a wide range of objects and situations.

Novel arrays of unaltered objects also affected response. Thus, if five or six coconut shells were stacked up in a pile, near another array that was left as it was found, the monkeys invariably responded to the former, and bowled the pile over.

In their behavior toward each other, the rhesus seemed to show less reaction to simple visual changes than was seen with inanimate objects. On different occasions, over 20 monkeys were dyed with bright dyes, and on several occasions I also observed males who had been in fights and had received large facial wounds which greatly altered their appearance. Members of the social group showed no unique reaction to those changed animals. Had the altered animals not been recognized as familiar, it is most likely that they would have been attacked, as nongroup members were.

Rather than always altering the objects themselves, I also presented identical objects in different locations, to see how the ecological context might influence response.[2] For example, one toy was placed in the open, and another next to a tree or rock. The differences in behavior were so great that even when the objects were presented simultaneously with as little as a two-foot separation, 86 percent of those animals showing detectable reactions ($N = 120$) directed their attention toward the one closest to the tree or rock. The monkeys either showed no response to objects that were in the open, or deliberately circled them, or (in those cases where approach did occur) would not approach as closely. In another variation on the same theme, a single novel toy was suspended from a limb of a tree, in such a way that the monkeys could approach equally closely from the ground or via the tree. The question was which route would be taken. Typically, monkeys who came along the ground and later approached the object glanced once, went to a nearby tree, climbed up, crossed to the tree containing the object, climbed down, and then hung within a foot of the object to stare. Sometimes they slapped or jerked at the string (thus moving the object) but avoided direct contact with the object. Other observations strongly supported the conclusion that there were gross anisotropies of approach distance between the vertical vs. horizontal planes, between above vs. below, and between the structure, for example, rock, tree trunk, or branch, on which the object was vs. a separate structure, for example, a parallel rock or branch. The three-dimensional space produced quite different results than would be seen in a one-dimensional runway (Miller, 1959) or a two-dimensional level area such as I used in Japan. These anisotropic effects were more pronounced with novel objects such as toys than with objects that had been gathered from the field. Table 4–1 shows the results of one such test. For this test, familiar and unfamiliar objects were placed singly on a long pipeway, near a tree and a vertical pipe support. The monkeys could make their approach (scored when an animal came within two meters) equally well by going to the adjacent tree, or climbing up from the ground beneath the object, or proceeding along the pipe. The familiar (control) object was a piece of coconut palm fiber rolled up so as to approximate the coontail in size and visual appearance. The monkeys frequently hopped over each other as they traveled the pipeway, in other words, these much smaller test objects were not physically impassable barriers for them. As

[2] Exactly where monkeys place the boundaries between "object" and "context"—or between "intrinsic" and "extrinsic" properties of an object—is, of course, unknown a priori. I make these distinctions anthropomorphically for purposes of description. To apply the zoom lens analogy here, the boundaries between object and context are subject to constant change; as the monkey's position in space and his visual field and attention vary, contexts can become objects and vice versa. (Allport, 1955, p. 106)

TABLE 4–1   *Percentage of monkeys showing various modes of approach to novel and familiar objects*

Object on Pipeway	Initial Approach Route				
	No. cases	Along pipe	Up from ground	To adja- cent tree	Step over object
Familiar Palm Fiber	44	56.4	20.5	23.1	59.1
Novel Doll	52	32.7	9.6	57.7	1.9
Novel Coontail	33	33.3	3.0	63.7	0.0

can be seen from Table 4–1, the mode of approach was typically horizontal (along pipe) for familiar objects, and typically from overhead or the side (to adjacent tree) and very rarely from beneath the object (up from ground) for novel objects.

Vertical vs. horizontal anisotropies were checked out in another way, by presenting two identical elongated objects, one placed upright and the other flat. Here I used 15 pairs of objects. These were gathered from the field and varied in size from one inch to ten feet. As predicted, the vertical objects received most of the attention (75 percent of 40 cases) and produced the most intense reactions. Smaller objects were manipulated by hand or stared at, but with larger objects side-by-side, the animal might simply sit on the horizontal to stare at the vertical, and then circle sharply around the vertical object, or (in the case of a tree branch) use it as a base for social play.

Context effects (see Hebb, 1958) could be seen very clearly in tests of this sort. For example, a pink conch shell was taken from the beach to the top of the highest hill on Cayo Santiago, and placed on a favorite resting rock. Whereas the monkeys had shown no reaction to such an object on the beach, some avoided the rock and all except two adult males of the total 17 animals who went onto the rock stared at the shell, smelled it, or tapped it away from them with the fingers, acting almost as cautiously as they would toward a novel toy (see Figures 4–3 and 4–4). Similarly, I took a bell-shaped sponge that had washed up onto the beach, and placed a bright red flower from a nearby bush into the cavity of the sponge. Over a dozen individuals circled this strange object before a juvenile finally stretched out cautiously and snatched the flower away. In the meantime, other sponges and flowers that were available in the vicinity received no detectable reactions. When everyday objects were placed out of context on branches or the long elevated water pipe that the monkeys used as a

FIGURE 4.3. *Juvenile rhesus stare at and smell a seashell that is placed out of context in the woods.*

trailway, over half of the monkeys that passed stopped to smell these objects, or poked at them and jumped away, and a few infants gave a big leap to get past.

Narrow passages that restrict the space available for getting around an object seem very important to response. Thus, monkeys, especially big males, at times passed within a foot of a stuffed toy or snake that was on level ground, with no display; but if the same object was on a branch or on the pipeway, they would stop at a distance and almost never cross over it (Table 4–1). Similarly, a doll in, or on top of, a bucket of food would keep any rhesus from reaching in, just as it produced avoidance in Japanese monkeys (see Figure 4–2). However, if the same object was placed on top of a pile of food on open ground, the monkeys would often take food that was in direct contact with the doll, or even hurl the doll aside.

These findings on spatial and contextual factors raise some troublesome questions. For example, what do we mean by "available space" and what are its metrics in the behavior of monkeys? I would like to think

FIGURE 4.4. *A juvenile eases up toward a stranger from the rear, after circling around the rock. Similar behavior is displayed toward people; several rhesus followed up by jabbing me in the back with a finger and racing up a tree.*

that we will eventually achieve what Hull called a "bonafide field theory," stating the concept of available space physicalistically in terms of multiple spatial gradients (Fraenkel & Gunn, 1961, Chapter XI; Hull, 1952, p. 241). But, how does an animal determine a spatial gradient in the first place? How do gradients of available space (that is, available to the animal) get projected around an object that lies at a considerable distance from the animal? Is there a single gradient that emanates from the object itself, as tropistic theories, Hull's diagrams, and Figure 4–1 in the present paper all suggest; or are there hundreds of gradients, each subject to biases of organismic perception at every step as the monkey moves through an object-cluttered space? Does every object in the world have a gradient around it, as some physicalistic accounts would suggest, or are not many objects irrelevant as the monkey (and attention) wanders? Why are distances and directions always ordered variables for behavior, and where does this order come from? So far as I know, there is still no adequate explanation of why ten yards produces a functionally different response than five yards, and why one yard to the left of an object is functionally equivalent to one yard to the right (assuming that it is, or, that laterality is unimportant) but only half a yard overhead. How does an animal integrate the normally-occurring multitude of gradients simultaneously to come out with the best spatial path, which goes far enough, but no farther than necessary, from a noxious object? Why does the monkey not retreat to an infinite distance? Are constancy phenomena really as ubiquitous and adaptive as perceptually-oriented psychologists would have us believe? How does perceptual constancy square with performance inconstancy? Why do juveniles, and occasionally even adults, go out of their way to come close to objects that they subsequently act cautious toward? Are approach and avoidance really dichotomous tendencies? All of these questions still puzzle me.

Another finding reminds one of the gestalt principle of "grouping" (Köhler, 1929). Sometimes, in varying my locations of testing, I placed a toy down next to a stone or a coconut shell that had simply been lying around. A common reaction was to stare for a moment, approach the toy to within about one yard, vacillate, stretch out a hand and jerk back, and then run over, grab up the familiar object that had always been available, carry it away, and sit under a bush and bat it around while staring at the novel object. When two or more novel objects were presented simultaneously, the monkeys responded quite differently than they did to single objects. In another test of grouping effects, I placed out a row of four identical toys, and varied the size of the gap between the objects. Characteristically, the monkeys approached from the end of the group and circled it. If any objects were touched, they were usually the ones most isolated from the rest of the group. Of the few (19 of 163 animals) who passed between the objects, 17 went through the largest gap. These were juveniles, and they made a game of leaping through the gap and returning to repeat the performance. Several subsequently crossed through a small gap.

The same sort of thing seemed to occur with a strange observer and a novel object as the related objects. For example, monkeys confronted with a raccoon tail would often stop and scan the area before checking the object further, and if they saw me, they would look back and forth between the object and me. This rarely occurred with everyday, inanimate objects. These behaviors could be enhanced by adding a further connection such as a loose string between the object and me. If I touched the string, the monkeys would withdraw from the object.

Eventually, I learned something in these experiments that is already clear to all perceptually-oriented psychologists, that is, the phrase, "object as such," is a convenient fiction. So long as he is free to move, all an animal has to do is turn his head or walk a few steps and the object might no longer exist for him. Especially when we operationally define a snake as a fear object, a toy as a plaything, or a banana as a positive reinforcer, we are apt to create more problems than we solve. Fear, sociality, play, edibility, positiveness, and negativeness are not characteristics of objects; they are inferences as to what the animal does or is capable of doing with that object. Simply by varying other factors, such as physical context, it is possible to get all of these reactions to the same object. Laboratory data on chimpanzees (for example, Mason, Davenport, & Menzel, in press; Menzel, 1964) indicate that the identical object can produce strong avoidance, threat, attack, wrestling, grooming, attempted copulation, tool using, or no reaction at all according to the circumstances of testing. For chimpanzees, a doll, for example, is much more than a "social surrogate." If one is determined to use such terms, a doll can be a surrogate for just about anything. The fundamental limits to its qualities are set by chimpanzees.

To a lesser, but still substantial, extent, one can see a similar lability of object-functions in wild rhesus, also. The following episodes with artificial fruits are illustrative of about 25 such tests. I was using these objects to examine social interactions around a class of objects that was visually familiar but otherwise novel. My particular concern was with social dominance factors and with the reactions of the adult males, who ignored my other test objects. These animals were rarely seen to obviously orient toward a toy, but if a plastic fruit of equivalent size and shape was taken out of my pocket, they seem to materialize out of thin air, along with the ubiquitous juveniles.

In one instance, a group of 80 was giving loud vocalizations of the sort they make for real food before I put a plastic orange down. Several adults and juveniles raced toward it. A top-ranking female won out, the others backing away as she approached. Ordinarily, most monkeys at this point would have grabbed up the plastic fruit and tried to chew it for a time, but as this female reached for it, she jerked back, peered closely, and gave a bark. That was the end of the food vocalization from the others. Everyone sat for a few minutes. About a dozen juveniles and a few adults came over later and stared at or smelled the object, as they would with a doll. An infant started to tap the orange around, but an adult female immediately ran over and pulled the infant away. Several minutes later the group moved away and another group of 50, that had been resting 15 yards away, came into the area. Two or three individuals glanced at the plastic orange as they passed by, but otherwise everyone ignored the object.

Such social context factors are ubiquitous and scarcely surprising. However, it can easily be seen that this particular sort of case did *not* mean that the two groups learned once and for all from the single individual that the object was not food. On this and other occasions, when a plastic food had lain ignored for hours, I walked over to the object, picked it up while the monkeys watched, placed it down again, and walked away. Several animals came over and checked it—as they checked many objects that any other monkey or I had been handling. This time they grasped it up immediately. Two juveniles started to play with the object. One broke away with it and ran, at which several infants in a tree gave "food vocalizations" again, and immediately about ten monkeys, including some adults, chased the one with the object. An adult female caught him, got the orange away, ran up a tree with it, chewed at it excitedly for a few seconds, and then threw it away. No one other than juveniles bothered with it again (until the next test), and the juveniles played with it. The object passed from one juvenile to the next, usually according to the age and size of the animal.

Learning is quite possibly involved here, but it is indeed short term, unreliable, and reversible. It would also take an enormous amount of research to separate learning from other aspects of the group performance. Here I find the group performance more interesting than the isolation of a single process. The object, the physical situation, and what other animals are doing all enter into the overall context, but no single factor is sufficient. For rhesus, social factors seem to be the most important in determining responses to an object, the physical situation is next in importance, and the characteristics of the object are merely a predisposing factor, especially if the entire array of things has any element of novelty whatsoever.

Observation

In the course of the experiments with the test circle in Japan, we had become aware that the macaques spent little or no time in the open test area unless food was there as a lure. The situation was excellent for photography and for measuring of distances unconfounded by three-dimensional spatial factors (which was, in fact, the reason that I as an experimentalist selected it), but it was obviously not ideal for monkeys (which piqued my curiosity as a naturalist). In other situations the animals also seemed to avoid open areas. They often stretched out on large rocks for resting and grooming, and the more I watched, the more I felt there were preferred loci on the rocks. But the rules were not obvious.

Whether these observations related to the topic of major interest to me—"responsiveness to objects"—I did not know, for I was as yet un-accustomed to thinking of boulders and large patches of ground as objects, or simply lying down as a sign of responsiveness. However, on Cayo Santiago I decided to look further and see if I could predict where a monkey might go. I felt that if I could make sense out of this problem, the earlier problems of adaptation to objects in space might appear in a clearer light. Accordingly, I spent some time looking over a group of boulders or a patch of woods or trail, squinting along the ground or through the trees at rhesus level, and simply watching where the monkeys walked, sat, and laid down. After two or three weeks, my success in prediction improved quite a bit, but it was even longer before I discovered some of the general principles on which I was apparently basing my predictions. Specific classes of things, for example, trees, buildings, rocks, open areas, were of secondary importance. The crucial element seemed to be simply objects, edges, and verticals in general. Figure 4–5 shows the scene that finally caused me to see the obvious. Since my speculative summary notes of that evening (October 11, 1965) express the details as well as I can express them now, I shall reprint them, adding in occasional references and examples from later notes.

> Probably because of the sun, few monkeys are on the cistern or shed roofs today, but all I've seen have been on the edge. This is true whether they walk, sit, or lie down, although generally it seems most true of lying. Other object-structurings of the space can change or modify this; for instance, adult male No. 107 and adult female No. 75 sit at 10:20 on the cistern away from the edge, but near a water pipe. They copulate. Between each of several mountings, one or the other sits with hands on the pipe.
>
> At the feeding areas, also, the rhesus tend to sit along the building,

FIGURE 4.5. *The use of edges in resting on top of a concrete structure. On naturally occurring rocks one must, of course, also take into account contours and configurations within the "object."*

or on the rim, especially by pillars. This breaks down to some extent if food is scattered or if other special incentives require the use of the open. It also breaks down if one animal orients at or sits next to another. In this case, however, one of the pair or group is still near something else most of the time. A monkey is without question the most important class of object for another monkey, but it is still an object and a spatial referent.

Many other things, of such an enormous size range seem to get most attention at the edges that the problem becomes what is an object in the first place, and what is an edge (for example, Allport, 1955; Gibson, 1958, 1966). The animals tend to stay near the side of a trail (Figure 4–6), the edge of a large clearing, the crown, base, or prominent ledge

FIGURE 4.6. *The use of edges in traveling along a trail.*

on a hill. Sticks and leaves are chewed most on the ends, small box seats for observers are sat on at the corners, novel objects such as a rope are smelled or touched first on an end, novel objects such as a coontail are approached cautiously from one end. A doll is smelled most frequently at the top and back of the head (see Figure 4–4), even though the initial approach might be from the front. With each other, face end and rear end are critical in most display patterns. I am most often approached and stared at from the back, and next most often from 120° or 210° by adults; juveniles approach most often from overhead in a tree (Figure 4–7). I'm given most latitude in front. A subject animal's judgment of available space would seem to take account not only of what is available to him, but also of what is visually available to the stimulus animal.

As noted earlier, several objects placed down at once often seem to form a "group" and are most closely approached from an end of

FIGURE 4.7. *While the rest of the group rests and grooms in the afternoon, three juveniles, who approached from overhead, play on a novel rope. Note also the adolescent female smelling the rope from the ground. Before the monkeys swung on the rope as they would on a vine, they spent some time staring, smelling, poking, grasping, jerking, and hanging on the rope—in that order.*

FIGURE 4.8. *Part of a traveling "group" of rhesus confronts a "group" of novel objects. The main line of travel subsequently flowed around either side of the row of objects. Several monkeys approached more closely, a few touched the objects, and one or two jumped through the large gap.*

the group (Figure 4–8). Monkeys trot down a row of trees in a smooth continuous path, not touching or swerving at each tree, but acting as if the trees constitute a "tree line" or "edge of the clearing." Do rocks form a "rock formation" and water a "shore line" for them? Judging again from behavior, this is at times a meaningful and convenient way to describe the effective stimulus. With infant chimps in the lab, a novel pile of gravel placed on a floor that is already covered with gravel is initially responded to with caution, and later with approach, slapping, threat postures, and eventually rolling around and jumping on the pile, whereas even while all this goes on, the loose gravel all around is walked on as before, and several individual pieces of the pile might be tapped off and carried around and played with freely. Might there not be three object-concepts—or "nonequivalent stimuli" (Klüver, 1933)—involved here simultaneously? Certainly there is a big difference, behaviorally, in the "ground" (loose gravel), the "figure" (the pile), and the "stimulus elements" (individual pieces of gravel), and these differences are seen in the identical time periods. There is no reason whatsoever that the same sort of thing cannot happen across time as an animal moves through space, especially since he then receives very different sets of visual information from the identical environment (Gibson, 1958, 1966).

Gestalts are not always the same gestalts, and in some cases the animal's attention would seem to zoom back and forth repeatedly, as well as to scan.

Even though the monkey does not obviously attend to minutiae, he is constantly taking them into account. For example, the direction of locomotion is constantly affected by patterns of light and shade. If several branches are on the ground in a row, an animal tends to walk or deflect his path along this line, and if he stops and orients in quadrupedal position for a moment, it will be with hands on the branch. Otherwise he will stop at a stone, a tree root, a bush, a rock, or even a crack in a rock, but rarely where there is no object. Possibly, this is partly for a better view, or for security, or for support. One could find, post hoc, a separate reason for every act listed above, but are the reasons not somehow related? The behaviors and the effective characteristics of objects seem more consistent and more simple than all the reasons we could conjure up, and specific reasons might be added on top of general reasons, rather than being quite independent. The size of the structuring units, or the objects that structure a larger unit, can vary enormously, but there is always a structuring there.

The probability of stopping a walk (and more so of sitting, and even more so of lying down, and even more so of lying supine rather than prone) is greater if *any* edge, rim, projection, cover, end, edge, or ledge is there. There is a definite hierarchy of behaviors with respect to objects. If another monkey already occupies a spot, so much the better. Often, one can see a series of monkeys displacing each other, in turn, from a rock or a root along a trail. Before they come out of the woods, the animals stop at the last tree, bush, or stone, just as they pause at the threshold before entering a building. Frequently, they "keep one foot on base" before stepping away from a rock or a fallen branch on which they have rested for only a few moments.

Are such acts completely unrelated to the territorialism that one sees in species other than rhesus; in other words, are these seemingly significant orientations toward objects the precursors of much more specific and stabilized restrictions on the free use of space? Monkeys do not defend an abstract concept of "territory"; they defend where they are; and the first problem is to find out why they are where they are. For that matter, *where are they*? What reference points are they using and in terms of what objects and parameters of objects do they recognize a familiar location?

The probability of running—especially if I stare too hard, or a jet plane passes overhead, or a large, unfamiliar monkey is nearby— definitely seems to increase as the animal gets away from a well-structured spot. It is as if one j.n.d. is added to his arousal level for each decrease in the amount of physical structure. Perhaps this is one thing that makes a strange, bare room in the laboratory so noxious to most primates.

Most threats are directed toward me from spots where the vertical element and visual cover are prominent. There is even a hierarchy of spots: a rock vs. a stone or a root, a tree vs. a rock, a tall tree or a leafy one vs. a small or bare one, and still further a rock near a tree vs. a rock in the open, and so on. If the animal is first in the open, he will nearly always move away from a large stranger. However, he might run to a rock or (more likely) a tree and *then* threaten. He does not always show a clearly avoidant response, and he does not move to a fixed metric distance. He goes to the nearest "unit of space" that is "far enough" away, and this is easier to predict on the basis of objects than on the basis of distance alone. The smaller the animal, the greater the likelihood that he will threaten, if at all, from overhead. Indeed, smaller or subordinate monkeys are less apt to sit in the open or on the pinnacle of a rock or a tree when alone (Draper, 1965). The juveniles and some females are by far the worst for threatening observers, and juveniles seldom, if ever, do so from the ground level. Females do, but with a big male nearby. (Question for field workers: Why call it a "protected threat" if another animal is nearby, but not if the threatener is behind a bush or on a rock or tree? In either case there is a "supporting object." No doubt the protecting animal introduces special elements because it, too, can act, but I strongly stress the fact that the same sorts of behaviors can be seen whether the stimulus objects are monkeys, people, rats, or toys.) One more word on threats: If the animal does perchance threaten from the ground, he will most often have his hands on a branch or root, and so forth. If I stare at a seated animal suddenly and he does not threaten, he will glance upward and reach for a hand support (Hunt, Landis, & Jacobsen, 1937) even if the "escape route" is only a twig or a one-foot stump (see Figure 4–9). This reaching for a support is, however, common in any sort of strange or arousing situation. Could it possibly stem from a pervasive and almost infantile tendency to clasp (any) objects?

In short, there are always objects guiding any reaction, even if we would not say the animal was especially responsive in the sense of manipulating, playing, or avoiding. These objects can be just about anything. The same object serves multiple functions and is attended to in quite different ways, sometimes as a thing in itself and sometimes as part of a larger configuration or relation. It is not exactly correct to say, as I did about *Macaca fuscata* (Menzel, 1966) that monkeys are "indifferent" to most everyday objects. We must at least remember that the substratum and objects of context are reinforcing and sustaining, and that the objects involved are vitally important as a physical frame of reference for performances involving other (focal or goal) objects (see footnote 2). The thing that distinguishes infants from adults is that they more often treat everyday objects as focal objects, to the extent that they respond manually, orally, and with more overt visual orientations, and look at the ground instead of the horizon. The adult, however, is

FIGURE 4.9. *An intergroup fight over an artificial feeding unit. The smaller adult male, who stands on a fallen palm branch to threaten, was from a large and dominant group. His challenges drove the other group from the feeder to the edge of the clearing. Note how the Number One male of the subordinate group circled to charge and how others use structures in various ways.*

far from being oblivious or unaffected, as is patently clear from responses such as sitting, walking, and the like. Why do objects deserve to be called reinforcers only if they can be eaten or handled? For that matter, do they have to be called reinforcers at all? To state the problem differently: When a monkey circles a rock, climbs one tree, crosses to another, descends a thin branch, and *then* touches another monkey, it is an observational inference and a convenient oversimplification to say only that his responsiveness was directed toward the last object. This is like describing operant conditioning only in terms of what happens at a food trough.

Needless to say, I could not satisfactorily check out all of these hunches and speculations immediately, and I still do not know whether all of them will hold true. However, as a *general set* of phenomena they seem to me to possess a considerable bearing on rhesus psychology and to be most pertinent to classical problems of psychology generally. They obviously "zoom in" on selected problems of habitat selection, behavior in space, and general ecology, extending the potential orderliness of behavior down to the level of micro-ecology and back toward the levels of traditional interest to psychology, or at least to the problems I had started with. They also greatly expanded my notions about "objects" and forever rid me of the illusion that no information can be gained about behavior unless the monkeys are responding in obvious fashion to each other or to test objects. The nature of the surrounding environment is never unimportant. A monkey's location is never accidental or trivial. We can probably extend this principle down hierarchically to the twig on the branch on the tree in the woods in the habitat, near the species and the group and the family and the mother. Then, once we get the "animal as a whole" pinpointed, we can ask where his hand and his eye and his tail might be. I am not at all convinced that one is being "precise" by jumping immediately into microscopic details, as some scientists urge us to do.

A complete analysis of physiological reactivity and posture would not, in fact, be precise *enough* for the naturalist. Such information is too encapsulated within the organism. It could not tell the naturalist anything about his first and most important problem: Where on the map are my animals? How can I best learn to find them and what is the nature of their effective environment? I therefore suggest that we think of "precision" in relativistic rather than absolute terms. Precision is *information* rather than minutiae; it is that which eliminates our uncertainty about behavior, or reduces it to a given degree. The more uncertain the environment, that is, the greater the number of alternative locations and reference points the animal might use, the more the potential information, and the less minute on an absolute scale need we become to achieve a given amount of information.

This attitude has an important effect on experimental procedures also. Within limits, the more free the behavior situation that we give our animals, the better, for insofar as we do not restrict them, we can test their behavior against more general and complete models of what might have been. The major function of refined, restricted, and physically controlled situations should be (a) to give us clearer and sharper ideas of how to set up the general model of "what might have been," and (b) to allow us to determine more accurately and by alternative procedures whether formal, descriptive information is meaningful, relevant, and valid.

A first step in checking out the substantive ideas here was to attempt to verify a reasonable number of the independent statements and to get a better idea of how various behavioral tendencies might hang together and relate to each other. On Cayo Santiago, I concentrated on simple frequency counts of where the animals located themselves and what they did.

In several weeks, I observed 224 cases (some counts probably involving the same animals) of sitting or lying on the top of structures such as sheds and cisterns. Of these, 205 (91 percent) were on the edges or corners, and most were on the corners. The slope of a roof definitely affected locations also: as the angle of the two halves of the roof departed from 180°, the monkeys used the upper ridge instead of the edge. No doubt, on a steeply pitched angle, most would locate on the top ridge, as indeed they characteristically did on one building.

On flat objects and rocks, even those less than 10 in. high and about 2 x 2 ft. on the top surface, the smaller animals used an edge in 19 of the first 20 cases, even though they perched in ordinary seated positions and did not drape their legs or tail over the edge. Because of their size, larger rhesus could not be tested here.

Along the wider trails usually used by human observers, I estimate from several weeks of checking and following monkey groups that there were at least five animals just off to the side of the trail for every one on the trail and few, if any, in the center third (dead center) of the trail.

Between the two tree lines along a stretch of beach (approximately 15 yds. wide and 100 yds. in length) that connects two parts of the island, 73 of the first 79 animals (92 percent) sat nearer to the trees than to the center.

All such *edge effects* increased considerably if I started to approach the animals or if disturbances occurred; but even when I observed from a considerable distance with binoculars, the tendency was still very definitely there. These formal counts were made only when the sun was not out, and when sun-shade factors would not be a biasing factor. (Of course, shade is a by-product of vertical structures and might be one factor underlying their attractiveness.) On several occasions, however, many monkeys were sunning in the early morning after a rain, and even though in the open, they remained close to edges and objects. Along a cliff top on two mornings, 26 of 30 sat on or immediately next to large rocks.

Further counts were made when the animals, for various reasons, sat in relatively open areas in the woods. In this case, I checked the tendency to sit by roots, stones, and so on. In 119 cases, 102 monkeys (86 percent) found some "structure," however small. However, these counts were difficult to make because of the ambiguity as to what might constitute an object. Therefore, I set up a simple experiment. Figure 4–10 shows the

FIGURE 4.10. *Sitting on or near objects when in the open. The concrete blocks were introduced experimentally.*

situation. Eight old cinder blocks that had been lying nearby were moved a few yards and set out in rows on a bare patch of ground. I noted where the first 100 animals who entered the predesignated area, bounded by blocks, sat down. In keeping with other observations, 68 rhesus sat on an object, 10 sat touching one, and 22 sat farther than one foot away. Thus, 78 percent of the rhesus used a mere fraction of the available area. A majority of the remaining 22 percent sat next to another animal, who was near an experimental object. Again, it is doubtful whether sitting next to a partner is a real exception to the rule. One might call the partner a mobile "home base surrogate," although it should be noted that if one wants a single criterion for predicting where monkeys will be, the best predictor of all would be social. Monkeys are found where others are found; they stay within the confines of their own closed social group rather than with just any aggregate. Within the group, they tend to stay with members of their family, and even within the family there are individual preferences and waxings and wanings of associational bonds, for example, as the animal matures (Imanishi & Altmann, 1965; Sade, 1965). The observer on Cayo Santiago uses such facts as his best guide for locating an individual.

On branches in the trees, the most common sitting places seemed to be near a projection, although the irregularity of the branches made counts difficult. Therefore, I placed several large branches on the ground, observed where the animals sat, rotated the branch to a new position in space, and found in all of 20 cases that the identical places on the branch were still selected. On a few buildings, there were artificial branches in the form of wooden beams. On these, the animals nearly always sat at the edge, or by a projection or an additional supporting object.

Further tendencies of the same general type were also noted, and although I judge them reliable, I can place no numerical estimate on reliability as yet. For example, in climbing the wire side of a building, rhesus ascend at an end or by a post, even though the former is inefficient, as it confronts them with the greater overhang at the roof corner, and they switch to one side to get up on the roof top. In walking between trees, rocks, or buildings, the monkeys pass closer to one structure than to the center. In battles between two groups, the lines are drawn along cliff ridges, tree lines, shore lines, and so on, as in Figures 4–11 and 4–12. In group travel, all members tend to remain on the same side of a hill, or in trees, where visual contact can be maintained; in other words, the top of the hill forms a group border. Old monkey trails on the ground

FIGURE 4.11.   *An intergroup fight on a cliff top: the beginning. The opposition is just out of sight on the other side of the bush line.*

FIGURE 4.12. *An intergroup fight on a cliff top: the end. This picture was taken about 30 seconds after Figure 4.11.*

seem to be lines connecting or just bypassing a series of structures such as trees, and are off from the centers of relatively open places.

Further field data bearing on the functional significance of such behaviors in reaction to other objects have been discussed in the preceding sections. The experimental data on reactions to novel objects would seem to fit in perfectly with what can be seen under these ordinary circumstances.

Observation and Experiment in Field and Laboratory

Where do we go from here? What can a laboratory psychologist do once he has been bitten by the bug of field work, and of what relevance are field studies to the behavior of primates in more precise experimental studies, such as might be conducted in the laboratory?

First and foremost, there is the matter of the experimenter's attitude. Before we get down to matters of technique, we must determine what sorts of questions we want answered, and we must decide to what we wish to generalize. I would say that what we are trying to reconstruct, analyze, and ultimately generalize to, is behavior as it might occur in nature without our interference. If our present theoretical biases and methodological inhibitions are so great that they obscure this fact, let us forget theory and method, put aside our apparatus for a spell, and try to approach behavior as if for the first time. To the extent that a common method of analysis can be applied in any situation, apparatus might be superfluous anyway. Working in this fashion, and trying to start as it were from scratch, it surprises me over and over again how well Darwin, Freud, Hull, Köhler, Lewin, Lorenz, and other naturalists of various stripes have stated the issues and formulated methods.

In the meantime, I am still trying to discover where an animal will go and what he will do in space, which inevitably is structured in terms of objects. Insofar as possible, the same techniques and vocabulary are used in all situations, that is, we pinpoint spatio-temporal events as accurately as we possibly can, while still trying to get a good qualitative grasp on what the data might show. The emphasis is upon getting a good account of objects and activities; drives, capacities, processes, and the like, can take care of themselves.

At present, I am working with individual animals in a 10 $\times$ 14 ft. indoor room, a 16 $\times$ 100 ft. cage, and a half-acre enclosure. Partly to test some notions developed there, Dr. John Morrison and I (1966) released an intact social group of over 50 rhesus onto a 350-acre island, and tried our hand at a grand-scale study of exploratory behavior, or whatever multitude of things you could call it when animals must adapt to an unfamiliar environment. (We are still trying to figure out what all might be involved in an indoor room.) Many aspects of group travel and social use of space can, I believe, be predicted from individual behavior in the simpler situations; and conversely, the laboratory data make even better sense as field behaviors become more clear.

The principle of some of the tests is to start out with a bare room and a single animal, and to add single objects and then combinations and hierarchical arrays of objects to this situation to see how and why the use of space is modified. Social interactions, approach and avoidance, following behavior, and learning are studied within the same context. I must admit that I still occasionally despair over this tabula rasa approach, this ecological counterpart to isolation-reared infants, naïve organisms, and mechanical robot models. The complexity of simultaneously taking into account even three or four variables is so great, and the number of alternative directions to follow in each successive experiment is so large, that the chances of ever working up to a reasonably complete account of behavior merely by zooming out seems very remote indeed. Nevertheless, as an experimental psychologist, I am convinced it is necessary to keep on trying.

Conversely, with other tests we start with an approximation to a natural context, or otherwise recognize the environment and the organism as parts of an open ecosystem whose boundaries are as yet unknown, and we try to work downward by subtracting variables a few at a time.[3] This approach can be applied to any ecological system, including the infant in a bare cage, but the rich environment makes the discovery of relevant variables and interactions easier at times.

Exactly how all these ends (naturalism and experimentation, laboratory and field, zooming out and zooming in, wild hunches and patience) will meet I do not know, but thus far I am impressed with how much I had been missing in the laboratory by ignoring the conceptual standards of a general naturalistic outlook. Stated otherwise, there is no such thing as a completely unnatural animal or nonfield situation. The amazing thing is how well many principles *do* hold up across many situations. To give one example, many of the edge effects and context effects described earlier are so strong in a small room that you can scarcely get rid of them, which after a while can be an appalling nuisance. After going over films of our isolation-reared chimpanzees, I would judge they are more, rather than less, apt to stay close to edges and verticals than wild rhesus or chimpanzees. For isolation-reared chimpanzees, walls rather than trees are most important—but note that even free-living rhesus orient toward walls and corners of artificial structures (and it is unlikely that they share our concern with artificiality and naturalness). All species I have tested or casually observed in the laboratory—including chimpanzees, gelada baboons, four species of macaques, galagos, squirrel monkeys, and callicebus—show a marked predilection for the corners and edges of cages, rooms, and outdoor compounds unless other verticals are provided. Also, of course, there are species differences as well as similarities in preferences along the vertical direction and in what constitutes an adequate vertical structure.

The characteristics of virtually all reactions to objects and animals within an indoor room are affected by such spatial biases, and even within

---

[3] Physiological research, for example, on brain lesions, usually follows this approach also. The brain specialist does not completely decorticate an animal and then add one factor at a time. He starts with an intact animal system and subtracts or adds. The chief difference between him and the naturalist is that the naturalist's system or gestalt is much larger; it includes the animal, its social group, and its physical environment (see K. R. L. Hall, in press). In fact, some naturalists might argue that the normal primate inherits his social group and his environment almost as strictly as he inherits his physiology.

a few minutes, one can see that an animal's location and activities are highly correlated. Entire sequences and patterns of behavior tend to occur repeatedly in identical portions of the room (cf. Guthrie, 1952). Nearly all resting takes place in corners of the room or on the edges of other structures, such as a perch. If an animal is in the center of the room (which is rare, except when we position an additional object or a social being there), he will usually be walking or running. The probability of entering each square foot of the room can be quite readily scaled according to the weighted distance of that sector from the walls and from other focal variables in the situation. In initial approaches to a novel object, monkeys usually move along a wall or cage wire, and they approach more closely thus than if they should move in from the open. If objects are portable, and if they evoke play, they are carried off to a corner or up onto a vertical structure. All these effects are enhanced when an animal is in a novel or otherwise arousing situation, and with habituation there are consistent changes in performances.

Before I had worked in the field, I was practically unaware that such things had gone on in my laboratory tests. Had I not seen dozens of direct parallels to these behaviors in the wild, I would no doubt agree with those of you who are thinking: "These are position habits, thigmotactic tendencies, or simple orientational behaviors that we have known about for years in the rat and cockroach (Fraenkel & Gunn, 1961). So what?" Now, however, I would like to know what lies behind the labels. What functions do the behaviors serve in the primates? How do they develop? What motor patterns, species variables and stimulus parameters are involved; and, do we not have more than a vague parallel to behavior in the wild? Can we not better understand territorial and social attachments, arboreality, social spacings and patterns of travel, resting, and exploration from laboratory data, and vice versa? What can quantitative spatio-temporal measurements tell us about the general behavioral organization of the species?

What will we think of even simple corner preferences once we finally stop viewing walls as merely walls, trees as merely trees, and cages as merely cages, and start analyzing what makes them so crucial to the animal? Here our own biases, which see certain features as fixed rather than as variable, might well be what has produced our present blasé attitude (E. T. Hall, 1966). The laboratory and the cage are the most unknown stimulus variables we have in psychology; they are introduced into virtually every experiment we conduct; and so long as they are not viewed as variables and examined as special cases of ecology that are possibly producing special breeds of primates, they will remain uncomprehended and our attempts at extrapolation to "behavior in general" will remain myopic.

It is most likely that a monkey's preference for a corner stems from the same orientation toward vertical structures and the edges of structures that we see in the wild. In nature, two large vertical structures do not ordinarily form a juncture. Tossed into a cage, the monkey does what he has in one way or another done since the moment of birth (for example, Cairns, 1966), namely, he locates himself with reference to the most prominent objects available, and thereby "acquires" what we call a corner preference. Figure 4–13, which was taken several minutes after about 30 members of a Cayo Santiago group were trapped from the field and placed in a holding cage, shows what I mean.

What, however, is a "prominent object?" Since little has been said about experiential factors in this paper, let us by all means give learning its due and go back to the point from which these field studies started: to the rearing experiment. For a neonate as helpless and undifferentiated as most primates are, we may take it for granted that some exposure to objects is required before specific classes of objects will become "prominent" and "reinforcing" in highly specialized ways (Mason, Davenport, & Menzel, in press; Menzel, 1964). Exposure to objects also obviously influences how some objects become prominent, and field experiments are rarely capable of enough control to isolate what mechanisms are involved here. But beyond this, our current primate studies of learning and early experience tell us surprisingly little. Especially as applied to behavior in the field, the concept of learning is often as specious and ill defined as the performances we would have to explain with it. Granted that learning is still important, is there anything else that might be involved in a performance that comes about as a result of object-exposure? What forms of experience are sufficient to produce a given performance in a given species? When does a primate learn, what does it learn, and why do different species living in the same geographical environment learn such very different things?

Why is it always *objects*, rather than relatively empty spaces, that receive the strongest aversions, cathexes, and preferences? Why do characteristics such as edges, textures, directions, sizes, movement, and distance produce affective reactions with essentially any form of object, including social beings? I am still looking for a completely neutral object, but this is much harder to come by than I ever thought. To what extent do specific classes of objects involve us in unique principles of behavior, and to what extent are specialized qualities of objects merely added to dimensions and qualities common to all objects? Why do certain behaviors, including lying down, sitting, walking, approaching (in varied fashions), and avoiding (in varied fashions) seem to occur in such predictable orderings across time and across stimulus conditions? To what extent are

FIGURE 4.13. *The use of verticals and edges in the response of a freshly trapped group of monkeys to a holding cage. All animals not in this corner were on an overhead perch, and about one-tenth of the available area was used. Although the whole aggregate (as well as pairs) would seem to be huddling for comfort, biting and screaming in fact resulted when the juveniles tried to crowd into preferred locations. Note also that sleep is one response to this form of stress.*

behaviors functionally interchangeable with spatial locations, and spatial locations with objects and social beings? Why does behavior go in ordered changes, rhythms, progressions, and cycles? Where does this order come from, and how does the order of rhythmical, cyclical, molar units of behavior affect the more molecular units that they include, whether learned or not?

Here I find myself back at the same ancient problem that sent me out to the field. This problem keeps proliferating itself and coming back in ever-different forms but it can never be stated fully or satisfactorily. As the naturalist might say: What is the nature of the organism, and how is its nature reflected in and shaped by the environment it selects and the behaviors it performs with respect to that environment? As the psychologist narrowly rephrases the same question: What is the stimulus; and what is the response? Or: What is responsiveness, and what is its object?

Summary and Conclusions

Through a review of my own research, this paper argues that experimental and naturalistic approaches to primate behavior not only can be, but *are*, intimately related and necessary to each other. Especially on the level of published reports of technique and data, the differences are at times considerable, but on a more realistic level, the similarities outweigh the differences. I shall now bypass the differences to summarize what naturalistic and experimental approaches have in common for me.

(a) The central problems of naturalistic and experimental research are identical, namely, what is the nature of living beings? Where does the environment leave off and the organism begin? Where does one organism leave off and another begin? How is the nature of the organism reflected in and clarified by behavior? Where did this organism or that behavior come from?

(b) Experimental *models*, whether they be physical or conceptual, are of vital interest insofar as they help us to understand *originals*, that is, organisms, environments, and behaviors as they are and have been for millions of years. In this sense, naturalists are often more literal-minded than is necessary. They forget that they, too, deal only with models and samples. At the same time, true inventions and artifacts in primate psychology would be anomalies and of no relevance whatsoever to our professed subject matter. The value of any sample or model (including "natural" models and samples) must continually be demonstrated by comparing it with further data. Apparatus, experimental stimuli, and the laboratory itself can be treated as special cases of ecology, and the behaviors that are seen in experimental situations are special cases of those that actually or potentially exist in normal events. They help us to more fully assess the adaptive potential of a species. Insofar as a common system of analysis can be applied to any situation, the experimenter uses specific situations and procedures principally to focus the animal's attention, to focus or alert his own attention, or possibly because we do not as yet have the technical skill to effectively use everything that is already available in the way of test stimuli and test behaviors.

(c) Often it is convenient and occasionally it is necessary to talk as if we already know what the stimulus and the response and the organism are, and where one leaves off and another begins. So long as we are discussing matters of technique, we can in fact define and measure these factors independently, by specifying the different operations that *we* employ. But what correspondence do our technical systems bear to the natural systems we are studying? Here lies the central psychological question. In a fundamental sense, stimulus, response, and organism are the central *unknowns* in animal psychology. An adequate understanding of them would exhaust our topic and extend far beyond it. The task of naturalist and experimentalist alike is to use their own creations and definitions as dispensable tools for discovering the creations, definitions, and classifications which (in at least one sense) are already extant.

(d) In any form of scientific study of behavior we observe animals, and through observation and reflection try to discover or verify meaningful, specific questions or general principles concerning organisms. This process can be deductive or inductive; it can become more or less selective and more or less explicitly focussed as prior information is already available and as special manipulative controls, sampling procedures, techniques and equipment are introduced; but it remains observation. General naturalistic data will no doubt be overthrown in behavior research as more explicitly experimental studies are done, just as astronomy overruled astrology, and chemistry overruled alchemy. Nevertheless, the new experimental data in themselves presuppose an untold amount of intuitive and unexamined experimenter's lore, and they must in turn be subjected to the same process of critical review, even from common sense. Experiments are a part of the naturalistic endeavor, and not a thing in themselves.

(e) No observation or experiment is ever a "complete description of the entire behavior of the whole natural animal" or a "completely objective, rigorously controlled, precise science," as some naturalists and experimentalists, respectively, seem to believe. What call is there, then, to stand in awe of Method? It is the human observer who attempts to freeze the constant spatio-temporal flow of natural events into "photographs" such as the ones I have presented in this paper. It is rare indeed that he chooses the critical instant and the right angle for his photograph. It is the observer who selects discrete lens settings or tries to zoom in or out for proper perspective. It is he who must say what is in a photograph, what is relevant and irrelevant, what is the subject, and what are objects. Moreover, single events are of little interest to science unless they have relevance beyond themselves. In trying to find the general principles which constitute science, and in trying to present these principles in an economical fashion, the observer must group many photographs into classes; successively reduce these photographs to maps, graphs, and eventually equations; calibrate his classifications against those of other observers; and perform the checks and controls that will permit him to judge whether his sampling procedures and his results are representative enough and precise enough to answer his questions. It is he who must defend the meaningfulness of both his questions and answers.

All of the thousands of photographs that I viewed in the course of my research would not suffice to completely explain a single one of the figures that appear in the text. Each of the photographs introduced as explanatory evidence would in itself require additional evidence in its own behalf, and so on *ad infinitum*. However, I am quite content with being something less than a pure naturalist or a pure experimentalist. Insofar as we can agree on the final outcome of these and further observations, experiments, and harangues, we share the glories of feeling that we are objective and recognize the obvious, and are looking at the same world; and in such a case it should not matter what academic title we give ourselves.

REFERENCES

Allport, F. H. *Theories of perception and the concept of structure.* New York: Wiley, 1955.

Altmann, S. Primate behavior in review. *Science,* 1965, **150,** 1440–1442.

Boring, E. G. The nature and history of experimental control. *American Journal of Psychology,* 1954, **67,** 573–589.

Brunswik, E. In defense of probabilistic functionalism: A reply. *Psychological Review,* 1955, **62,** 236–242.

Cairns, R. B. Attachment behavior of mammals. *Psychological Review,* 1966, **73,** 409–426.

Carpenter, C. R. *Naturalistic behavior of nonhuman primates.* University Park: Pennsylvania State University Press, 1964.

Davenport, R. K., Jr., Menzel, E. W., Jr., & Rogers, C. M. Maternal care during infancy: Its effect on weight gain and mortality in the chimpanzee. *American Journal of Orthopsychiatry,* 1961, **31,** 803–809.

DeVore, I. (Ed.) *Primate behavior: Field studies of monkeys and apes.* New York: Holt, Rinehart & Winston, 1965.

Draper, W. A. Free-ranging rhesus monkeys: Age and sex differences in individual activity patterns. *Science,* 1966, **151,** 476–478.

Fraenkel, G. S., & Gunn, D. L. *The orientation of animals.* (Rev. ed.). New York: Dover, 1961.

Gibson, J. J. Visually controlled locomotion and visual orientation in animals. *British Journal of Psychology,* 1958, **49,** 182–194.

Gibson, J. J. *The senses considered as perceptual systems.* Boston: Houghton Mifflin, 1966.

Guthrie, E. R. *The psychology of learning.* New York: Harper, 1952.

Hall, E. T. *The hidden dimension.* Garden City, N. Y.: Doubleday, 1966.

Hall, K. R. L. Social learning in monkeys. In P. Jay (Ed.), *Primates: Studies in adaptation and variability.* New York: Holt, Rinehart & Winston, in press.

Hebb, D. O. *A textbook of psychology.* Philadelphia: Saunders, 1958.

Hediger, H. *Studies of the psychology and behavior of captive animals in zoos and circuses.* New York: Criterion, 1955.

Hinde, R. Some recent trends in ethology. In S. Koch (Ed.), *Psychology: A study of a science.* Vol. 2. New York: McGraw-Hill, 1959. Pp. 561–610.

Hull, C. L. *A behavior system.* New Haven: Yale University Press, 1952.

Hunt, W. A., Landis, C., & Jacobsen, C. F. Studies of the startle pattern: V. Apes and monkeys. *Journal of Psychology,* 1937, **3,** 339–343.

Imanishi, K., & Altmann, S. A. (Eds.) *Japanese monkeys: A collection of translations.* Alberta: University of Alberta Press, 1965.

Klüver, H. *Behavior mechanisms in monkeys.* Chicago: University of Chicago Press, 1933.

Köhler, W. *Gestalt psychology.* New York: Liveright, 1929.

Mason, W. A. Naturalistic and experimental investigations of the social behavior of monkeys and apes. In P. Jay (Ed.), *Primates: Studies in adaptation and variability.* New York: Holt, Rinehart & Winston, in press.

Mason, W. A., Davenport, R. K., Jr., & Menzel, E. W., Jr. Early experience and the social development of rhesus monkeys and chimpanzees. In G. Newton (Ed.), *Early experience and behavior.* New York: Charles C Thomas, in press.

Menzel, E. W., Jr. Patterns of responsiveness in chimpanzees reared through infancy under conditions of environmental restriction. *Psychologische Forschung,* 1964, **27,** 337–365.

Menzel, E. W., Jr. Responsiveness to objects in free-ranging Japanese monkeys. *Behaviour,* 1966, **26,** 130–150.

Menzel, E. W., Jr., Davenport, R. K., Jr., & Rogers, C. M. Some aspects of behavior toward novelty in young chimpanzees. *Journal of Comparative and Physiological Psychology,* 1961, **54,** 16–19.

Miller, N. E. Liberalization of basic S-R concepts: Extensions to conflict behavior, motivation, and social learning. In S. Koch (Ed.), *Psychology: A study of a science*. Vol. 2. New York: McGraw-Hill, 1959. Pp. 196–292.

Morrison, J. A., & Menzel, E. W., Jr. Adaptation of a rhesus monkey group to artificial group fission and transplantation to a new environment. Paper read at meeting of American Association for the Advancement of Science, Washington, D. C., 1966.

Nissen, H. W. Description of the learned response in discrimination behavior. *Psychological Review*, 1959, **57**, 121–131.

Polanyi, M. *Personal knowledge*. Chicago: University of Chicago Press, 1958.

Postman, L. The probability approach and nomothetic theory. *Psychological Review*, 1955, **62**, 218–225.

Sade, D. S. Some aspects of parent-offspring and sibling relations in a group of rhesus monkeys, with a discussion of grooming. *American Journal of Physical Anthropology*, 1965, **23**, 1–18.

Schneirla, T. C. The relationship between observation and experimentation in the field study of behavior. *New York Academy of Science*, 1950, **51**, 1001–1122.

Schneirla, T. C. An evolutionary and developmental theory of biphasic processes underlying approach and withdrawal. In M. R. Jones (Ed.), *Nebraska symposium on motivation*. Lincoln: University of Nebraska Press, 1959. Pp. 1–42.

Schrier, A. M., Harlow, H. F., & Stollnitz, F. (Eds.) *Behavior of nonhuman primates*. New York: Academic Press, 1965.

Skinner, B. F. A case history in scientific method. *American Psychologist*, 1956, **11**, 221–241.

5

Naturalistic Method and the Clinical Approach

HAROLD L. RAUSH

SOME TWENTY YEARS have elapsed since clinical psychology began its recent history. This science has historically had its moments of drama and crisis, and more of such moments will undoubtedly come. The viability of clinical psychology has become a fact, but where it stands as a discipline within psychology is less certain, and this uncertainty is reflected in the concerns of clinicians about their identity. Identity problems are ubiquitous these days to the point of tediousness, and it is not my aim to cry pity for the poor clinical psychologist. But, of all the psychologists it is the clinicians who are so often called upon—by themselves even more than by others—to answer the question of whether they are to be scientists, practitioners, or artists; or indeed whether they are to be all of these simultaneously or at different times. Although the difference may be solely a qualitative one, the clinician, compared to other psychologists, is or feels himself to be somewhat more marginal in his stance within psychology. This is particularly so in relation to research.

Sometimes we can understand problems more clearly by studying them at their margins, and it is from this vantage point that I wish to examine some of the dilemmas about research that confront the clinician. That is, I am here less interested in the problems of the clinician per se than in what these problems have to tell us about his relation to psychological research in general. My argument shall be that the clinical psychologist's dilemmas about research derive from his failure to understand and respect his own methods as a scientific naturalist. From this failure come, in turn, both the failure to develop and refine his methods and the failure to develop modes of public contribution of research findings. Again, my aim is to highlight issues more general than those of clinical psychology, particularly the issues of method that confront the psychologist as investigator.

122

The Clinician as Naturalist

Let me contrast briefly two views of the clinician as research investigator.

CLINICIAN VERSUS RESEARCHER

The prevalent view sees the daily work of the clinician as divorced from research. In this view, clinical work may stimulate thinking and the development of hypotheses. Furthermore, clinical experience and training may help in suggesting the population, for example, schizophrenics rather than college students; the instruments: Rorschach rather than rotary pursuit; and perhaps the variables: sexual identification rather than retroactive inhibition. From this conception of clinical psychological research, some clinical experience may be useful, but a little is enough. One who continues to engage in clinical work must be thought of as an applied scientist, one who applies "general psychological principles" to specific cases. The view then extrapolates toward proposals to separate academic and professional degrees, drawing analogies to the relations between physics and engineering, or between physiology and medicine.

The ambivalence that characterizes this common view, contrasting clinical work and research, is perhaps most often seen in the treatment accorded to Sigmund Freud. On the one hand, Freud is recognized as contributing to and influencing current views and research in the psychology of personality, in developmental and social psychology, and in perception and memory. On the other hand, his findings are often relegated to the status of mere, though sometimes good, clinical hunches. Even those most actively investigating psychoanalytic notions will take the position that Freud contributed *insights*, but that it is the job of the *scientist* to test these. Yet, we seldom devote the effort of systematic verification or disproof to the comments of our next door neighbor, our garage mechanic, and our barber, who also have clinical hunches and insights. Strangely enough, psychologists have attended to what Freud had to say and have accorded his views that scientific dignity signified by continued discussion and continued efforts at verification or disproof.

My point is not in the least to defend Freud. He himself is not blameless for the fact that he is treated one time as a bright social commentator, and another time as an empirical scientist. But whether correct or incorrect in their various specifics, many of Freud's ideas were stimulating and productive of further work. That is, they had the heuristic effects we expect of good theories based on good empirical work. It is because

Freud was an empirical scientist who, like Darwin, observed much, modified his modes of observation, and molded and changed his theories in the light of what he observed, that we have given him such serious attention. Certainly, Freud's contributions to psychology are not primarily good case histories, at least no more than were Darwin's contributions to biology nor Piaget's contribution to child development primarily case histories.

There is no doubt that some research, proceeding from a conception that splits off clinical work from scientific investigation, may be good research. It is equally obvious that such research partakes very little of the everyday process of clinical work, in which the relationships among phenomena emerge only in the course of a long and intensive series of interchanges between clinician-investigator and client-subject. The differences between the two poles have been described sympathetically by Loevinger (1963) who speaks of the "conflict of commitment in clinical research." Loevinger notes some of the absurdities committed in the name of research when those clinicians who are lacking in elementary notions of scientific limitations and scientific canon attempt to become "researchers." But it is not surprising that, since he must disassociate himself with his primary source of data, the clinical psychologist must often become a poorer scientist as a "researcher" than he is as a clinician. It is in part an awareness of this discrepancy between clinical data and the data of traditional research design that induces so many clinicians to withdraw progressively into private clinical activities, against a background of not very meaningful exhortations that the clinical psychologist "should also do research." Loevinger proposes that the functions of the clinician and those of the research investigator be kept separate and that, given a tolerance based on mutual understanding, these functions can complement one another.

There is a parallel here to typical ideas about naturalistic studies, that is, you get your hunches in the field, then test them in the laboratory. Implied is that the formal characteristics of the laboratory test must differ sharply from those of naturalistic observation.

CLINICIAN AS RESEARCHER

The alternative view, which I accept, sees the clinician as a naturalist, as an explorer in the realm of human events and as an organizer of those events and their implications. Like other naturalists, he is an observer, and if his observations are to have scientific merit, he must be a disciplined observer. Yet, he is not only an observer. Unlike some, though not all, naturalistic investigators, he is also a participant in the events he chooses to study. The strategy of participant-observation has its scientific risks, which training and discipline can reduce, though not completely eliminate. But, this same strategy is also the source of the clinician's power as scientific investigator. Like any other personal contract between people, such as marriage or student-teacher relationships, the contract between client and therapist legitimizes a special class of interventions. Unlike most other contracts, however, the therapy relationship empowers the therapist to intervene for the purpose of studying the client and, even more important, of studying the relationship itself. The contract thus embodies a research collaboration, so to speak, in the service of the client's aims for change. The position defining the participants as colleagues engaged in a search was represented in Freud's great clinical leap from the method of hypnosis to that of free association, and the position has been re-emphasized and extended by Sullivan (1953), Rogers (1951), and Bugental (1965).[1] In the remainder of this paper, I shall try to articulate some assumptions of naturalistic research and of clinical work in ways that will allow us to view the clinical investigator as a scientific naturalist.

ARTIFICIALITY

To think of the clinician as naturalist may raise questions about the clinical situation. After all, the physical and temporal boundaries of the clinic and consulting room are highly artificial, and the rules and limits of the clinical relationship are by no means usual ones. The structure of the clinical situation is an artificial one, created for those who are suffering and who are seeking a very special form of help in the alleviation of their suffering. The paradox here, as Bordin (1965) notes, is that the clinic, an artificial creation, is a natural habitat for those who need and seek the kind of help it may offer.

It may be instructive to follow the question of what is or is not a natural situation a step further, for we may be led to a clearer understanding of what naturalistic investigation implies. The paradox of the simultaneous artificiality and naturalness of the clinical situation exists for other human situations. A schoolroom is similarly an artificially created structure and similarly a natural habitat for certain forms of teaching and learning. So, too, does the paradox of artificiality and natural-

---

[1] Here and throughout this paper, it is the clinician's work as therapist that is considered. Activities in therapy not only make up the greater part of clinical practice, but are the major source of clinical knowledge about people. The arguments may, I believe, be extended to diagnostic work, with only minor modifications.

ness exist for the cocktail party, the athletic field, the hospital ward, the children's camp, and the family dining room. And one can even muster statistical evidence that serving as a laboratory subject in a psychological experiment is a natural situation for the college sophomore who is taking his first psychology course. Surely, then, so far as human subjects go, we cannot delimit naturalistic investigation by requiring that the situation proposed for investigation be free from human artifice.

The issue of artificiality obscures matters that are much more salient for the naturalistic investigator. One such issue has to do with representativeness and another is the matter of interference by the investigator.

Representativeness

REPRESENTATIVENESS AND ECOLOGICAL DISTRIBUTION OF SUBJECTS

Most of our present statistical methods deal with questions of drawing inferences from limited samples of subjects. So much has been written about this matter that extended discussion here would be superfluous. Yet, a distinction needs to be made between naturalistic and experimental approaches. The logic of inference is well defined for ecologically oriented studies in which generalizations are made from limited samples to specified populations. That is, if we are interested in studying political attitudes, spending behavior, reading habits, or socialization practices of a specified segment of a population, we have procedures for estimating the adequacy of our subject sample. Insuring adequacy of sampling for inferences to the population may be difficult or expensive, and investigative procedures apart from sampling may be fallible, but the issue of representativeness of subject sampling is empirical rather than logical. The sampling issue does not differ here between Transducer methods, that is, noninterfering methods, and Operator methods, or, methods by which the investigator imposes himself into the data stream (see Barker, 1965). The logic of subject sampling is the same for such Operator methods as the questionnaire survey and such Transducer methods as ecological studies of animal behavior. In both types of studies, the first level of data analysis is essentially a descriptive account of specified variables in the behaviors of subjects who are presumed to represent a defined but more general population. A second level of analysis examines the relations among variables, often drawing inferences from these relations to theories about relations among population parameters.

The logic of subject sampling changes as we enter into the realm of controlled experiment. In a sense, the estimation of population parameters becomes irrelevant. Under ideal conditions of perfect experimental control, one subject would suffice. Subject sampling has no intrinsic interest here; it is simply necessary because of uncontrollable error. What is sought is not representativeness, but assurance that error does not obscure the interpretation of the immediate findings. And the question of a sufficient N is answered in terms of whether the results would be likely to be similar if the experiment were repeated with the same subjects under the same conditions, rather than in terms of whether the findings are likely to represent the diversity existing in a defined population. The design provides no logic by which we may jump beyond the peculiarities of a particular sample—for example, college sophomores registered in a particular psychology course at a particular university and volunteering for a particular experiment—to generalize to a population of broader interest. The leap is one of faith. Obviously, that faith is not entirely misplaced. The history of science tells us that one does not need a representative sample of all humans to study the human circulatory system or neurological functions. But I know of no a priori rules by which we can judge when generalization to a population is justified from a controlled experimental study.

At one extreme, then, we have studies in which the ideal is a representation of the ecological distribution of a species with respect to some phenomena of interest. At the other extreme are studies in which the ideal is an elimination of individual and group variance with respect to some phenomena of interest. Respectively, these are the ideals of purely ecological and purely experimental models. Few studies, particularly as they involve humans and complex phenomena, can meet either of these ideals. Experimentalists, or those who devise and control the conditions of investigation, come to recognize increasingly the likelihood of an interaction between variation in the phenomena under investigation and individual or subgroup variation. Thus, they come to select or classify individuals or groups in multivariate designs so as to clarify the phenomena. Naturalists, or those who observe events as they occur in the "real" world, also come to the same point. In order to clarify phenomena under investigation, they come to select individuals or groups, a particular Indian tribe, for example, or a delinquent subculture, or a social or political group. To the extent that investigations aim neither at a purely ecological descriptivism, at one extreme, nor at a kind of *in vitro* abstractionism at the other, the problems of subject sampling and its basis for inference tend to coalesce for the experimenter and naturalist despite their differences in approach. The resolutions to problems of subject sampling depend not so much on whether one labels oneself as experimenter or naturalist, but rather on the aims of the investigation. Barker and Wright's *One Boy's Day* (1951) is a naturalistic study despite the fact that the sample is limited to one child. I shall return to the matter of sampling later in discussing "event" versus "subject" laws.

REPRESENTATIVENESS AND ECOLOGICAL DISTRIBUTION OF SITUATIONS

A frequently mentioned criterion for naturalistic investigation is ecological representativeness. As noted by Brunswik (1947), a particular situation, chosen as a focus for an investigation, may or may not be representative of other situations. There is no foregone conclusion that results obtained under one set of environmental conditions are transferable to another set of environmental conditions. To the extent that people are consistent and to the extent that situations share conditions, some overlap can be expected; to the extent that situations are heterogeneous and to the extent people make differentiations, differences can be expected. Roger Barker, in particular, has argued cogently for ecological studies of human behavior in diverse settings (1960, 1963). We are certainly lacking a psychology of everyday life; we know far too little about the range of environmental situations and their effects on behavior; we lack concepts and vocabulary for describing environments. These deficiencies limit our knowledge of development and change for both individuals and cultures. On this point, Milgram (1965) says:

> Ultimately, social psychology would like to have a compelling *theory of situations* which will, first, present a language in terms of which situations can be defined; proceed to a typology of situations; and then point to the manner in which definable properties of situations are transformed into psychological forces in the individual. (p. 74)

The same point may be made for other fields of psychology. Naturalistic studies are strongly needed in order to develop a vocabulary of, and concepts about, situations.

What I have said above about subject sampling holds equally for situational sampling. Again, the logic of inference differs, depending on whether one is interested in describing the world or in defining principles, and again the logic is more problematic in the latter case. Again, we may note an increasing tendency for experimental and naturalistic studies to coalesce with respect to situational sampling. Ideally, the experimenter selects the single situation that will maximize his opportunity for studying a phenomenon of interest, and ideally he would eliminate all situational variance except for the stimuli he controls as the independent variable. In practice, as he comes to recognize the likelihood of interaction between variation in the phenomena under investigation and variation in situations, the experimentalist tends to be directed toward multivariate situational designs. On the other hand, the naturalist who is interested in a special class of phenomena must often move away from the ideal of ecological representativeness of situations, simply because the phenomena may not occur in most situations with sufficient frequency for study. Thus, if one is interested in such matters as behavior in crises, environmental transitions, reactions to provocation, and responses to rumors, one becomes highly selective about the natural situations he chooses to study.

OTHER ISSUES OF REPRESENTATIVENESS

Before turning to what I consider the essential distinction between naturalistic and experimental approaches, it is worth noting that issues of representativeness, other than those involved in subject and situational sampling, may be raised. For example, phenomena and their interrelations may change with stages in the life cycle of an organism. Conclusions relevant for one developmental phase may not generalize to another. Thus, developmental representativeness must be a matter of concern for both naturalistic and experimental studies. Similar issues exist with respect to a representativeness of states of the organism; conclusions for states of low motivation (or low arousal, fatigue, and so on) may not generalize to other states. Again, temporal representativeness is seldom considered; diurnal, seasonal, and physiological (for instance, estrus) cycles can influence the findings of naturalistic and experimental studies.

Evidence can be adduced for the effects of each of the above dimensions of representativeness. What becomes clear is that no single investigation can stake a claim to be representative of all the dimensions that are likely to be salient for its findings. Every investigation, then, reflects a decision by the investigator as to which dimensions of representativeness are critical for explicating the phenomena he wishes to study. Unfortunately, the bases for such decisions are logically obscure.[2] Successive

---

[2] To the extent that the phenomena being studied can be viewed as part of a system that is relatively independent of and impermeable to other systems, problems of representativeness recede. Experimental control can suffice to yield the order in the system. Systems that are evolutionarily more primitive seem to show lesser variability and lesser interdependence. They can be studied with less confounding by issues of representativeness. Perhaps this is one reason that the experimentalist is tempted to regress ever to more "basic" physiological studies.

investigations or multivariate designs can expand the decision so that results can be plotted, so to speak, in the multidimensional space of the various aspects of representativeness.[3]

REPRESENTATIVENESS OF INPUT
AND OUTPUT REPERTOIRES

By the somewhat awkward phrase, "representativeness of input and output repertoires," I refer to what I believe is the major difference between experimental and naturalistic approaches. On this criterion, the naturalist can be as *selective* as the experimentalist in his sampling of subjects and situations and still remain a naturalist.

Consider the experiment in contrast to the field study. In the laboratory experiment, the investigator defines and restricts the ranges of both stimuli and responses. For example, in a narrow case, the stimuli may be a red and a green light, and the response the pressing of one button or another. Some additional stimuli may be noted (instructions for the subject, feedback about his responses, and so forth) and some additional response variables may be investigated (autonomic measures, response delays, and so forth), but the modalities of the subject's experiences and actions are sharply limited in accordance with data-gathering procedures. A polar contrast is the purely naturalistic study in which the investigator attempts to exercise no influence over the range of stimuli or the range of responses; it is the subject who selects and defines the repertoire of both stimuli and responses. Even in those less extreme cases in which he interferes with an ongoing course of events—introducing a special stimulus or a new condition—the naturalist leaves the definition of the stimulus and the mode of reaction to the subject.

The naturalist faces the knotty problem of defining and classifying input and output repertoires. Altmann (1965) presents some logical suggestions for categorization, but no matter how crude or how refined the categorization, the aim of the naturalist is to include as grist for his scientific mill all of the events in the realm of his investigation. The situation or the field of investigation may be narrow, but the definition of data is broad. The naturalist's lack of control over the subject's stimulus and response repertoire is apt to attenuate the precision of his findings, but it increases their generalizability. In contrast, the experimentalist's

---

[3] A good example is given in Milgram's studies of obedience and disobedience to authority. Each subject sample was carefully balanced for age and occupational types, four orders of experimental conditions were employed, the institutional and social contexts for the studies were varied, and other variations explored other dimensions of representativeness.

control enables him to make precise statements, but he has no basis for knowing whether his statements are important or trivial in relation to the extra-laboratory aspects of the topic of investigation.[4]

Intermediate between those studies which, on the one hand, restrict both input and output variables and, on the other hand, restrict neither, are studies which delimit one side (either input or output) but allow free range for the other side. This intermediate mode of investigation is suggested above in the selection of special subject samples or special conditions. It is represented in Milgram's study quoted above, in which the stimulus situation is defined by the experimenter, but in which the subject's entire range of responses is of interest. It is also represented in current studies that my colleagues and I are engaged in, in which conflict situations are defined for our subjects, but in which their responses are allowed to range free. Other studies may limit the output side, investigating the effects of a wide range of inputs. An example is a voting poll in which decisions are made about a very limited number of candidates, but where a wide range of inputs affecting these decisions may be examined.

Intervention

The matter of intervention by the investigator can thus be brought into the context of representativeness. *Intervention* is a constraint on either the inputs or outputs to the subject, or both, in other words, a limiting of the possibilities in his repertoire. It is through such constraints and the observations of their effects that we, whether as experimenters or naturalistic observers, achieve information about the relationships among events. This is as true in our daily lives as it is in laboratory or field studies; nature is a far greater intervener in the course of ongoing events than is any psychological investigator. It is true, as Barker (1963) points out, (a) that some interventions are *interferences*, that is, activities that disrupt or destroy the very phenomena we think we are studying, and (b) that we must be sensitive to the issue of whether our investigative techniques distort our analyses. The question then becomes one of whether the constraint imposed by an intervention yields information about the phenomena under investigation or whether it yields information primarily about the effects of disruption. In this sense, any investigator who is interested in the generality of his findings must ask himself to what extent

---

[4] For example, the conditions of operant conditioning can be stated and tested with precision, but whether the operant model represents a modal, optimal, or trivial form of learning is obscure.

the interventions which he imposes on the subjects represent those that occur in nature. Again, I do not know how one can make an absolute judgment about this. Certainly, Menzel's interpositioning of objects in a field situation for the purpose of elucidating phenomena of "edging" (see Chapter 4 of this volume), or DeVore's throwing a piece of food between two baboons to elucidate dominance (Hall & DeVore, 1965; see also DeVore, 1965, p. 627) seem to me legitimate attempts to delimit, for the purposes of investigation, classes of events found in nature. To go a step further, Milgram's efforts to study obedience to authority through the imposition of commands to punish others represent, it seems to me, (unfortunately) quite natural interventions, but less natural than some of the examples above. On the other hand, I find it hard to say what the constraints set by such arrangements as the Skinner box, the T maze, or some experiments on communication in purely ad hoc groups, represent for the phenomena under investigation. These evaluations are subjective ones, but I know of no logic that enables us to go beyond such subjective judgments.

How these issues of representativeness and intervention relate to the clinical situation is my major concern in what follows. The clinical situation occupies a peculiar position on the issue of representativeness. It is, on the one hand, a single and highly artificial situation. On the other hand, its structure allows the verbal representation of a wide variety of human experiences. It is not *ecologically* representative with respect to behavior; to predict everyday behavior from the events of the consultation room leads to bad mistakes. Yet, I can think of no situation which is so representative, *psychologically*, of subjective experience and human concerns.

With respect to the issue of intervention, the clinical situation and the clinician's activities obviously represent purposeful interventions in the client's life and in his stream of behavior. However, I believe it would be a mistake to think always of such interventions as interferences in the sense discussed above. Rather, they are aimed at elucidating and clarifying the communications between client and clinician. Texts on psychotherapy, whether client-centered (Rogers, 1951) or psychoanalytic (Fenichel, 1941), issue ample warnings against interference by the therapist.

Clinical Psychology as Method

Although analogies relating clinical psychology to engineering or medicine are facile, their legitimacy is questionable. Unexamined too often are some peculiar assumptions about the words *basic* and *applied*. For one thing, there are few basic propositions in psychology that are stated with sufficient specificity so as to enable clinical application. Consequently, most clinical psychologists would be hard put to state explicitly how they apply specific principles to their work, although they might speak of psychological positions that serve as guideposts in particular instances.

To say that specific principles of behavior are rarely applied directly does not preclude the application of methods and techniques of data collection and analysis. In fact, what clinical investigators most often apply in particular cases are not general principles of behavior but generalized techniques and methods of observation. In essence, this is little different from other areas of psychology, for instance, from the use of psychophysical methods in studying hearing, electronic or tissue sectioning methods in studying physiological functions, statistical methods and polling or questionnaire techniques in studying attitudes. Some methods require more training than others and some require special cautions and have special limitations, as for example, those of clinical psychology and those of brain surgery. Some probably require certain natural aptitudes. But in each case the methods are seen as requisite for certain kinds of studies. By themselves, the methods are not science nor, for that matter, art. They are simply tools. It is the orientation of the investigator and the purpose to which the methods are put that determine whether the results are basic or applied. Even if the initial orientation is to apply principles and help someone, observations may be basic to the extent they impinge on general principles. Dittmann and I (1954) have discussed the data-gathering and analytic method of psychoanalytic investigation in some detail, but a brief example may press home the point.

> If a patient responds to a variety of self-described situations or to the therapeutic situations with anger (or it may be twitching or weeping or withdrawal or descriptions of these), the therapist then forms a hypothesis which would relate these situations. By further observations, questions, and interpretations, he proceeds to check, modify, and extend his hypothesis. Thus he may observe that the behavior (or again, the patient's description of his behavior) of anger follows situations (or descriptions of situations) where affectionate feelings are aroused in the patient. He hypothesizes this relationship to be invariant. If the patient then expresses anger toward him, the therapist checks with the patient as to whether an unverbalized feeling of affection toward the therapist did not precede the angry outburst. Where his hypothesis fails to be confirmed, it is either completely or in some respect in error. Thus the therapist may, for example, modify the hypothesis to the form that there is an invariant relationship for this patient between affection-

producing situations and anger in relationships with women but not with men, or through further checking, the modification may be of invariance in the case of women who behave in a seductive manner, but not toward those who behave in a nonseductive manner and not toward men. (p. 395)

ASSUMPTIONS OF THE CLINICAL METHOD

Behind any method are values and assumptions about what are worthwhile realms for study and about the nature of the phenomena under investigation. Of course, values and assumptions are not tested, per se. They can at best be judged by the products they lead to. I shall forego any direct discussion of values, although they are no doubt implicit in what is to follow. For a major and very salient discussion of values as they relate to research, I would cite Chein's recent article (1966) in the *American Psychologist* on "Divisiveness among Psychologists," and particularly to the section on the clash of subcultures, where he discusses positions labeled as *scientism* and *clinicalism.* For present purposes, I would rather look at some assumptions of clinical methods as compared to other methods of psychological investigation. There are differences. And although these differences are likely no greater than between, let us say, the methods of social and physiological psychology, some comment is necessary, simply because there is so much confusion.

The Scientific Legitimacy of Life Situations.   First, there is the assumption, held in common with many other areas of psychology, that behavior, experience, thoughts, and so forth, and/or *reports* of behavior, experience, thoughts, and so forth, as they occur in actual life situations, are legitimate sources of data. This particularly naturalistic bias contrasts with the assumption that we can have no firm source of information about phenomena other than from a controlled laboratory situation. According to David Bakan (1956), this latter notion derives from "the postulate of epistemological loneliness," which says that we can know nothing about the mind of another. Bakan contrasts this postulate, which he attributes ultimately to Hume, with another assumption that says, "after all, we are all pretty much alike." The clinician's assumption is the latter—that we can and do, often, though not always, understand something of one another's actions, communications, and so on, in the natural process of ordinary observation.

The Assumption of Change.   A second assumption, held by clinicians in common with some other investigators, is that psychological phenomena can be studied through attempts to modify the phenomena, or through observation of modifications as they occur more or less naturally. Like the laboratory investigator who interposes an experimental procedure and studies its effects, the clinician is both an agent and a student of change. In this he differs from the transductive orientation of the pure observer. However, the clinician's interventions seek to preserve and to test the character of an open-field situation, and in this respect he differs from the laboratory experimenter (see section on *Intervention*).

Context versus "Objectizing." A third assumption, and one that is more difficult both conceptually and methodologically, is that contextual factors have a major influence in determining the nature of psychological data. There are, of course, various aspects to the notion of context. One may, for example, speak of physical or sociological contexts. The corollary that is particularly relevant for the clinician is the assumption that some psychological phenomena are best studied in an interpersonal and sometimes intimate context.

More than physical or institutional contextual factors, the clinical situation emphasizes motivational and interpersonal context. On the motivational side, the assumption is that some phenomena are best studied under conditions of natural, intrinsic, and sometimes high, motivation. The interpersonal aspect is even more relevant. Increasingly, studies have shown that test results are influenced by the personalities of the investigators, that the effects of teaching methods vary with the personalities of the teachers, that attitude surveys are influenced by class or racial differences between subjects and interviewers. And now, recent investigations by Rosenthal (1966) tell us that the results of experimental studies may be highly biased, in spite of all obvious controls, by the attitudes and hypotheses of investigators.

Such studies and their illustrations of confounding surprise and perturb us. We prefer to maintain what I would call the fiction of *objectizing*—not objectification, but objectizing. By objectizing I mean a peculiar form of repression that allows us to conceive of people as rather inert chemical substances, and allows us to think that people can be put on shelves, can remain unaffected by the surroundings, and, if handled with usual laboratory precautions, can be taken down later, unchanged.[5]

Sequences of Events. A fourth assumption, fundamental to the clinician as naturalistic researcher, says that events occur over time and

[5] Approaches to bringing context into study design are suggested by: Barker (1960, 1963); Campbell (1963); Campbell & Fiske (1959); Hursch, Hammond, & Hursch (1964); Raush, Dittmann, & Taylor (1959b); and Raush, Farbman, & Llewellyn (1960).

that a sequence of events is analyzable. The clinical psychologist often deals with single subjects over long periods of time. His observations and inferences are based on successive samples of events and on the effects of his interventions in modifying events. The study of events over time with single subjects demands that such a set of events contain sufficient variability to enable relationships to emerge. It also demands confidence in the working principle of potential generalizability—that "after all, we are all pretty much alike." Of course, the questions of sufficient variability and of sufficient generalizability to other cases need continuous exploration and testing. Dittmann (1952) noted these problems in his study of the efficacy of different interpretive approaches utilizing data from a *single* therapist-client pair. Nonetheless, he was able to find sufficient variability and sufficient replication among the statements of one therapist to examine consequences in the one client's responses.

With the psychophysiologist studying vision or audition, the clinician thus shares the bias that fundamental functional relations are discoverable or testable through the intensive use of a few subjects. He shares with some students of learning the notion that the distribution of events over successive time intervals may demonstrate a coherence expressing general laws. The assumption about the relevance of sequences of events leads directly to questions about the study of process.

The Study of Process

There is no aspect of experience that is more compelling than its temporal quality. Not only are physical and psychological development temporally organized, but all ongoing psychological functions—thought, memory, perception, affect—are ordered in time. Our communications with one another are certainly so ordered. Scramble the paragraphs in an article or book, sentences in a verbal communication, words in a sentence, or letters in words, and see how much information is conveyed when the *sequence* of events is ignored. Or, observe the scrambling of memories in some senile psychoses. In a sense, recent experiments in films and novels show the power of temporal arrangements by their disconcerting efforts to subvert these arrangements. The development of constancies and conceptions of conservation in infancy and childhood would seem dependent on a phasing over time, for example, that which is here *now* is the same as that which was there *then*, the object which is long *now* is the same one that was round *before*. Relationships, even those with clear role definitions, do not emerge full-blown, but evolve with each step having reference to a previous and a future step. Our lives may not be predetermined, but they certainly do not run backwards.[6] We know what we know by the ordering of events and by the contingencies we observe or infer through their arrangements in time; and we know what we know not by the stability of events, but by their systematic change over time.

The ordering of phenomena over time, or an awareness of this ordering, even if it is not handled in systematic analysis, is, I would say, a major and an essential data source for the naturalistic study. And it is from observation of the chaining of events that the clinician derives, modifies, tests, and refines his hypotheses. There is nothing very special about this. Certainly, from early childhood our inferences about our worlds derive in large part from the temporal ordering of events.[7] Yet, it is this ordering in time which is most likely to be ignored when we move into formal scientific methods.[8]

The raw material of naturalistic studies are events as they occur over time. Observational protocols, or codings of observed events, are gathered in a temporal order simply because events occur that way. Most often, however, in the process of conversion to data for analysis, the ordering of events is lost or ignored (see Barker, 1963).

I may illustrate this loss through a series of observational studies done by my colleagues and myself with disturbed and normal children (Raush, Dittmann, & Taylor, 1959a, 1959b; Raush, Farbman, & Llewellyn, 1960). By examining the frequencies of various categories of acts by the children toward peers and adults, we were able to demonstrate: (a) that the disturbed children changed in treatment; (b) that the changes were

---

[6] One would apologize for such truisms except for the fact that we tend to ignore them in both formal psychology and in informal thinking. A striking example is given by the game, "Twenty Questions." We are generally astonished by the ability to delimit a single event from the world of events through only twenty yes-no questions. An information-analytic approach (Attneave, 1959; Bendig, 1953) clarifies why so few questions should have such great power. What is not made explicit, however, is that the power derives from the fact that the questions are successive. Each question delimits the classes into which the event might fall, but the player must *remember* the delimitations established by previous questions. Within the game itself, the solution is not a matter of learning in the usual sense, that is, Bendig (1953) finds no learning over three games. Solution depends rather on remembering what went on previously and on utilization of past information in selecting the next move.

[7] And conversely, should not any given inference system lead us to questions and hypotheses about the temporal ordering of events which led to that system? In this sense the genetic "prejudices" of clinicians and their clients are "natural"; the question of "How did it come about?" resolves into a question of temporal order.

[8] One might compare the naiveté of criterion studies of success or failure of psychotherapy with the sophistication of the approach by which Lehrman (1964) defines the sequence of steps which determines whether or not the ring dove will incubate an egg.

not simply a function of maturation; (c) that social settings had a powerful influence on interpersonal behavior; (d) that the influence of the setting was greater for normal than disturbed children; and (e) that this influence increased as the disturbed children approached normality. Our results were significant statistically, and, what is more, they illuminated some phenomena of normal and pathological development.

But, so far we had ignored the temporal order of interactive events. If we looked at process, it was inferentially rather than directly. Fortunately, and I say fortunately because it was not clearly foreseen in the initial design, we were able to take a second look from the viewpoint of process. We could do this because the raw protocols described events in the order in which they occurred and because the codings from the protocols were similarly entered in a sequential order. Thus, with the aid of informational and Markov analyses, we were able to examine sequences of events (Raush, 1965).

Through such reexamination we could study how pathology and social settings influenced not only the frequencies of categories of events, but also how they influenced the processes of interaction. For example, we could see that the behavioral pathology of our hyperaggressive sample consisted not at all in their reaction to hostile gestures, nor did it consist solely in their higher level of initiation of aggressive acts. A major factor of difference between normal and hyperaggressive boys was that although the disturbed children were like the normal children in response to hostile gestures, they, unlike the normal children, responded with aggression to friendly gestures. Moreover, normal children acted as though they could foresee the consequences of a chain of events and they exercised control so as to improve eventual outcomes. In contrast, the chaining of acts among very disturbed children suggested a progressive decline in control over a series of interactions. We can say, then, that these groups differed from each other not only in the classes of events they produced or elicited, but also in the way they organized events sequentially. Social settings seem to work in much the same way, influencing not only the likelihood of specific events, but also the way in which events are patterned.

Such findings are not remarkable. For example, the potentials of the very disturbed children for escalation of aggression and for progressive loss of control were well known to all who worked with them. What is interesting is that we could capture, in a systematic way, the process by which we, as clinicians or as human beings, draw inferences from repeated observations of sequences of events over time. With such methods, there is hope (a) that we can move from a psychology premised on static states to one more capable of dealing with both structural continuities and continuous change, and (b) that we can illuminate and document the kinds of sequential phenomena that provide the inference base for our clinical and everyday views of human behavior.

Problems of dealing with sequences of events and of describing process are not solely the naturalist's concern. As early as 1949, Miller and Frick noted their relevance for experimental psychology:

> The central idea in the preceding discussion (of approaches to serial dependencies) is the *course* (italics mine) of action. If interest is confined to individual responses and no attempt is made to describe and discuss sequences of responses, experimental psychology may have difficulty in meeting many problems posed in clinical and social areas. Some such concept as the *course* of action (italics mine) seems inevitable. (Miller & Frick, 1949, p. 322)

THE CLINICIAN AND PROCESS

The clinician draws his inferences from repeated, ongoing sequences of events, as described in the client's retrospective reports and as they occur in the moment-to-moment relations between client and clinician. The clinician's interventions are directed toward enabling exploration of connections among events by sometimes expanding and sometimes delimiting the possibilities. It goes without saying that this approach to inference has its scientific risks. Some criticisms of the approach are worth noting, since similar criticisms are sometimes made of other naturalistic approaches.

Clinical Data Are Private Rather than Public. True, historically, but not true, necessarily. Rogers and others, even before the advent of modern tape recording, have shown that raw data may be made public while protecting clients' rights to privacy. Broader availability and interchange of materials can protect clinicians' rights to privacy. Likewise, naturalists' protocols, photographs, and films can be as public as scores and statistical indices.

The Clinical Approach Is Intuitive Rather than Objective. No more so than the choice of any problem or the development of any hypothesis is intuitive. Canons of scientific method have little bearing on the sources of scientific ideas. Even bad philosophies, as in the case of Fechner, have led to good scientific work. What counts is that the findings be empirically demonstrable.

Clinicians Consider Dissection, Reduction, and Classification as Bad, Per Se. The question is rather what is dissected and classified. Some classifications prove scientifically negligible, although they may consume much time and labor. The analytic efforts of the alchemists bore little scientific fruit. Many clinicians believe that the current psychiatric classifications are similarly scientifically unproductive. On the other hand, the developmentally oriented classifications of Erikson have had wide acceptance among clinicians. Certainly, scientific efforts must move toward particularization. But, the main test of any structurization of entities is an empirical one; that is, does it work and is it productive of further knowledge.

The Clinician Searches for Ultimate Causes Rather than Being Satisfied with Functional Relations. Loevinger (1963) criticizes clinicians for failure to delimit their theories, for derogating noncausal laws, for failure to accept chance variation, and for indulging, far beyond the reaches of evidence, in a regressive search for causal constructions. Indeed, the criticism is too often justified. Philosophical speculations (as, for example, Freud's notions on Eros and Thanatos) have at times failed to be differentiated from constructions which, whether good or poor, are confrontable by evidence. Yet, it is not justifiable to equate inadequacies in the education of many clinical practitioners as philosophers of science with the scientific utility of clinical methods. By associating clinical work with Lamarckism, Loevinger confounds six issues: philosophical speculation, bad research, vitalism, the choice of operational units, the handling of error, and an orientation to process. It is unnecessary to comment on the first three. However, the last three require at least brief further comment.

(1) The question of selecting units of maximum scientific utility is one that plagues all of psychology. Concepts such as relationship, interaction, and transaction are not scientific anathema, per se. Relationships, interactions, and transactions are certainly classifiable into discriminable categories. Whether or not classifications of this order are worthwhile depends on the inferences suggested by the classifications and on the empirical examination of these inferences.

(2) The variation one investigator attributes to chance is scientific meat for another investigator. The study of individual differences, for example, derived from what had earlier been considered random variation; the error terms of Newtonian physics became investigative data for Einstein. Clinical investigation, with its emphasis on multiple determinacy, indeed considers as data that which other investigative methods would call error. But the reverse is also true. For example, whether the subject has 20/20 vision may be a relevant datum for a perceptual study; it is chance variation for the clinician. A more serious critique drawn by

Loevinger has to do with errors of bias and with the contamination of two sets of measures, whose relation is being examined, by a mutual, biasing influence. These violations of ordinary scientific canon are particularly prevalent when the clinician moves toward what he imagines is *the* research orientation—the testing of an hypothesis via subject sampling. Clearly, some research ideas demand such testing, and under these circumstances the clinician must either learn the trade or stick to his role as practitioner and occasional suggester of interesting possibilities for researchers to follow up. It is not that biasing and correlated errors do not occur in the clinical situation dealing with multiple events examined over time, but the situation provides some good opportunities for such errors to be corrected. For one thing, while folies à deux are not unknown, the two participants may, since they are unlikely to share the same bias over an extended period, exert a corrective effect on one another. Second, unlike the situation in the normative, subject sample study, results are cumulative and are not limited to the disconfirmation or maintenance of a single hypothesis. That is, initially, a multiplicity of hypotheses are equally tenable; through repeated observation and through testing by means of a variety of interventions, progressive selection among and modification of hypotheses may occur. The initial uncertainty, the repeated observations, and the wide latitude for response variability in the situation are apt to temper the likelihood of correlated errors. Third, a hypothesis is judged, not so much by the fact that it is not disconfirmed, but more by its suggesting hitherto unrealized connections that are then subject to examination. In its openness to unexpected data, and in its complex criteria for acceptance of an hypothesis (Fenichel, 1941), the clinical situation gives some protection from correlated biases. Fourth, a major goal of clinical supervision and psychotherapy—where it is part of training—is to attenuate correlated error; countertransference is the clinical term for such error. None of these buffers in the clinical situation guards entirely against the possibilities of correlated error, but they do provide some protection.

(3) The third issue of criticism—orientation to process—brings us back to the main topic under discussion. The clinician's orientation toward process leads him to opt for qualitative rather than quantitative analyses. The choice is not a matter of logic; it is a pragmatic one. If the clinician as naturalist has been resistive to quantitative treatment of data, he has had good reasons. For one thing, appropriate quantitative methods have been few and far between; for another, psychologists have usually been taught only those methods that are entirely inappropriate to the clinical situation as we have described it. Recognizing the inadequacy of usual statistical models for his work, the naturalistic clinician has often taken

a defensive antimathematical position.[9] The dilemma the clinician has faced is between choosing to favor the data and reject the statistical methodology of his psychologist preceptors, or alternatively, to favor the methodology he has learned and reject the data. With the former choice, he is apt to retreat from scientific interest to the warming glow of the ineffable richness of experience; choosing the latter course, he retreats from knowledge, substituting sacrificial gestures at the cold altar of science.

Yet, the model descriptive of the daily work of the clinician and of his interest in process is by no means unique. The learning theorist who applies stochastic methods to study successive trials, the student of communication who deals with the mathematics of information flow, the physiologist who requires a mathematics by which he can judge the recurrence of heart rate cycles in a single subject, the comparative psychologist who is interested in the contingent probabilities in a temporally organized sequence of events, and the experimentalist who employs a Bayesian approach in decisions about procedure, all study process and provide far more appropriate models for data analysis than does the sampling researcher. My own biases are that the methods of informational and Markov analyses may help us improve the study of sequences of events that are of interest to clinicians. But, the state of the field is such that it is appropriate qualitative studies that need to be encouraged, rather than inappropriate quantitative ones.

EVENT VERSUS SUBJECT LAWS

In talking about process, I have been implying a need to distinguish between two sorts of laws. *Subject* laws are descriptive of normative phenomena and are based on sampling of subjects. Examples are statements concerning effects of childrearing practices on children's behavior, Freud's belief in the universality of the Oedipus complex, or his suggestions on the relation between paranoia and homosexuality. *Event* laws are descriptive of intrinsic relations among events and are based on sampling of events. Examples are Skinnerian principles of operant behavior, Freud's description of the succession between anxiety, repression, signal anxiety and defense, or his description of the process of dream formation.

---

[9] Relevant is Bakan's statement: "When, as is evident, the press of observations forces us towards a view that there exists a realm of phenomena for which the scientific approach is inappropriate, then we must conclude that the inappropriateness is inherent in that which we conceive science to be. In other words, the fact that the present conception of science forces honest, astute, and conscientious investigators to look elsewhere for guidance must be interpreted as a shortcoming in the current conceptions of the scientific approach." (1956, p. 656)

Let me give a simpler example. A child growing up learns about his mother. His learning is initially of the form: If I do *X*, Mother does *Z*. Failures in prediction lead to more differentiated learning: If I do *X*, when *Y*, Mother does *Z*. The sequences of eventualities may be progressively extended, and the events may become organized into sets: There is a class of events which, if I engage in under a class of conditions, leads to a class of consequences. The child thus learns laws that describe the ordering of events in his relations with mother. He may not be able to state the laws explicitly and he may be unconcerned about whether his laws hold for the relations between other children and their mothers.

If he grows up to be a scientist seeking *event* laws, he improves his methods somewhat, he tries to be explicit about his findings, he aims at a union between the utmost precision and the utmost generality, he may be observer rather than participant, and his concerns may be less parochial and less personal than those of relations to his mother. But, his approach has not changed essentially; he is still interested in ordering the connections among events, and his sampling is of events. In contrast, the scientist seeking *subject* laws is less interested in connections among events than he is in differences among people. He must, therefore, sample subjects so as to show that one class of subjects differs from another, or that a class of characteristics is associated with certain persons rather than others.

The sampling emphasis for the subject-law investigator must be on the issues of subject representativeness noted above. The sampling emphasis for the event-law investigator must be rather on issues of representativeness of input and output repertoires. There is no question that event laws need to be checked across subjects. But, this is not the same as the issue ordinarily thought of in relation to subject sampling. For example, in any event-law study, a failure to confirm the relationships with a second subject demands ideally either a revision of theory or a questioning of method. Checking across subjects is thus similar to (and as necessary as) replication of experiments.[10]

By virtue of his method, the clinician is most often occupied with the realm of relations among events. Although the clinical situation limits the control he can establish, it gives him power to study these relations. The limitation is serious, although other psychological methods have equally serious limitations. But nothing is solved by confusing the two realms of discourse, or by using cross-sectional, normative, subject-sampling methods for discovering, verifying, or disproving notions based on temporally distributed, intra-subject, event-sampling methods.

---

[10] Of similar relevance is the question of replication across situations.

Conclusions

I have described the clinical investigator as a naturalist studying relationships among events in a situation evocative of highly personal and interpersonal expressions. His methods of investigation are based on assumptions about: (a) the relevance of life events and experience; (b) the relevance of modification and change; (c) the relevance of contextual circumstances; and (d) the relevance of the chaining of events. I believe that the clinical approach to psychological phenomena shares these assumptions with other naturalistic methods, though it may emphasize particular ones and de-emphasize others. No doubt, too, there are assumptions which have been omitted here.

My emphasis has been on clinical psychology, not as a body of content nor as a way of instigating personal change, but as a method of investigation. Some have suggested that the method is appropriate for voyages of discovery but not for trials of proof. Perhaps so. I, myself, can make no certain judgment of this.[11] I am convinced, however, that clinicians as well as nonclinicians need to recognize and accept the clinical approach as a naturalistic research method which, like other methods in science, demands training, caution and rigor, and is subject to error and limitations, but is nevertheless legitimate for scientific exploration, discovery, and even verification. I would remind us again that Freud developed his theories of psychic functioning primarily from his own dreams, that Piaget developed his concepts of cognitive and perceptual functioning initially through a series of games with his young children, and that present-day computer simulation methods may have a primary base in the introspections of the designers (Newell, Shaw, & Simon, 1960; Reitman, 1965). None of our students would be so daring about using his own clinical findings as research, although he might not hesitate to quote from the clinical findings of others whose training has involved fewer inhibitions.

So far, the clinical method, like other naturalistic methods, has been primarily qualitative. It has been so because of its concern with process, that is, concern with the relations among events, rather than with classes of subjects. We need not be especially self-conscious about this. Particularly, we need to be careful not to dissipate the strength of the method by forcing it into inappropriate statistical molds. Nor should we regress to simpler problems. We must, on the other hand, search for the rigor that will extend our investigative powers. Data analytic techniques for investigating the

---

[11] For example, Lorenz (1966, see especially Chapter 1 and 2) implies a reverse order from the one usually suggested. That is, he seems to do laboratory studies to develop hypotheses, which he then tests in the natural environment.

complex stream of events that characterize our experience are developing. Learning to use these investigative tools, rather than having them use us, can extend the contributions of clinical and other naturalistic approaches to psychology.

REFERENCES

Altmann, S. A. Sociobiology of rhesus monkeys. II: Stochastics of social communication. *Journal of Theoretical Biology*, 1965, **8**, 490–522.

Attneave, F. *Applications of information theory to psychology.* New York: Holt, Rinehart and Winston, 1959.

Bakan, D. Clinical psychology and logic. *American Psychologist*, 1956, **11**, 655–663.

Barker, R. G. Ecology and motivation. In M. R. Jones (Ed.), *Nebraska symposium on motivation.* Lincoln, Neb.: University of Nebraska Press, 1960. Pp. 1–49.

Barker, R. G. (Ed.) *The stream of behavior.* New York: Appleton-Century-Crofts, 1963.

Barker, R. G. Explorations in ecological psychology. *American Psychologist*, 1965, **20**, 1–14.

Barker, R. G., & Wright, H. F. *One boy's day.* New York: Harper & Row, 1951.

Bendig, A. W. Twenty questions: An informational analysis. *Journal of Experimental Psychology*, 1953, **46**, 345–348.

Bordin, E. S. Simplification as a strategy for research in psychotherapy. *Journal of Consulting Psychology*, 1965, **29**, 493–504.

Brunswik, E. *Systematic and representative design of psychological experiments.* Berkeley, Calif.: University of California Press, 1947.

Bugental, J. F. T. *The search for authenticity.* New York: Holt, Rinehart and Winston, 1965.

Campbell, D. T. Social attitudes and other acquired behavioral dispositions. In S. Koch (Ed.), *Psychology: A study of a science.* Vol. 6. New York: McGraw-Hill, 1963. Pp. 94–173.

Campbell, D. T., & Fiske, D. W. Convergent and discriminant validation by the multitrait-multimethod matrix. *Psychological Bulletin*, 1959, **56**, 81–105.

Chein, I. Some sources of divisiveness among psychologists. *American Psychologist*, 1966, **21**, 333–343.

DeVore, I. (Ed.) *Primate behavior.* New York: Holt, Rinehart and Winston, 1965.

Dittmann, A. T. The interpersonal process in psychotherapy: Development of a research method. *Journal of Abnormal and Social Psychology*, 1952, **47**, 236–244.

Dittmann, A. T., & Raush, H. L. The psychoanalytic theory of conflict: Structure and methodology. *Psychological Review*, 1954, **61**, 386–400.

Fenichel, O. *Problems of psychoanalytic technique.* New York: The Psychoanalytic Quarterly, 1941.

Hall, K. R. L., & DeVore, I. Baboon social behavior. In I. DeVore (Ed.), *Primate behavior.* New York: Holt, Rinehart and Winston, 1965. Pp. 53–111.

Hursch, C. J., Hammond, K. R., & Hursch, J. L. Some methodological considerations in multiple-cue probability studies. *Psychological Review,* 1964, **71,** 42–61.

Lehrman, D. S. The reproductive behavior of ring doves. *Scientific American,* 1964, **211,** 48–54.

Loevinger, J. Conflict of commitment in clinical research. *American Psychologist,* 1963, **18,** 241–251.

Lorenz, K. *On aggression.* New York: Harcourt, Brace, & World, 1966.

Milgram, S. Some conditions of obedience and disobedience to authority. *Human Relations,* 1965, **18,** 57–76.

Miller, G. A., & Frick, F. C. Statistical behavioristics and sequences of responses. *Psychological Review,* 1949, **56,** 311–324.

Newell, A., Shaw, J. C., & Simon, H. A. Report on a general problem-solving program. Paris: *Proceedings of the International Conference on Information Processing* (UNESCO), 1960. Pp. 256–264.

Raush, H. L. Interaction sequences. *Journal of Personality and Social Psychology,* 1965, **2,** 487–499.

Raush, H. L., Dittmann, A. T., & Taylor, T. J. The interpersonal behavior of children in residential treatment. *Journal of Abnormal and Social Psychology,* 1959, **58,** 9–26. (a)

Raush, H. L., Dittmann, A. T., & Taylor, T. J. Person, setting and change in social interaction. *Human Relations,* 1959, **12,** 361–379. (b)

Raush, H. L., Farbman, I., & Llewellyn, L. G. Person, setting and change in social interaction: II. A normal-control study. *Human Relations,* 1960, **13,** 305–333.

Reitman, W. *Cognition and thought.* New York: Wiley, 1965.

Rogers, C. R. *Client-centered therapy.* Boston: Houghton Mifflin, 1951.

Rosenthal, R. *Experimenter effects in behavioral research.* New York: Appleton-Century-Crofts, 1966.

Sullivan, H. S. *The interpersonal theory of psychiatry.* New York: Norton, 1953.

6
Nonreactive Assessment
of Attitudes

LEE SECHREST

ALTHOUGH THERE IS GENERAL AGREEMENT in psychology about the meaning of the concept *attitude*, there are nonetheless differences in usage of the term that threaten its usefulness as a scientific concept. For example, for a considerable period of time in psychology there was much controversy about the relationship between attitudes and behavior, as if the two were conceptually and operationally distinct; and one still encounters statements implying such a distinction. However, as Campbell (1963) has so clearly shown, the concept of attitude can only be used in a meaningful and operational way to refer to an acquired behavioral disposition, or as he put it originally, a social attitude is a "syndrome of response consistency with regard to social objects" (Campbell, 1950, p. 31). Green (1954) has also noted that the basic definition of attitude involves the idea of response covariation.

Obviously, attitudes must be inferred from some behavior, whether it be verbal, postural, motoric, or whatever, and since they are inferences from behavior, there cannot be "inconsistency" between an attitude and behavior. If an individual's responses do not covary in a theoretically coherent manner, then all that can safely be inferred is that the individual does not have an attitude in the area in question.

Careful consideration of the definition of social attitude given above will indicate that there is no single class of responses that has priority or superiority as a basis for inferences about attitudes. However, in practice, an individual's verbal self-report has been relied upon almost exclusively for inferences about his attitudes. It is interesting, for example, that despite Green's (1954) assertion that attitude involves response covariation, his chapter in the *Handbook of Social Psychology* is devoted entirely to a consideration of various kinds of attitude scales dependent on verbal response, whether oral or written. In fact, it is probably fair to say that most users of attitude scales have not actually used them so much to *infer* some attitude (a process suggestive of some transformation or interpretation) as to *measure it directly*, for example, by assuming a monotonic, linear relationship between scale values and attitude strength.

Nonetheless, an attitude is usually regarded conceptually as a unitary and unifying variable, even if of a "latent" nature as Green (1954) puts it. It then follows that an attitude may manifest itself in a variety of ways, verbal statements being only one of the myriad of possibilities. It is the task of the individual who would assess an attitude, whether he is a scientist doing formal research or an individual attempting to discover his position vis à vis his social milieu, to look for "outcroppings" of the attitude in a way analogous to what Webb *et al.* (1966) have described as the process of scientific inquiry. The difficult part of the task is to imagine manifestations of an attitude that have a reasonable probability of occurrence, that permit objective assessment, and, at least for the researcher, that lend themselves to quantitative treatment. Verbal statements are, of course, one of the important manifestations of many attitudes, and they offer many advantages for research and other purposes. However, when they form the sole basis for inferences about an attitude, there are serious threats to the observer's understanding and future predictions. Illustrative of the limitations on purely verbal measures is a recent experiment reported by Doob and Gross (1967). They used two automobiles, a luxury model and an older, inexpensive model, to block traffic momentarily at the change of a signal light from red to green. They were interested in differential aggression toward high and low status figures, and their response measures were latency of honking and frequency of honking. The low status car produced both faster and more frequent honking. However, when a separate sample of subjects was given a questionnaire measure about their responses in the same situation, people *said* that they would be more likely to honk at the high status car.

Not all manifestations of an attitude are equally likely under any given set of circumstances, or as Campbell (1963) has more elegantly put it, the different indicators of an attitude have different thresholds for appearance. Some manifestations of a social attitude are easy or have low thresholds in the sense that only a relatively weak attitude, that is, disposition to behave, is necessary for them to occur. Other indicators are difficult or have high thresholds—an attitude must be very strong before they will occur. It follows that some thresholds may also be characterized as medium in strength, which will allow manifestation of some strong attitudes but inhibit weaker ones. It is the failure to appreciate the foregoing considerations that led to the conception of attitudes "inconsistent with behavior." A verbal statement of a disposition to respond may not be an inevitable accompaniment of the actual response because, in part, it may be easier to say one will do something than actually to do it. To take a well-known example, and following Campbell's (1963) analysis, La Piere (1934) found that about 92 percent of business establishments to which he wrote said that they would refuse service to Orientals. Yet, of 250 hotels and restaurants actually visited, only one refused service. Apparently it is much easier to say "No" to minority groups by mail than it is to do so in person, or at least it was back in the 1930s before Civil Rights legislation made such commitments on paper rather risky.

Of course, verbal statements may or may not be consistent with other forms of response. People may be inclined to show more prejudice than they will admit, but they may report very faithfully their voting inclinations on a school bond issue. "Consistency" will depend on such factors as the visibility of various responses, the sanctions attached to different forms of response, and so on. Thus, an apparent attitudinal discrepancy may occur if one can make some responses in secret but must make others in public or if penalties are attached to some responses but not to others.

An illustration of consistency between verbal responses and other behavioral indicators of an attitude is provided by the work of Church and Insko (1965) and some hitherto unpublished research of my own. Employing a semantic differential measure, Church and Insko showed that students of Chinese and Japanese ancestry in Hawaii differ from Caucasian students in their attitudes toward sex. I then made systematic observations on the campus of the University of Hawaii and focused on the degree of physical contact within opposite-sex couples. Four degrees of contact were noted, ranging from "no contact" to "kissing." As shown in Table 6–1, couples of Oriental extraction (it was not possible to distinguish between Chinese and Japanese) displayed a lower degree of physical contact than did Caucasian couples. Moreover, for racially mixed couples, the amount of contact was apparently intermediate. It may be worth noting that the greatest amount of contact is associated with Caucasian females and the least with Oriental females. In any case, with respect to attitudes toward sex there is some degree of consistency for these student samples between verbal and other manifestations.

If we take prejudice as an example, we may examine the various manifestations of prejudice in the order of their probable appearance as an attitude gains in strength. In fact, we may restrict the situation to one in which an individual is riding on a public conveyance and abruptly finds

TABLE 6–1   *Physical contact and ethnic background of pairs of University of Hawaii students*[a]

Degree of Contact	Caucasian male Caucasian female	Caucasian male Oriental female	Oriental male Caucasian female	Oriental male Oriental female
No physical contact	28	39	12	206
Holding hands	7	2	3	5
Arm in arm	10	3	2	1
Embrace	3	0	0	0
Kissing	4	0	1	0

[a] χ^2 based on 4 × 2 (contact-no contact) table = 70.30; $p < .001$

that a target of his prejudice has occupied the adjacent seat. Perhaps the first indication detectable under any circumstances would be some sort of autonomic reactivity such as the GSR. Incidentally, McGuire (1966) considers the use of physiological measures of attitude an encouraging trend. Even if there were measureable autonomic reactivity, the direction of the attitude might remain in doubt. A pretty girl might elicit the same level of GSR that a target of prejudice elicits. An individual might be able to admit to himself that he was uncomfortable in the situation before he could admit it to anyone else, although we should never know about it. However, at a relatively weak level of prejudice the individual might disclose his discomfort to a trusted friend who shared his own attitude, and at a stronger level, he might make the same disclosure on an attitude measure used for "scientific" purposes. At still stronger levels, he might make a public complaint, might get up and change his seat, or at still higher levels, he might even make a physical attack on the victim of his prejudice. Ideally, we should be able to develop a Guttman scale indicative of perfect consistency in the sense that every individual at any given level would show all weaker manifestations and would not show any stronger ones.

It should not be supposed that it is always possible to tell in advance just what the order of difficulty of a set of attitude manifestations is going to be. Under some circumstances an individual might well find it easier to change seats on a bus, under some pretext, than to admit his prejudice to another person. Pettigrew (1961) has pointed to the pressures for conformity in the South, that is, toward the public expression of segregationist sentiments, which might make considerable difference in the ordering of attitude indicators between Northern and Southern communities.

Attitude Expressions in Artificial and Natural Situations

It is most unfortunate that, at least for scientific purposes, attitudes have been assessed almost exclusively by questionnaires and interviews. Cook and Selltiz (1964) and Webb, *et al.* (1966) have detailed the considerations which make dubious, at best, the total reliance on one very limited method of assessment. Not the least of these considerations is the loss of a great deal of the complexity and richness of social attitudes that can manifest themselves in so many ways but which are assessed only in terms of voluntary verbal statements. Moreover, questionnaires and interviews have the prime disadvantage of signalling all too clearly to the respondent just which attitude the researcher is interested in, thus almost inevitably producing a bias in response. The great amount of research on the bias in responses produced by the characteristics of the experimenter or interviewer, the particular phrasing of the question, and the situation under which the attitude statements are collected all attest to the caution needed in interpreting the responses of persons who are being tested and know it and who know for what they are being tested. (The same caution is needed in the interpretation of many behavior-observational measures.) And what of the person who does not respond at all? When the cooperation of the subject is required, there is a definite risk that cooperation will be denied and that a biased subset of respondents will be excluded from the research.

The especially troublesome limitations of tests and interviews become apparent in studies of attitude change. First, tests or interviews done a second time are clearly not comparable to the initial administration, and special controls have to be employed to make certain that whatever changes are found are not attributable to the effects of repeated testing. Many test items and interview questions derive at least part of their effect from surprise or novelty, and when that is missing, the character of the measurement device is changed considerably. Moreover, testing itself may produce changes in whatever is being measured, as witness the report of Crespi (1948) that one of the outcomes of polling is to reduce the number of persons not having any opinion on a matter. A second problem in studies of attitude change is that the questionnaire or interview may sensitize the subject to whatever efforts are being made to change his attitudes, so that whatever the results, they are generalizeable only to those persons, who, like the experimental subjects, are exposed to the testing or interviewing. Campbell and Stanley (1963) have discussed this problem and point out that it represents a possible interaction between the testing procedures and the experimental treatment.

Cooperation-Free, Nonreactive Measures

What are needed in the study of social attitudes, as in other areas of psychology, are measures which (a) do not require the cooperation of the subject, (b) do not permit the subject's awareness that he is being measured or treated in any special way, and (c) do not change the phenomenon being measured. The above three provisions may be taken as an operational definition of *naturalistic* measures. Most such measures will, of both choice and necessity, occur outside the laboratory and in the real world.

There are any number of ways in which an attitude may manifest itself, and, with one exception (autonomic response measures), the manifestations are not limited to the laboratory. It is the stimulus situation, not the response, that defines a naturalistic method. For example, the verbal self-report is one possible manifestation of an attitude. In fact, it is the one ordinarily depended upon in interviews and questionnaires. However, people frequently make verbal statements from which it might be possible to infer attitudes, and most such statements are made outside a laboratory or research setting. Conceivably, one might collect a sufficient sample of an individual's verbal emissions in order to justify some inference about his attitudes toward, say, high school dropouts. The main problem is that what Webb *et al.* (1966) call the "dross rate" is much too high, in other words, the amount of freely emitted speech one would have to record would be prohibitively great. The point, however, is that verbal emissions may be studied as cooperation-free, nonreactive measures.

There is not space here to exhaust the list of possible manifestations of social attitudes, but it might be well to sample from, and thus illustrate, the response universe involved. Already mentioned is the possibility of using autonomic response measures, and for certain purposes such measures are likely to be quite useful. However, because of the need for hardware, such measures are not likely to be possible outside the laboratory and without the cooperation of the subject. Moreover, they may well involve a great many reactive effects. Nonetheless, it might be worth pointing out that the effects of some autonomic responses are visible to the unaided eye and are regularly used in everyday life to diagnose important attitudes, for example, blushing, profuse perspiration, and pupillary dilation may give important clues concerning attitudes to the sensitive observer. Similarly, many aspects of speech other than its content (rate, pauses, hesitations, volume, errors) all afford possible clues to attitudes, although their interpretation is not without its difficulties. Postural and gestural cues may also be used (Ekman, 1965). Hess (1965) has shown the great potential of pupillary measures if problems of obtrusive instrumentation can be surmounted.

A wide variety of locomotor responses may suggest the nature of an attitude, but undoubtedly the simplest is movement along some approach-avoidance gradient. In general, we expect that people will try to place themselves in some spatial proximity to those things toward which they feel positively and that they will retreat from things toward which they have feelings of antipathy. Thus, spatial distance provides one possible index of attitude. Those who have observed the shrinking behavior of someone seated beside another person repugnant to him will grasp immediately the possibilities for exploiting spatial measures in some kinds of social attitude research. Hall (1959, 1966) and Sommer (1967) have been especially imaginative in their studies of the use of space and the meaning of space in social relationships. There are other responses which, if they do not involve actual locomotor responses, are symbolic of spatial alignments, for instance, joining an organization may be seen as conceptually similar to moving toward a group of people.

A good many researchers have made use of naturalistic measures in social attitude research, but the principal use of such measures has been as validating criteria in the development of attitude scales or interviews of one sort or another. Admittedly, the development of attitude scales is an important enterprise, for they have many important uses, and it is also true that an attitude scale may prove to tap an attitude better than any of the criteria against which it is validated. Still, I suspect that cooperation-free, nonreactive measures have been neglected as measures in their own right. They have the advantage of verisimilitude; indeed, they very often *are* the behaviors in which we are interested. And they can be exploited in conjunction with each other or with other measures. Finally, there are often naturalistic measures available for single individuals, but also for entire populations in which we may have an interest (see Webb *et al.*, 1966).

Opportunities for Nonreactive Measurement

Some of the procedures which may be exploited in naturalistic measurement have been detailed elsewhere (Campbell, 1963; Sechrest, in press; Webb, *et al.*, 1966), and I cannot go over all of them here. However, it might prove instructive to indicate some of the opportunities which exist for obtaining attitude measurements of a cooperation-free and nonreactive sort.

Tailing requires that an individual be followed over a period of time and all his behaviors be noted that are relevant to measurement purposes. This is scarcely feasible in attitude research, and it is unlikely that it could be done without producing any number of reactive effects. However, it is a model for other kinds of assessment efforts. Instead of tailing an individual, if one is interested in a population, one may try to approximate tailing by observing, for example, watching, listening to, a random sampling of individuals from the population in a random sampling of situations, recognizing in both instances that randomness is usually a desideratum rather than a reality. The problem with tailing is that the dross rate is usually inordinately high. Even for such salient problems as peace and war or civil rights one must overhear a great amount of conversation to hear anything at all that is relevant.

An approximation to tailing is *situational sampling* in which observations are made only in those situations that have a reasonably high probability of yielding data of interest. For example, if one is interested in attitudes toward Negroes as reflected in spatial distance, there is not much point in observing all-white suburbs. Arrangements should be made to observe in certain situations in which whites and Negroes have a high probability of encountering each other. Even so, there can be much wasted effort involved in waiting for exactly the right sort of situation to occur. Therefore, there is often much to be gained, both in terms of efficiency and control, by setting up *contrived situations* in which the experimenter can manipulate events so that the critical one in which he is interested will occur. For example, Lefkowitz, Blake, and Mouton (1955) were interested in the probability that pedestrians would violate "Don't Walk" street signs as a function of the behavior of high and low status models. Presumably, they could have waited with incredible patience for exactly the right sort of situation to occur. However, they found it expedient to contrive to have appropriate models, at appropriate times, behaving in appropriate ways (appropriate from an experimental point of view). Doob and Gross (1967) did much the same thing in their horn-honking elicitations. Such strategies are commonly called field experiments.

Depending on the nature of the response and on the environment in which it occurs, it is quite possible that a trace of the response may endure long after its occurrence. For example, the cigarette butts in the ashtray reveal the smoking habits of the occupants of a room, and worn stair treads indicate the ambulatory habits of generations of students. These two examples respectively illustrate two general categories of behavioral traces: *accretion* and *erosion*. Probably relatively few social attitudes result in the laying down of durable traces, but there are certain possibilities, one of which will be explored later. At this point, it is sufficient to note that under the proper conditions behavioral dispositions may be diagnosed after the behaviors themselves have ceased to occur or are no longer visible.

Some Naturalistic Measures of Social Attitudes

As stated previously, relatively few investigators have employed naturalistic measures as the prime measures in investigations of social attitudes. However, in the presentation that follows, no distinction is made between studies in which given observations are employed as predictor or criterion variables. The emphasis on covariation in responses makes all measures equal in status until some other conclusion is empirically justified.

One area in which a naturalistic method has been used on several occasions, as a focus of interest in the investigation, is the diagnosis of political liberalism-conservatism, and the method employed has been to examine verbal emissions or voting records of the subjects of the study. Politicians have most often been the population studied, but one investigator was interested in news columnists. Gage and Shimberg (1949), MacRae (1954), and Dempsey (1962) are among the many who have developed indices of political liberalism-conservatism on the basis of Senatorial voting records on presumably critical bills. In each case, the measure derived was used in its own right rather than as a criterion against which to validate some other measure. Webb's (1962, 1963) study of political liberalism-conservatism of newspaper columnists made use of two kinds of congressional records. First, individual Congressmen, both Senators and Representatives, were given liberal-conservative scores based on their voting records, and then the *Congressional Record* was searched to discover which Congressmen were having the writings of which of twelve influential political columnists inserted into the *Congressional Record*. The results coincide rather well with independent judgments of the columnists.

Anderson has studied some of the determinants of congressional voting and has found that Congressmen apparently do not simply follow the wishes of their constituencies. For example, there is greater consistency in the voting record from a given constituency when it is represented by the same man in two different Congresses than when it is represented by two different Congressmen in the same Congress (Anderson, 1964a), a finding consistent with those of Froman (1963), who concluded that Congressmen vote their own beliefs. Of more direct interest here is that when an issue is highly controversial, when attitudes are presumably strong and polarized, the voting of Congressmen tends to be unidimensional (Anderson, 1964b). That is, few predictors are needed to foresee the vote on controversial issues.

Of course, it cannot be maintained that voting records, speeches in Congress and the like are nonreactive, although they are cooperation free. In fact, they are highly reactive, in one sense, because the responses are produced in a very deliberate way, "for the record." However, the behavior involved is so critical that there are distinct limits on the variation which is possible. A Congressman, for instance, cannot afford very often to vote in opposition to his conscience and his constituency merely in order to build a particular image of himself. Moreover, the responses are produced without prior knowledge by the Congressman of the exact use which may be made of them. It is unlikely that any Senator anticipated that Dempsey (1962) would examine his pattern of voting in order to study party loyalty. Thus, the behavior involved is very real behavior and is not produced as a result of the specific stimulus of the research use to which it will be put.

Ethnic and racial prejudice is another area in which there have been some interesting investigations employing unobtrusive measures. Stuart (1963) studied the Grievance Board records of a garment workers union for indices of conflict among minority groups. While such records are not totally unreactive to the circumstances under which they are obtained, again they represent important attitudinal indicators. Stuart found clear indications of the mutual hostilities between members of different minority groups. Campbell, Kruskal, and Wallace (1966) studied the seating patterns of Negro and white students in college classes on the premise that where choice of seats is voluntary, it should be possible to determine the extent to which acquaintance and friendship cross racial lines. Their study was carried on in three schools, which were thought, on an a priori basis, to differ markedly in social attitudes, and they showed the expected difference in aggregation by race. Moreover, the study utilized data collected in 1951 and again in 1964 at one of the schools. However, a somewhat expected decrease in racial aggregation was not obtained. Sechrest (1965) has reported two investigations showing seating aggregation by race in elevated trains and in lunch counters. More recently Davis, Siebert, and Breed (1966) have studied interracial seating patterns in the New Orleans Public Transit system and have discovered a number of variables related to the level of integration achieved on a given vehicle. For example, integration is apparently more likely among youthful passengers. All in all, it would appear that spatial aggregation may provide a rather good and definitely unobtrusive measure of social attitudes that can be expressed on an approach-avoidance continuum.

Sommer (1967) reviews a number of investigations in which it appears that closeness of approach along a spatial gradient is related to attitude toward the approached object. Following a somewhat different line of investigation, Bratfisch (1966) has found that those objects with which one is emotionally involved have a shorter subjective distance. In current research in our own laboratory (Patterson & Sechrest, 1967), we are finding that the distance at which an actor places himself in a social interaction is a strong determinant of the impressions others have of him.

Two other investigations have made use of group membership or participation in group activity that has some bearing on the question of racial attitudes, but in neither case was the unobtrusive measure used as an independent attitude index. Maliver (1965) attempted to validate a scale of anti-Negro feeling to be used with Negro subjects, and he found, as anticipated, that Negro students who were members of CORE and who had participated in civil rights demonstrations were lower in anti-Negro bias. Interestingly, that was not true of NAACP members. Gore and Rotter (1963) had students in a Negro college indicate their willingness to participate in civil rights demonstrations in a situation conducive to the belief that they were actually committing themselves. Gore and Rotter were interested in such commitments to social action as a function of the level of belief that one's destiny is in one's own hands.

An additional investigation of interest here, and also one that is relevant to the issue of agreement between verbal and other attitude indicators, is a study of attitudes of students toward two different teaching methods, or internation simulation vs. case study, in a political science course. Robinson *et al.* (1966) found that the verbal reports of their students tended rather strongly to favor the case study method of teaching. However, they also noted a number of other behaviors which might seem to reflect attitudes toward the two measures, and they seemed at variance with the verbal reports. All the other behaviors seemed to involve some degree of commitment and effort on the part of the student. Thus, students being taught by simulation more often visited instructors to talk about the course, and they were more faithful in attendance at class sessions. Moreover, a check of library records showed that they more often checked out books assigned as collateral reading. Perhaps teaching by simulation requires too much effort from the casual student, thus leading to a preference for a less demanding method of learning.

Finally, in relation to prejudice, we studied graffiti, writings on toilet walls, in four types of institutions of higher education, and, as expected, we found indications of Negro-white and Jewish-Gentile conflict in those institutions that were integrated but which also were characterized by a generally high level of hostile expression (Sechrest & Olson, 1966). In a current investigation, I am studying graffiti of all kinds, on outdoor walls as well as in toilets, in places characterized independently as high or low in racial strife and with different proportions of racial groups in residence. By recording the extant wall writings before and after specific racial incidents, it may be possible to determine whether such recordings vary systematically with the level of racial tension in a community. It might be noted here that in other studies (Sechrest & Flores, 1965; Sechrest & Olson, 1966), we also found it possible to study attitudes toward homosexuality by means of the traces left on toilet walls.

Attitudes toward criminals and toward current problems in law and justice are of obvious interest and importance, but very little beyond the usual questionnaire survey research seems to have been done. However, in an ingenious experiment fraught with social significance, Schwartz and Skolnick (1962) prepared four employment folders for a hypothetical unskilled laborer. The four folders were identical, except that information pertaining to a criminal-court hearing was varied. In one folder, the man was described as convicted, in the second, as acquitted, in the third, as acquitted with an excusing letter from the judge, and in the fourth, there was no indication of any criminal-court record. One of the four folders was assigned randomly to each of 100 employers, who were asked whether they could use the man described. Any indication of a court record of any kind, even acquittal with a letter from the judge, resulted in a drop in the proportion of employers with any interest in the man. We are reminded here of a similar, although more reactive, study which showed that the terms used to justify being in psychiatric treatment had a differentially biasing effect on employment counselors, with the term "personal problems" being less unfavorable than "mental illness" (Rothaus et al., 1963). Further studies need to be done in such areas and the less obtrusive techniques may offer the best hope of meaningful findings.

Conclusion

The inference of a social attitude can only arise from observation of some behavior of the individual, and there are no categories of behavior intrinsically superior to others as a basis for inference. Thus far, the field of attitude measurement has relied almost exclusively on verbal behaviors, mostly of the self-report variety, but it is clear that other approaches are badly needed in order to supplement verbal measures and to compensate for some of their weaknesses. The major problems to be avoided are those stemming from the high level of reactivity of verbal self-reports. Several investigators have shown considerable ingenuity in exploiting natural measures such as spatial distance in assessing important attitudes or have engaged in the arduous task of mining the public archives involving such things as voting records. Still other investigators have created experimental situations likely to produce behavior relevant to the attitude in question but without the obviousness of the typical laboratory experiment. The field of attitude assessment can only profit from additional and more intensive unobtrusiveness.

REFERENCES

Anderson, L. F. Individuality in voting in Congress: A research note. *Midwest Journal of Political Science*, 1964, **8**, 425–429. (a)

Anderson, L. F. Variability in the unidimensionality of legislative voting. *Journal of Politics*, 1964, **26**, 568–585. (b)

Bratfisch, O. A further study of the relation between subjective distance and emotional involvement. Report from the Psychological Laboratory, University of Stockholm, #208, 1966.

Campbell, D. T. The indirect assessment of social attitudes. *Psychological Bulletin*, 1950, **47**, 15–38.

Campbell, D. T. Social attitudes and other acquired behavioral dispositions. In S. Koch (Ed.), *Psychology: a study of a science*. Vol. 6. New York: McGraw-Hill, 1963. Pp. 94–172.

Campbell, D. T., Kruskal, W. H., & Wallace, W. P. Seating aggregation as an index of attitude. *Sociometry*, 1966, **29**, 1–15.

Campbell, D. T., & Stanley, J. C. Experimental and quasi-experimental designs for research on teaching. In N. L. Gage (Ed.), *Handbook of research on teaching*. Chicago: Rand McNally, 1963. Pp. 171–246.

Church, J., & Insko, C. A. Ethnic and sex differences in sexual values. *Psychologia—An International Journal of Psychology in the Orient*, 1965, **8**, 153–157.

Crespi, L. P. The interview effect on polling. *Public Opinion Quarterly*, 1948, **12**, 99–111.

Davis, M., Seibert, R., & Breed, W. Interracial seating patterns on New Orleans Public Transit. *Social Problems*, 1966, **13**, 298–306.

Dempsey, P. Liberalism-conservatism and party loyalty in the U. S. Senate. *Journal of Social Psychology*, 1962, **56**, 159–170.

Doob, A. N., & Gross, A. E. Status of frustrator as an inhibitor of horn honking responses. Unpublished mimeo, 1967.

Froman, L. A., Jr. *Congressmen and their constituencies.* Chicago: Rand McNally, 1963.

Gage, N. L., & Shimberg, B. Measuring senatorial progressivism. *Journal of Abnormal and Social Psychology,* 1949, **44**, 112–117.

Gore, P. M., & Rotter, J. B. A personality correlate of social action. *Journal of Personality,* 1963, **31**, 58–64.

Green, B. F. Attitude measurement. In G. Lindzey (Ed.), *Handbook of social psychology.* Vol. 1. Reading, Mass.: Addison-Wesley, 1954. Pp. 335–369.

Hall, E. T. *The silent language.* Garden City, N. Y.: Doubleday, 1959.

Hall, E. T. *The hidden dimension.* Garden City, N. Y.: Doubleday, 1966.

La Piere, R. T. Attitudes vs. actions. *Social Forces,* 1934, **13**, 230–237.

Lefkowitz, M., Blake, R. R., & Mouton, J. S. Status factors in pedestrian violation of traffic signals. *Journal of Abnormal and Social Psychology,* 1955, **51**, 704–706.

MacRae, D. Some underlying variables in legislative roll call votes. *Public Opinion Quarterly,* 1954, **18**, 191–196.

Maliver, B. L. Anti-Negro bias among Negro college students. *Journal of Personality and Social Psychology,* 1965, **2**, 770–775.

Patterson, M., & Sechrest, L. Physical distance and personality impressions in social interactions. Unpublished mimeo, Northwestern University, 1967.

Pettigrew, T. F. Social psychology and desegregation research. *American Psychologist,* 1961, **16**, 105–112.

Robinson, J. A., Anderson, L. F., Hermann, M. G., & Snyder, R. C. Teaching with inter-nation simulation and case studies. *The American Political Science Review,* 1966, **60**, 53–65.

Rothaus, P., Hanson, P. G., Cleveland, S. E., & Johnson, D. L. Describing psychiatric hospitalization: A dilemma. *American Psychologist,* 1963, **18**, 85–89.

Schwartz, R. D., & Skolnick, J. H. Two studies of legal stigma. *Social Problems,* 1962, **10**, 133–142.

Sechrest, L. Situational sampling and contrived situations in the assessment of behavior. Unpublished mimeo, Northwestern University, 1965.

Sechrest, L. Testing, measuring, and assessing people. In E. Borgatta & W. Lambert (Eds.), *Handbook of personality research.* Chicago: Rand McNally, in press.

Sechrest, L., & Flores, L. The handwriting on the wall. Unpublished mimeo, Northwestern University, 1965.

Sechrest, L., & Olson, K. L. Graffiti in four types of institutions of higher learning. Unpublished mimeo, Northwestern University, 1966.

Sommer, R. Small group ecology. *Psychological Bulletin,* 1967, **67**, 145–152.

Stuart, I. R. Minorities vs. minorities: Cognitive, affective, and conative components of Puerto Rican and Negro acceptance and rejection. *Journal of Social Psychology,* 1963, **59**, 93–99.

Webb, E. J. How to tell a columnist: I. *Columbia Journalism Review*, 1962, **1**, 23–25.

Webb, E. J. How to tell a columnist: II. *Columbia Journalism Review*, 1963, **2**, 20.

Webb, E. J., Campbell, D. T., Schwartz, R. D., & Sechrest, L. *Unobtrusive measures*. Chicago: Rand McNally, 1966.

7

Psychological Naturalism
in Cross-Cultural Studies

DAVID GUTMANN

STUDY GROUPS of granting agencies are typically suspicious of cross-cultural designs in psychology. To them, such designs suggest intellectual medievalism, and a joyride at the granting agency's expense. What are commonly called naturalistic approaches are less suspect, and claim at least sentimental allegiance despite their subjectivity. Even hard nosed experimentalists admit that valuable hypotheses often germinate as vague impressions from unfocused observation of natural phenomena. Accordingly, I would like to begin with a brief discussion equating naturalistic and cross-cultural methods, in the hope of finding a new legitimacy for the cross-cultural approach.

For me, the crux of the naturalist's method is that it does not treat nature as passive. The naturalistic assumption, in any field, is that intrinsic orders exist "out there" and that these regularities will organize and drive events even though our theories take no notice of them. By contrast, the experimentalist's implicit assumption is that nature is passive; that it exists because theories exist, and that the role of environment is to supply data that will either demonstrate theory or refute it. To the theory-oriented experimentalist, nature is interesting because he has a theory about it. The naturalist also constructs and defends theories, but he comes to them via a different relation to his data and to his chosen segment of nature. His a priori theories tend, like his methods, to be conditional; they are ways of getting into the phenomena, ways of jogging nature into a response, so that it will declare itself and make explicit the terms in which it can best be understood. Thus, the techniques and instruments of the naturalist are aimed at bringing out, at highlighting some implicit order in the domain of his interest, and toward turning the implicit order into explicit data. Where the task of the theorist is to explain data, the special task of the naturalist is to generate data. What was hitherto unattended, cognitively neutral, is suddenly seen as the signature of some important principle—it becomes data.

Freud, for example, made the hitherto unattended phenomena of dreams, fantasies, slips of the tongue, and free associations available to scientific study and imagination. They were recognized as the indicators of man's persistent unconscious strivings, and so became data. Now, even Freud's opponents try to refute him via the kinds of data that he created.

In this volume, Dr. Menzel (see Chapter 4) has also given us an example of data generation. The previously unattended position of the chimp, his proximity to edges, became crucial data for predicting his behavior towards other objects.

Referring back to the dialectic relation between theory-centered and data-centered science, I admit that the cross-cultural approach in psychology is troublesome as a theory testing method; but I would assert that it is an important method for creating new domains of data. The major objections against cross-cultural tests of psychological theory are pretty much justified: there are too many uncontrolled variables, we can't be sure that our instruments are equivalent across cultures, it is hard to assess the effect on indigenous populations of foreign investigators, we don't know if our questions mean what we think they mean, distortion is created when we translate our protocols, and so forth.

But, while deficient on the side of theory testing, cross-cultural work supplies crucial experiences for data generation. How do we generate new data? Most generally, by removing ourselves from or interfering with accustomed, established behavioral formats and sequences. Established action patterns, enacted in familiar settings, pull us toward stereotypy of behavior and perception. We act, another reciprocates in kind, we reciprocate in ways that match the now alerted expectations and action potentials of the other, and we are soon prisoners of the escalating game—be it the mating, teasing, disciplining, or competing game—that we have set in motion. There is little possibility of new data now. The only data that engage us are the familiar behavioral and affective cues relevant to the game. Accustomed action is antithetical to wide-ranging, data-generating forms of attention.

It follows that we are most likely to stimulate new attention and to generate new kinds of data by stepping out of accustomed action frameworks, and by waiting for unexpected regularities to announce themselves. Then the agents implicated in these inferred regularities, and the events that summate to them become, more and more explicitly, our data. We have not declared in advance what the data should be; rather, in our experience, it has *forced* itself on our attention.

In effect, we create data by stepping out of our accustomed ecologies, and by changing our relation to them. We cannot usually objectify as new data that which is reciprocal or *ecological* to us in a close-knit, umbilical way. We truly *experience* the fact that we are air breathers, and "air" becomes an objectified datum, only when we first fall into the water. By the same token, man only learned to fly in airplanes when he stepped outside of the usual, accustomed relationship with the air and air currents.

We can similarly view psychotherapy as a data-generating process. The psychotherapist turns the patient's unconscious motivations into more objectified data by refusing to supply the patient with his expected and comfortable psychosocial ecology. He doesn't join the patient's preferred mating or punishing dance, he doesn't react as the patient predicts, or take a role in his psychodrama. Ideally, the patient begins to discover that his motivated predictions or expectations are distinct from the environment that they predict to; they become the *data* of his subjective awareness.

Like psychotherapy, cross-cultural experience also gets us out of our social skin, out of our accustomed psychosocial ecology. In the foreign setting, our most deeply ingrained and motivated expectations, actions, and cognitive styles do not link up to, or mortise into, a reciprocal habitat. That is to say, many features of the new environment do not easily fit the glossary of categories into which we routinely process our experience and through which we buffer ourselves against too much stimulation. The world now lacks neutralizing names, and we do not know which cues portend which events. We are temporary psychic cripples, heavy with that awareness of disorientation and unreality sometimes called "culture shock." This shock has some idiosyncratic roots: we miss familiar people, familiar scenes, familiar comforts. But we are not only the product of our private history and private arrangements; to the degree that we are sane we are also the standard product of those experiences regularly provided by our own culture. Thus, "culture shock" ultimately means that two discontinuous cultural systems have come into contact, and the surplus, unintegrated experience provided by the new culture seems disorganized only because it corresponds to regularities discrepant with our own. Accordingly, such troubling surplus experience can be converted into data for understanding those regularities of the new milieu which distinguish it from our own. We turn culture shock into data by asking ourselves questions like: "Precisely where and when do I feel most estranged in this place? What kinds of things make me feel temporarily at home, on familiar ground? What are the persistent differences between those things that I find strange and those things that I find familiar in this environment?" By constantly asking questions of this sort, the naturalist will begin to discern commonalities and persistent modalities among the characteristic features of the new habitat. Approached in this way, the structure of the new habitat begins to reveal itself, and the first approximation to these defining regularities comes from the investigator's subjective response to them.

There follows an example of this process taken from my own experience in a Lowland Mayan village of the Yucatan, where I collected projective materials from middle-aged and older village-dwelling corn farmers. I also collected data bearing on the typical personality of this group. I did not begin as a naturalist. Working from psychoanalytic bias and theory, I conscientiously made data out of parent-child interaction, weaning, toilet training, disciplining practices, and the location of the child's hammock relative to the parent's hammock. Whenever I wrote about these people, however, I always seemed to start with more banal, but also more truly ecological comments. It seemed important that all women dressed alike, or that pigs could wander freely through the house, or that there was a relative absence of straight lines and sharp boundaries in this environment. All these phenomena seemed to be data that were calibrating toward some regularity distinctive of this village, a regularity that set it off from my own accustomed urban American ecology.

My initial approximating statement gives a sense of some of the things that became data for me:

> In the Yucatan, the eye gets trained to flatness and to lack of variation. The eye is constantly pulled horizontally, along the scraggly but generally unbroken line of the bush, over the regiments of hennequen plants, and along the straight extension of the road ahead. The North American eye gets hungry for opposition of line, color, form—for verticals to oppose the horizontals, for clearings in the dusty uniformity of the bush, for stream or lake to contrast the chalky texture of limestone and soil.

> In the village, one finds a world whose major events take place at or below the eye level; save for the church, nothing asserts itself with much distinctness, individuality or angularity either against the sky or against the land. Most buildings are alike and have much the same ground plan within their plots, the same conical straw roof, the same white-washed and rounded contours, and much the same uneven boundary walls of white-washed stone. Within the village, the roads meander to avoid an outcropping of the limestone here, a tree there. They do not cut through the landscape, but rather accent it; and at their margins the paths merge, via gradations of underbrush, into the surrounding bush. The domestic habitat is similarly mingled with the terrain; neither the exterior nor the interior of the typical house is sharply distinguished

from the natural surroundings. The two realms, the natural (or "vege-table") and the domestic, are interpenetrated; the house floor is of packed dirt, the roof is of thatch. Piles of corn, fodder, and wood at hearthside represent the world of bush and *milpa*. Chickens, dogs, and even pigs move freely from outdoors to indoors and out again, in their search for scraps.

Thus, there is relative lack of distinction between nature and house, between house and house, and, finally, between person and person. That is, dress is not used by the Yucatan Maya to portray individual themes or differences, nor are faces or bodies very expressive of emotion. The men's costume is simple and practical, and relatively invariant from *campesino* to *campesino*; the women's huipils are clean, simple (save for slight touches of embroidery) and similarly invariant.

Summing up, then, I do not know what effects these characteristics of the Mayan ecology have on the form of Mayan character, but I can say that there is little in the visual experience of the Mayan habitat to suggest individual differences and unique properties. Both the natural and the man-created world suggest uniformity, homogeneity, and the blending together of elements which, in other settings, might manifest themselves in contrast and opposition.

Thus, I began to sense that, just as my ego was the internal reciprocal of a more boundaried and differentiated world, the Mayan ego might be the internal reciprocal of a world that provided experiences of connection and interpenetration in all manner of ways. In other words, the Mayan ego functions seem to be isomorphic with the prevailing organization of space, time, and boundary in their accustomed habitat.

New Interviewing Approaches

These hunches began to generate data; they suggested new things to look at, new questions to ask, and new ways of thinking about the replies. As this process took hold, it was registered in a changing interview style that shifted from a precoded schedule to more open and responsive procedures.

Most subjects were monolingual, middle-aged and older men, and interpreters were usually required. The original schedule represented a priori interests in the psychological aspects of the aging process; that is, respondents were questioned about old men's feelings, how men changed over the life span, how old men dealt with others, how they advised their sons, how their sons regarded them, and so forth. By and large, respondents understood my questions, and answered them, but without much involvement. The data were static, and after about the fourth interview, one could predict their course; "Young men respect old men and old men give young men good advice" was the standard message.

Accordingly, I shifted from a data-accumulating to a data-finding approach. I decided that my task was not to review specific topics that might or might not be of interest to my subjects, but to promote an atmosphere in which subjects would be free to report on whatever interested and involved them, and on how they handled these matters. I tried to provoke free communication about subjective states, to see where the subject was psychologically located vis à vis his fellow villagers, and then to see if the psychological styles native to the village also discriminated age groups within it.

Typical criteria of standardization rule out this kind of idiosyncratic interviewing. However, our usual definitions of standardization are based on superficial and external criteria; for example, the rather obsessive-compulsive notion that if we keep our instructions, questions, gestures, and inflection constant from subject to subject, we somehow establish equivalence across situations. Because our behavior remains the same, we assume that we somehow magically, ritually, maintain the surrounding universe constant. As I see it, standardization and equivalence reside in a *condition*, a condition of rapport, and not in some specific behavioral formula. Relaxed, trusting communication is the desirable standard interviewing condition, and it is reached in each case via different routes, depending on the subject's reaction to the interviewer and to the interview.

While it is fairly easy to generate rapport and "clinical" communication of wishes, fantasies, significant memories, and so on, with clients who have sought out treatment, it is not easy to generate such communication across racial, linguistic, cultural, and status barriers with psychologically naive subjects. However, the field worker who wants to get significant depth interviews does have some advantages on his side. By and large, regardless of cultural barriers, people do want to talk to us about matters that are vitally important and troubling to them. Given facilitating circumstances, they will attempt the kind of discussion that routinely goes on in the psychological clinics of our own culture. Thus, the task of the psychological naturalist is to replicate, in the field, some functional equivalent of the clinical situation.

Most importantly, this clinical milieu is not organized by social norms; it is *extra-cultural*. As mentioned earlier, the clinician does not respond in conventional ways to conventional overtures; he asks about unconventional matters and he proposes unconventional explanations. He frees communication by suggesting, through all the experiences that he provides, that the confession of socially tabooed material will not have the usual, feared, and expected social consequences. In another sense, the clinician creates a dyadic culture whose norms sponsor the expression of emotions and attitudes that are important to the patient, but which the patient cannot communicate to his significant community.

Thinking and experimenting along these lines, I found that I could sometimes provide such extra-cultural experiences for preliterate Mexican and American Indian informants, and that I could thereby initiate depth interviews with them. It is important to note that this procedure is not an extension of anthropological techniques. The anthropologist does not gain interviewing leverage by drawing attention to his alien origins and qualities. Instead, he learns about his area of concern, the social system of the society that he studies, by participating as much as possible in that social system. His method is to become the familiar and even honorary kin of his informants. As his circle of intimates and his web of kinship ties grows, so grows his knowledge of the subject society. My experience suggests that the psychological naturalist, the student of *internal* matters, should avoid being enlisted into the external social systems of his informants. Once he becomes a social object in the conventional sense, his informant's revelations to him automatically have social consequences, and the precondition for the clinical dialogue is compromised. Thus, in order to maximize his effect, the naturalist-clinician should not try to play down the real social, racial, and linguistic discrepancies between himself and his subject. But, if he does not minimize social distance, he must also assume that his subjects will, in varying degrees, suspect and fear him. Thus, in order to maximize the methodological usefulness of foreignness, the investigator must allow his informants to express and to reality-test such preconceived fears and suspicions. Accordingly, at the beginning, I routinely invite the informant to interview me, suggesting that before he answers my questions, he probably has questions of his own to ask. I demonstrate the sincerity of this offer by urging the respondent to ask more than polite questions, or I try to reflect and sharpen the meaning of allusive, roundabout enquiries: "Señor, I think you want to know who besides me will hear these tapes"; or, "I think that you are wondering if I will make a lot of money from this interview."

When asked a blunt or hostile question, I congratulate the informant on his frankness, and answer the question as honestly as possible. Thus, I try to reward straight communication, trying to convey the idea that directness is more important than politeness. Finally, this technique of the *invited interview* can supply to the informant the experience of the new, socially atypical situation. The subject does not expect an authority figure, and a white man at that, to concede to him the power role, the questioner's role, by giving him the right to ask questions. I suggest that a priori expectations do not apply, that this is a new situation, and that new forms of communication can be attempted in it.

Incidentally, the data generated by the informant's invited interview are valuable in their own right; the respondent's questions are more reliable indicators of his persistent concerns and categories than are his answers. For example, the questions asked by older men are notably different than those asked by younger men within the same society, and the variation falls along lines predictable from a general theory of aging.

As a general rule, it is wise to regard any persistent theme developed by the respondent at the outset of the interview as reflecting his untested doubts and implicit questions of the investigator. For example, an aged Navajo medicine man spent the first half hour reciting incidents of white predation against the Navajo: a white official squandered money meant for the Navajo schools; another agent cuckolded Navajo men; Washington tries to steal the treaty lands "between the four sacred mountains"; and yet another white cheated the informant's father out of his policeman's job. I commented that the informant was probably wondering if I, another white man, was out to cheat him. The anti-white tirade continued until I countered that I had my land, my work and my woman, that I needed nothing that belonged to Navajos, and that all I wanted from my informant was his story. After this, the informant talked more directly to my questions, and finally revealed a more yearning and vulnerable side of himself.

Closely related to the attempted honesty and candor in answering, as well as to the attempted candor in explaining what I want from the respondent, is another principle to which I try to adhere in the process of establishing my credibility: I make no promises—I take every opportunity to point out that the respondent can expect no tangible benefit from the encounter. Not only does this affirm my interest in his story alone, but it also keeps me out of the outsider's and white man's role to which the respondent may be accustomed and removes some possibilities for lies on my part and disappointment on his part.

Depth communication is also achieved through the emphasis on the uniqueness of the subject. When we demonstrate our regard for them as unique persons, we evidently motivate our informants to bring up the personal concerns and fantasies, the special and determinant events, that distinguish them from their fellows. Thus, I inquire at length about the details of early life, the sequences and special qualities of orienting figures, and the history of education, employment, and migration. By asking for a detailed account of personal, idiosyncratic history, and by taking this account very seriously, I try to convey my interest in those aspects of the subject's life that are unique to him. In a sense, the process of gathering what we often call case histories serves the *procedural* purpose of facilitating the invited interview.

The sense of individual concern is also conveyed through the open-ended format of the interview. There are standard questions that I try to cover in each case, but these are not asked in any fixed form or sequence. To repeat, the naturalist should not worry about covering his list or schedule of a priori questions. His real job is not to get a quota of responses. Rather, his task is to find out, *from the respondent*, what questions to ask. Thus, I try to question around the themes and topics emphasized by the respondent, and I indicate that this is a serious enterprise by following up and asking for clarification of obscure points: "You say that you are happy when you herd sheep. But I have never herded sheep, so I do not know how that would make a man happy. Could you tell me what things happen when you herd sheep that make you happy?" I also try to demonstrate to the subject that his implicit messages are getting through. Thus, when I think that a theme has been identified, I try to make it explicit: "I think you are telling me that you are sad that nobody comes around any more to learn your medicine songs."

When the interview is going well, we inevitably touch on covert emotions, troubling to the informant. The resulting anxiety can lead to breakdown of communication. At these junctures, I try to estimate the content of the troubling wish or attitude, and through my resultant questions or comments, I try to convey my tolerance—better yet, my zest—for the covert material. In effect, I *sponsor* the underlying feeling. As a result, the informant might sense that I do not share his distrust of the covert wish or attitude, and he is better able to resume communication around the hitherto troubling topic.

For example, a 60-year-old Navajo man told me that his family had suffered much from a witch who envied their wealth in sheep and horses. He was rather vague about the identity of the witch, and became notably anxious when I asked if he was angry at this person. He replied that anger is bad, a moral shortcoming. I pressed for more details of the witch's depredations, and the informant reported that his son had talked of killing the suspect, but had been restrained by the parents. At this point, genuinely puzzled, I asked, "Why did you stop your son from killing this witch?" thereby conveying the idea that anger and ideas of revenge seemed fairly reasonable under the circumstances. The informant was then able to provide a much more detailed account of the witch's activities, the arguments for and against killing him, and the resolution of the problem: "He's been exposed, his witch-craft is out in the open where everyone can see it, and so it doesn't work any more."

Thus, by appearing to sponsor the subject's latent aggression, I obtained a clearer picture of its behavioral consequences (exposure of the enemy, rather than murder) and I obtained a detailed ethnography of one case of Navajo witch-craft.

Subjects approached in this manner are not likely to be "opened up" to the point where lasting psychological pain or damage results. It is not a rationalization to insist that subjects are not passive recipients of methods that "open them up," "pierce their defenses," and hopefully "close them up" again. To repeat, the subject actively *chooses* to "open up" if his preconditions for significant communication have been met; at best, we supply experiences which will make that choice more likely. By the same token, the subject "closes himself up" when he has gotten what he wanted from the interview—usually, a chance to let off steam without fear of retaliation. But the subject's choices of what to reveal and how to reveal it also give me what I want, namely, data for estimating the subject's psychological location.

The Distributed Self

Some of the more formal findings concerning the psychology of aging men in preliterate communities are reported elsewhere (Gutmann, 1966, 1967). The remainder of this paper will present some unexpected data and impressions regarding preliterate ego process, generated by the naturalistic interviewing approaches described above.

Generally speaking, in preliterate Mexican and American Indians, the sense of self seems to be much more distributed, or fractionated, than is the case in literate, urban communities. That is, the Mayan *campesino* or the Navajo sheepherder find data that have immediate, direct implication for themselves in those agents that we would consider to be completely distinct from them, and beyond the boundaries of the self. For example, the sense of self is distributed into aspects of the natural world that bear on survival: a Navajo woman complains that government-enforced herd reduction has caused drought, because the "bleating of the sheep brings the rain."

Here, the subject's own sense of deprivation is experienced in the bleating of her sheep, and the rain that could satisfy such thirst is conceived as being directly responsive to that thirst. Similarly, the agrarian

Maya experience their fields and the physical environment to some degree in terms of subjective states, particularly at crucial times in the agricultural cycle. The men of Aguacatenango, a Highland Mayan village, routinely saw clouds in the Rorschach "trying to rain" during the dry period when clouds were just beginning to pile up over the hills. Freudian theorists might interpret these responses to drought as representing a depressive, maternally deprived state—drought is a metaphor of the dried up breast. Or, they might note the urethral implications. This might be so, but it should also be noted that unconscious libidinal needs of whatever sort are experienced through one's field and livestock and tillage, and at a time when *fields* and *herds*, rather than the *informant*, are dry and parched.

Even more concretely, the highland Maya believe themselves extended into nature and beyond their own skin. They believe, for example, that their own existence is intimately tied up with the fate of their *nagual*, an animal spirit, whose life—though passed in the distant mountains—is coterminous with theirs:

> "In my dream, the bulls almost reach me by the horns, and I grab them by the horns and this force makes me awaken." (What do these dreams mean?) "I don't know, perhaps it is the spirit that frightens me." (Are they *naguales*?) "There are no *naguales*. It is just because of my hot head. If they were *naguales*, then something can happen to me later on. But, since they aren't *naguales*, nothing happened." (And do you have a *nagual*?) "If I did, I would be dead now." (Why?) "If one sees his *nagual* then he dies, because if the *nagual* gets killed, the man dies as well. The *naguales* get together and fight, then whichever *nagual* dies, his corresponding person dies too. If a man doesn't have a *nagual*, he doesn't die."

In the preliterate community, you are like the other people who are so clearly like yourself; that is, those who speak your tongue, wear your costume, obey your authorities, and often share your name. What you do is what they do, and what they do is indisputably what you *should* do. Thus, the sense of self is also distributed into the community, and into the norms and customs that develop out of a long and shared history of similar people doing similar things, for similar purposes. In the preliterate community, there is little seam or boundary between motive and action, especially conventional, norm-governed action. There, custom and convention are seen to initiate and explain action, and not the inner, subjective variables that *we* call "needs" or "motivations." The Highland Maya, for example, do not understand questions such as, "Do you like to work?", or "How do you feel about serving your turn in the town government?" These questions refer to conventional activities, and conventional behavior is its own rationale. They answer, "Of course I like it señor—it is the custom here." Asked about what they like, these men report the conventional things that they *do*.

These preliterate men do have a subjective life in the sense that they have idiosyncratic wishes, fantasies, and fears. The difference between our subjectivity and theirs is that they do not distinguish idiosyncratic from conventional thoughts. Thus, men with rather unusual perceptions of events routinely assume that these perceptions are justified by the nature of the situations to which they refer. Accordingly, they tend to confuse their perceptions of projective stimuli with the structure of the stimulus itself. Thus, an elderly Mayan shrinks away from the sight of "demons" on the Rorschach and then extends his fearful conceptions of the card to me, their owner: "You show me so many demons. Is the demon your *santo?*" By the same token, if circumstances force men to recognize that their behavior has been grossly deviant, this deviance will not be referred to some covert, subjective aspect of themselves, but to an external sponsor: "It is the liquor that makes my head go mad."

This lack of boundary—between man and man, between motivation and custom, between motivation and action, and between action and custom—seems to be tied to preliterate conceptions of causality. In our boundaried world, if agent A is to have an effect on agent C, then A must touch C, or there are other, definable "messenger" agents, $B_1 \ldots B_n$, which transmit the influence of A to C (and from C back to A). In our culture, we have "domino" theories. The dominoes support each other, or they knock each other down; but even as they affect each other, they keep their separate identity. Indeed, it is by virtue of being separate that objects have their effect in our systems. By contrast, preliterate Indians have "resonance" theories. If object A pertains to object C, even in (what we consider) allegoric, metaphoric ways, then A will affect C. These objects belong together in the same universe of discourse, and consequently they affect and *touch* each other (from our "domino" perspective) in concrete and physical ways.

Thus, the Navajo and the Maya believe that evil thoughts within the mind of one man can, unaided, provoke sadness in the mind, illness in the body, and misfortune in the life of a victim. Here, an Aguacatenango man explains the death of his children:

> "We don't know why they die. Some are envious, that's why they die . . ." (How does envy kill?) "Well, just because of *their* envy. *We* are not to blame, we just continue working and that's what takes place . . . we work for a living so there will be food for our children and then suddenly one might die." (What do the envious ones think about?) "Well,

they don't want to work and they think we should be the same as they, but we won't have enough to eat and so we work and make the effort . . . Sometimes one might better himself. And then he dies."

Here the cohesion between the witch and the victim is, from our perspective, almost purely mental; the witch's evil thoughts *pertain* to his victim, and therefore affect him. Consequently, questions such as, "How does A affect C, how does envy kill?" do not elicit Mayan or Navajo answers that make sense in our domino terms. These people can tell you in detail what sorcerers do, but the effect of the act is implicit in the sheer fact of its performance, and in its intent.

Psychodynamic theorists usually explain witch-craft fears in terms of the linked mechanisms of aggression and projection of unconscious hostility into others (Kluckhohn, 1944, especially pp. 83–102). True enough, but any university faculty can be a hot-bed of both hostility and projection, and yet when scholars become ill, they do not routinely believe that their colleagues' envious thoughts are doing them in. Fully developed witch-craft beliefs probably require unconscious hostility and projection, but also that peculiar confounding of equivalence and causation fostered by the intimate preliterate community. There, objects are experienced as extensions and reciprocals of each other; there, the other's envy of your good fortune blurs into your own self-condemnation for the same good fortune.

By the same token, the Navajo and the Maya believe in ghosts, and the usual theoretical explanation makes the expected "motivational" point: the ghost represents the believer's wish to be rejoined with the dead (see Krupp & Kligfeld, 1962). Again, the motivation alone does not account for the phenomenon; we also grieve for the dead, but we do not routinely believe in ghosts. Like the belief in witches, the belief in ghosts requires supportive consensus, plus an individual ego that locates aspects of the self in the objects that have been reciprocal to it. For this ego, objects external by our standards are *portraits* of the rage, fear, or love that they connote in the observer. Strong feelings towards significant people do not end with their death; hence the ghost. In the Mayan village and in the Navajo sheep camp, the dead continue to exist as social beings, maintained in their "ghost" status by the undiminished feelings of the bereaved.

It could be argued that these self-distributive modes of experiencing and explaining reflect culture, rather than more intrinsic, structural ego qualities. That is, it can be said that people give the explanations that they have been taught to give. However, it appears that this unboundaried mode represents more than social convention, for it is found across a range of cultures, where specific beliefs and conventions vary greatly. Then, too, preliterates apply this conceptual modality to novel phenomena, for which no prior, conventional explanation exists. For example, a philosophic old man in Aguacatenango offers his *personal* explanation of early mortality:

> "I don't know why we are not well formed here. The church is only half completed, it's not whole, we wanted to finish it, but he who finishes it dies. I don't know why the church was never finished. It's not well built. A long time ago there was another church behind where the present one stands and then there was an earthquake and that temple was ruined. They began to build it again and they didn't make it the same size. The people were to blame because they didn't have enough money so they said it wasn't necessary to build it the same length as it was before: 'You can leave it just like this.' Then the mason who was doing the work said, 'All right, I'll do as you say, but then I'll never return to my land, I'll die right here.' And that's what really happened, he died right here. That's why I believe that the men don't live very long here."

What Heinz Werner (1957, especially pp. 59–103) calls the syncretistic mode of thought comes through clearly in this speculation. A short church *is* a short life; a church finished too soon *is* a man that dies too young. Society may have sponsored this form of thought in the respondent, but this particular explanation represents a private solution, a personal conviction, and a personal relation to experience. It represents ego as much as it represents society.

Implications for Future Work

More examples of the *autocentric*[1] ecology of village and sheep camp could be cited, but I think the point has been made: Cross-cultural work gets at ecological data and ecological variables. Cross-cultural exposure can highlight the relevance of ecology for psychological processes, and it can shed light on the nature of specific ecological fits. Eventually, such work could lead to larger propositions, about the nature of the fittedness per se. Understanding something about these fits, we begin to look for

[1] The terms "autocentric" and "allocentric" were introduced by Schachtel (1959, pp. 81–84). For him, these terms refer to distinct modes of relating to objects. The autocentric mode is a self-serving use of the object; the allocentric is a mode in which the properties and needs of the object per se are recognized. As used here, these terms refer to the personal implications of social organization, that is, the autocentric social organization gives each individual recurrent experiences of being a focus, a center, of communal events and ties; the allocentric order conveys to the individual the sense that the centers and sources of organization, social bonds, and initiatives are extraneous to him—or that his alignment with such centers is not final and secure. For further discussion of the relation between ego functions and psychosocial ecologies, see Gutmann (1965).

data where we never looked before, and we have a new context for understanding data already available.

Nothing has been proven by these data and impressions, but despite its subjective and naturalistic[2] origins, the theory of the fit between autocentric ecologies and self-distributive ego functioning accommodates much available data, and it can be subjected to the impersonal, detached arbitration of scientific procedures. To this end, my next field work will entail a study of ego functioning among men, matched for age and located at strategic points along the folk-urban continuum of an ethnically, linguistically, and religiously homogeneous region. Presumably, changes in ego process can be observed, particularly in regard to the boundary functions, as one moves from the autocentric village setting to the allocentric urban setting. But this is a tentative hypothesis; after some field work, I expect to have different and hopefully better ideas about these matters.

REFERENCES

Gutmann, D. Women and the conception of ego strength. *Merrill-Palmer Quarterly*, 1965, **11**, 229–240.

Gutmann, D. Mayan aging—a comparative TAT study. *Psychiatry*, 1966, **29**, 246–259.

Gutmann, D. Aging among the highland Maya: A comparative study. *Journal of Personality and Social Psychology*, 1967, **7**, 28–35.

Kluckhohn, C. *Navaho witchcraft.* Boston: Beacon Press, 1944.

Krupp, G. & Gligfeld, B. The bereavement reaction: A cross-cultural evaluation. *Journal of Religion and Health*, 1962, **1**, No. 3 (April).

Schachtel, E. *Metamorphosis.* New York: Basic Books, 1959.

Werner, H. *The comparative psychology of mental development.* New York: International Universities Press, 1957.

[2] "Naturalistic" in the specific sense discussed above.

Part III
ARGUMENTS FROM THREE PROGRAMS OF RESEARCH

COMMENTARY

IN 1966, in a paper entitled, "Ecological Constraints on Mental Health Services," James G. Kelly argued that planners of community mental health services and preventive services should adopt an ecological perspective because (a) mental health services must have whole populations as their targets; (b) without this perspective, the transactional, that is, person-in-habitat, nature of pathology is disregarded; and, most important, (c) the perspective will lead planners to consider the ways in which an intervention in one part of a social system might produce costs and disruptions in other parts. In terms of research, Kelly viewed assessment of the relation of adaptive behavior to both its proximal and broader ecological context as the primary task. One need that this argument points out is an extensive program of research on the processes of selection for individual and group behavior in its ongoing system of niches, its ecology, as well as the adaptive value of such behavior to the individual. Consistent with his own argument, Kelly embarked upon a series of paradigm studies, focused on the inter-dependencies among population mobility in high schools and the behavior of students and teachers. Chapter 8 is a progress report on this research. Not only does Kelly present some suggestive findings on the correlates of population mobility, but he gives the reader the benefit of being rather candid about some subtle methodological issues. Perhaps most salient and controversial among these issues is his treatment of the interaction between the investigator and the situations he studies. Viewed in the usual way, Kelly is simply reinforcing a pessimistic evaluation of naturalistic observation; that it is often difficult, if not impossible, to standardize observation techniques and hold them constant across situations. However, Kelly would have us view this phenomenon with optimism. He would have us recognize that being forced to use different observational techniques in different settings, or the investigator's feeling of *constraint* in adopting differing strategies, may itself be a source of information concerning the phenomena under study. This stance flies in the face of some of the most sacred cows of methodology. However, if one will recall the shifts in procedure that the Brelands (1961, 1966) felt obliged to make—and actually made—in their attempts to correct and forestall failures due to instinctual drift, in dealing with animals, one will remember that these procedural shifts and the reasons compelling the Brelands to make them contributed greatly to their understanding of animal behavior.

Paul V. Gump has been closely identified with ecological psychology and his work has been highly productive in discovering issues involved in naturalistic research (see Chapters 1, 2, and 3 of this volume). In Chapter 9, Gump discusses his recent research on third-grade classrooms, which follows in his ongoing concern with children in relation to their naturally occurring habitats. This concern has led him to study games, playgrounds, gyms, camps, classrooms, schools, and even sets of schools. As far back as his studies of games (Gump & Sutton-Smith, 1955; Gump & Kounin, 1959–1960) and his studies of camping activities (for example, Gump, Schoggen, & Redl, 1963), Gump has spoken of molar, complex, system-like *activity structures* that children inhabit, with a special eye to how these structures, rather than discrete stimuli, affect behavior. When a classroom is viewed as such a system or activity structure, although the teacher can be viewed as a major source of organization and patterning for the system, she is still seen as only one component of it. This conceptual step and what it implies for both the substance and methodology of a research program were discussed by Gump in a paper on "Environmental Guidance of the Classroom Behavioral System" (1964). There, Gump delved into (a) why classroom research tends to focus on dimensions of individual personality and performance of classroom inhabitants; (b) why the personality approach is defective and incomplete; (c) a view of classrooms as behavior settings, that is, system-like environment-behavior units; (d) the importance of studying classrooms as such units; and (e) empirical means for studying the structure and flow of events in such classroom systems. In Chapter 9, Gump discusses some aspects of his recent program of research that has followed from this point of view. Not only does his essay offer data relevant to the process of education, but it also demonstrates an assertion made earlier by Sells and Barker (Chapters 1 and 2 of this volume): the environment of behavior is patterned and its patterning can be documented empirically, even at a molar, group level.

Several years ago, J. L. Kavanau (1964) made a set of far-reaching assertions about the experimental conditions and subject populations typically used to study the behavior of rodents in the laboratory:

A few generalizations emerging from ethologically oriented laboratory studies of wild rodents have important bearings on the rationale and
design of experiments on learning and reinforcement. Depriving animals
of natural outlets for activity by confining them in small and barren
enclosures greatly influences their behavior. Thus, when given the means
to modify their environment in ways that do not subject them to great
stress, captive rodents exercise this control repeatedly. These animals
find it rewarding to attain and to exercise a high degree of control over
their environment, perhaps in partial substitution for the freedom of
action enjoyed in the wild but denied by confinement. . . . The initial
responses of rodents in laboratory enclosures *do not reflect the preferences
or behavior of animals adapted to the experimental situation, but rather
those of animals forced to endure unnatural and completely arbitrary conditions and schedules of confinement and experimentation.*[1] The time
required for animals to adapt to the "insults" of laboratory experimentation is measured not in minutes or hours but in days or weeks. Thus,
even in experiments for which the design and analysis do not penetrate
beyond regarding the animal as a convenient experimental machine or
black box, the responses to daily short experimental sessions generally
give information only about the initial, and often rebellious, reactions
of the "machine" to abnormal and enforced working conditions. . . .

Using such atypical species representatives as domestic rats and mice
for laboratory studies of behavior narrows the animal response spectrum to
a point where its significance for adaptation, survival, and evolution becomes highly questionable. The selectively inbred animals are hundreds of
generations removed from the wild. Their bland behavior tells us mainly
how animals react to experimental regimes after many of the characteristic
adaptive responses of the species have been largely or completely lost.
Domestic animals remain convenient vegetalized strains for physiological
studies, but only wild animals provide the full range and vigor of responses
upon which solutions to the central problems of behavior must be based.
(p. 490)

These statements suggest a dilemma: (a) If one is concerned with generalizing to the naturally occurring, extra-laboratory behavior of rodents,
then the usual *techniques* of experimental study will not yield appropriate
data. (b) If one waits for animals to adapt fully to the conditions of the
laboratory, one is then left with *animals* that will not yield appropriate
data. In Chapter 10, Kavanau presents data and arguments from his own
ethologically oriented laboratory studies to support his earlier assertions
concerning the dilemma. Consistent with the ethological tradition, Kavanau
has generated experimental conditions that approximate the normal environment more than is typical and has selected experimental animals for

---

[1] Italics not in original—Editors.

heterogeneity rather than homogeneity. By these means, but within a laboratory framework, Kavanau strikes at the very core of the issue of generalization, and he is able to uncover a number of specific factors that jeopardize generalization from the laboratory.

REFERENCES

Breland, K., & Breland, M. The misbehavior of organisms. *American Psychologist*, 1961, **16,** 681–684.

Breland, K., & Breland, M. *Animal behavior.* New York: Macmillan, 1966.

Gump, P. V. Environmental guidance of the classroom behavioral system. In B. Biddle & W. J. Ellena (Eds.), *Contemporary research on teacher effectiveness.* New York: Holt, Rinehart and Winston, 1964. Pp. 165–195.

Gump, P. V., & Kounin, J. S. Issues raised by ecological and "classical" research efforts. *Merrill-Palmer Quarterly*, 1959–1960, **6,** 145–152.

Gump, P. V., Schoggen, P., & Redl, F. The behavior of the same child in different milieus. In R. G. Barker (Ed.), *The stream of behavior.* New York: Appleton-Century-Crofts, 1963. Pp. 169–202.

Gump, P. V., & Sutton-Smith, B. The "it" role in children's games. *The Group*, 1955, **17,** 3–8.

Kavanau, J. L. Behavior: Confinement, adaptation, and compulsory regimes in laboratory studies. *Science*, 1964, **143,** 490.

Kelly, J. G. Ecological constraints on mental health services. *American Psychologist*, 1966, **21,** 535–539.

8

Naturalistic Observations in Contrasting Social Environments

JAMES G. KELLY

THE PORTRAIT QUALITY of naturalistic data has been presented persuasively by writers such as Lorenz (1952), DeVore, and Hall (1965), and others. However, the issues involved in deriving hypotheses from direct and sustained observations of natural settings, uncontaminated by the interventions of an experimenter, have been presented by only a few psychologists (Barker, 1965; see Washburn and Hamburg, 1965). Investigators who employ a variety of methods for naturalistic observation often work from the shibboleth, "Look and ye shall find." I prefer the more restricted use of naturalistic methods as a supplement to the process of theory development and theory confirmation. To put it categorically, in my work I observe naturalistic events, but I am not necessarily a naturalist.

Naturalistic observations in my research are a consecutive series of observations of social settings, where the observations are designed to be unobtrusive. The focus of this research has been upon adaptive behavior by persons in different social settings. The theoretical goal is to develop propositions on how individuals become effective and survive in varied social environments (J. G. Kelly, 1964, 1966a), and the long-range purpose of the research is to contribute toward the construction of an ecological theory of intervention in social settings. The study of natural environments and how persons with different coping preferences interact with them is crucial to this work and naturalistic observations will continue to be important to its development.

Background

I assume that social environments vary in the functions they provide their members, and I am concerned more with the functions and activities that are dominantly provided in different environments than with the structures that are established for maintaining the societies. In other words, my aim is to define the activities provided and the needs met by institutions for their members, rather than to study institutions as such. From this point of view, which is similar to Goldschmidt's (1966) position regarding anthropological study, the purpose of inquiry is not only to define the formal properties of an institutional environment and the hierarchical order of the environment, or to describe the nature of social interaction, but to focus on the range of activities and needs that are met by a diverse number of functions in that institution. This point of view assumes, for example, that the behavior of both teachers and students in a school will depend in part upon the unique functions ongoing within that school, even though some aspects of the social structure may be similar, or even identical, to those of another school.

Measurement of institutional environments from this point of view includes assessment of normative functions, rules that define social behavior, social controls for managing deviant behavior, and institutionalized channels available to members for mastering the environment. The major premise is that as an environment varies in function, such functions will affect the generation and control of normative values, requirements for adaptation, and the expression of relevant coping styles by members. Adaptation is viewed as specific to a particular social setting, and as dependent upon the congruence between the particular coping styles, that is, individual preferences for mastering the environment, and the normative requirements of the environment. Thus, a particular set of coping styles will be relevant to adaptation in one environment but not in another. The research task is to specify the environmental conditions for adaptive and maladaptive behavior in different settings.

The specific type of setting I have elected to study is the high school. High schools were chosen on the belief that school life for the adolescent has pronounced, even encompassing, effects upon the behavior of the student, even when he is not physically in the school (Coleman, 1961; Rosenberg, 1965; J. G. Kelly, 1966b). But in developing observations of behavior in high schools, I have become increasingly impressed by the relevance to them of work on the behavior of subhuman primates (Jay, 1965). In a Panamanian field study of the behavior and social relations of howling monkeys in 1930, C. R. Carpenter, one of the early investigators of primates, observed that naturalistic observations vary in the extent of the observer's concealment as well as recording methods, for instance, from direct observations under complete concealment or blind conditions to indirect observation via photography. He verified that choice of technique *does* affect the range of data collected as well as the reliability of reports. For example, one of the cues that he used to assess the effects of his own presence on a group of monkeys was whether animals dropped limbs or fecal matter at his approach (Carpenter, 1964, pp. 18–21).

Naturalistic observation of human subjects presents a challenge in this respect. The challenge is to identify the direct and indirect effects of observers on the observed, and the frequently symbolic modes subjects employ to communicate to an observer, especially when these modes and responses are unique to specific settings. As my own work has progressed, I have been particularly impressed by the different modes and intensities of response in different environments to what I imagined were uniform behaviors of observers. For example, in the work with two contrasting high school environments, students in a school with a high rate of exchange of students seemed almost oblivious, even indifferent, to being observed, while students in a second school, which had a very low rate of population exchange, appeared to suppress public behavior, to become more covert and less verbal in their expressiveness as a function of being observed. The theoretical, interpretative challenge here was to understand what functions these situations and students' responses to them served in the two schools. The challenge to the strategy of observation was to adopt techniques that would yield the kinds of data we wanted in order to make reasonable statements about the schools. In the school with high population exchange, the solution was to determine reliability of recording by having several observers sample each segment of observational time. In the school with low population exchange, the solution was to have fewer observers sample the same setting at many points in time. The different responses to observers by students in the two schools are worth noting, and in themselves constitute an additional set of data that describe the cultures of these schools, the uniqueness of the environments, and the ways in which they affect the lives of their inhabitants.

Schaller (1965), in discussing the relevance of naturalistic observations for research on primates, has specified a workable ecological orientation for the naturalistic observation of social environments. First, he proposes a survey of as much of the primate's range as possible, with emphasis on diversity of habitat, distribution and abundance of the species, and similarities or differences in group size, composition, and food habits between populations of the species. This taxonomic orientation for human subjects has been represented most comprehensively by Barker's work (Barker, 1960; Barker & Gump, 1964). By studying the diversity of settings, it is possible to infer basic functions of specific environments and to define the limits for adaptation in each setting. One of the early tasks in my research was to consider the range of settings for each of the high schools in order to answer such questions as: Do different high schools have the same range of settings, and do the same settings serve the same functions across schools?

The second approach advocated by Schaller is a series of detailed observations of the social life of selected groups of the total population, concentrating on the repertoire of each species' behavior. This orientation has relevance for the study of human subjects, since, with multiple methods, it is possible to give a representative account of the behaviors that are normative for each of the settings that make up an organization. Documenting the uniqueness of social settings by multiple methods is a necessary antecedent to planning interventions and preventive services. Much of our current knowledge for planning preventive services is incomplete, in that it derives primarily from the study of selected individuals rather than from analyses of larger social units. I have attempted to modify this custom by focusing on groups of students who express different preferences for coping with the environment *in conjunction with* analyses of the social functions of the schools.

Schaller's third principle advocates an intensive study of specific aspects of behavior with joint field and laboratory experiments to clarify more complex relationships. These three guidelines provide mutually complementary methods for either the development or confirmation of hypotheses. They also provide the basis for a research cycle that allows the investigator to begin with a natural setting and end with a series of new questions about the behavior in that same habitat. I have chosen to establish initial meaning for concepts by means of naturalistic studies and to verify these findings by future experimental testing of hypotheses derived from observations of naturally occurring adaptive behaviors.

Theoretical and Empirical Context

I have been dealing with two high school environments, one characterized by 42 percent of the entrants leaving within a school year, and a second by less than 10 percent of the entrants leaving during the school year. I have termed these two types of environments *fluid* and *constant*, respectively, and I chose them on the premise that the styles of living and requirements for adaptive behavior would be clearly different. These expected differences are summarized in Tables 8–1 and 8–2, and are elaborated upon below.

I predicted that in an environment with rapid pupil turnover there

TABLE 8–1 *The ecology of adaptation: Major variables*

Ecological Variable	Environmental Functions⟵	⟶Environmental Effects upon Members	Individual Variable
Rate of population exchange	Status differentiation	Type of competences	Socially adaptive behaviors
	Modes of socialization	Mode of social participation	
	Maintenance of social norms	Coping performance	

TABLE 8–2 *The ecology of adaptation: Selected hypotheses*

Variable	Environment "Fluid"	Environment "Constant"
ENVIRONMENTAL		
Status Differentiation	Multiple	Unitary
Mode of Socialization	Personal development	Position location
Social Norms	Changing	Unchanging
Basis for Norm Violation	Organizational means	Organizational goals
INDIVIDUAL		
Valued Competence	Mastery of environment	Absorption by environment
Social Participation	Active participation in multiple settings	Specialized participation in few settings
Selected Coping Performance	High exploration and high internal control	Low exploration and high external control
Adaptative Role Functions	Change agent and innovator	Citizen and adapter

would be multiple bases for stratification and that social groupings would change from time to time. One of the consequences of living in a rapidly changing social environment was expected to be the emergence of a dominant value for personal development, in other words, an individual's functional competence would be primary for societal membership. In the constant environment, where there is very little turnover, a monolithic society with few and unchanging status differentials was predicted to arise. The primary ethos here would be for members of the community to locate themselves rather than to develop. The regulating units of the society rather than the individual would be the primary source for defining standards, and would mediate these standards by affirming what is *not* acceptable. In this way, constant environments are expected to be pre-occupied with deviant behaviors, since the orientation of these settings continuously underscores what *is* by focusing upon what *is not,* or *should not be.*

These ideas about the informal social structure can be classed as intervening variables to link the ecological structure of the society with the adaptive behavior of its members. For example, work on this project to date suggests the hypothesis that persons high on exploratory behavior (preference for novel experience), as measured by tests we have developed, will improve their general coping effectiveness more in a fluid environment than in a constant environment. Conversely, persons who have a low preference for this kind of behavior will be better adapted to a constant environment. The rationale for these predictions is that each society will develop a different repertoire of adaptive roles or niches for members. The fluid environment will generate roles that emphasize innovation and variation among individuals, while the constant environment will generate roles that emphasize solid citizenship and conformity. It is assumed that these classes of roles will differentially select for varied coping preferences by individuals. Fluid environments, with an orientation toward innovation and variation, can accommodate persons with a high preference for exploration. Constant environments, with a positive value for adaptive roles that emphasize citizenship and conformity, will accommodate persons who have lower preferences for exploration.

In the fluid high school, with the multiple bases for status generation, there should be an equal probability of occupying a high-status position for the person who is a competent athlete, debater, academician, or social leader. Furthermore, the bases for status will change from time to time. At one time, high status can be attained for dancing ability, at another time for cycling prowess, athletic competence, or ability to negotiate with faculty. In contrast, in an environment with little population movement, there will be fewer bases for status differentials and established differences will be maintained for relatively long periods of time.

Another distinguishing feature expected for the two environments is the type of normative structure that evolves. In the fluid environment, emphasis is upon standards that relate to individual performance and personal development, while in the environment with minimum population movement, normative standards focus upon expectations for position or social status. In a changing environment, it is believed that there are more divergent events and activities taking place that generate opportunities for personal development. The informal social structure that emerges facilitates an individual's participation in this society with a value for help and support. In the environment with very little change, implying a society with a fixed membership, the primary orientation is toward locating a person in the society, independent of his competence. Life revolves around society's requirements for membership and not around the diverse, individual concerns of the members.

There are other hypothesized outcomes for the two environments. In the fluid environment, there should be high variability in individual behavior over time and across settings, while in the constant environment there should be less variability, both across settings and over time. There should also be a difference between the two environments in their assimilation of newcomers. The fluid environment is expected to be more responsive to newcomers and to allow for more individual variation in their initial responses to the school. The constant environment, on the other hand, should be less tolerant of new members and should require them to alter their behavior to fit the society.

We also assumed that a fluid environment encourages more public, expressive behavior, since there should be more consistency between public statements of behavior and private beliefs. In a constant environment, where there are fewer settings for the expression of personal opinions, overt behavior becomes stereotyped and ritualistic. We would predict that maximum variability in individual behavior in a constant environment would be observed in the most private and personal settings, settings that usually are out of bounds for even the nonobvious observer. For the fluid environment, personal, and private settings should be prevalent and individual differences publicly channelled.

It is interesting to note that many of the predicted correlates of fluid and constant environments correspond to what other investigators have predicted and found for small and large high schools, respectively (see Barker, 1964; Willems, 1967).

Measurement Scales, Observations, and Interviews

The three main sources of data to date have been the correlates of measured coping style, field notes of three observers over a four-week period, and interview material gathered in 20 small group sessions from a stratified sample of 120 students in each school.

MEASUREMENT OF COPING STYLES

So far, a major portion of the work has been concerned with the development of a scale measuring adaptive behavior, or coping style (J. G. Kelly, 1966b). The total scale has four parts, each consisting of 30 self-report items. The four parts have been termed *Anticipation, Exploration, Locus of Control*, and *Social Effectiveness*, and each refers to a postulated style of environmental mastery. *Anticipation*, a concept similar to a major postulate in G. A. Kelly's Personal Construct Theory (G. A. Kelly, 1955), refers to the extent to which persons think about future social situations and includes such items as: "I don't usually plan what I'm going to do right after school," and "It often works out better just to do things rather than try to think about them first." *Exploration* refers to a preference for novel social experiences and participation in diverse social settings and includes items like: "I like staying home and keeping friendships with people I've known a long time," and "I don't like it when a special TV program takes the place of the one I usually watch." *Locus of Control* is a modification of Rotter's Internal-External Scale developed for adolescents (Rotter, Seeman, & Liverant, 1962; Rotter, 1966; Lefcourt, 1966), and includes items relating to confidence about environmental mastery, for example, "Some students are just lucky when it comes to good grades," and "Often no matter what I do I can't please anybody." *Social Effectiveness* refers to a person's perceived power to change the behavior of others: "I hesitate to speak up in a group," and "I can usually get a date to go where I want to."

Results of three preliminary studies involving high school students and college freshmen indicate that the Exploration and Anticipation scales are uncorrelated, and that neither is related to social desirability. However, as might be predicted, they correlate significantly and negatively with Srole's measure of anomie (Srole, 1956).

OBSERVATION SITES

Four types of observation sites were selected as having the highest probability of representing the effects of population change. Each site was selected on two dimensions. An *Environmental-Personal* dimension was defined as the extent to which behavior was affected by the setting (environmental) or the individual inhabiting the setting (personal). The second dimension was termed *Public-Private*: the extent to which behavior was open and spontaneous or restricted and covert. The four sites originally chosen as examples of these combined, orthogonal dimensions were the principal's office (personal-public), lavatories (personal-private), hallways (environmental-private) and cafeterias (environmental-public).

As work began, we quickly found that observations of behavior in a lavatory could be accomplished in the fluid environment but not in the constant environment. There was no easy way for the observer to become assimilated into the lavatories at the constant school, and thus, for this particular study, no lavatory observations were collected. In retrospect, I would surmise that the lavatory in a constant environment is one of the few places for expression of personal, private behavior, so that the site becomes literally and completely private for its members, while in the fluid environment, there are specific norms established for the expression of personal behavior in public places, with the result that there is little need to seek out and identify space that is genuinely private. This difference between schools again illustrates that environmental response to the process of data collection itself not only varies, but can also provide an integral basis for confirming hypotheses about the environments.

Observations on the three remaining sites in each school were achieved by having a pair of observers sample the same setting every other day for a four-week period. Slightly different methods were developed for each setting. First, for the cafeterias, the observer teams were supplemented by four student volunteers. Three types of behavior were recorded: (a) the number of table relocations between lunch periods, (b) the frequency of table-hopping within each lunch period, and (c) the proportion of males and females seated at each table. Second, the observations at the principal's office focused upon the number of entrances by faculty and students into the outer or main office, and the proportion of these entrances that resulted in going into the principal's private office. Finally, the hallway observations were focused on the size and amount of change of group membership as students exited from classrooms and upon dress and general behavior patterns. Here, the observers were again aided by high school student volunteers.

The observers went through a prior two-week period of training in observing similar settings in other, comparable high schools. After achieving 90 percent reliability among the observers for three sites, hand counters were used to tabulate behavior for the specific categories listed above.

INTERVIEWS

Interviews were conducted with a random sample of students at each high school, stratified on the basis of sex, mobility history, and leadership.

The purpose of these interviews was to clarify the modes of adaptation identified in Tables 8–1 and 8–2, to define the requirements for leadership at each school, to describe the type of faculty-student interaction and modes of faculty and student response to deviant behaviors by students, and to describe processes for assimilating newcomers. The interviews, each lasting a class period, were conducted by the author and at least one graduate student and undergraduate assistant in each school.

Some Findings and Impressions

The observations, interviews, and measures of coping offer a basis for statements concerning some, though by no means all, of the hypotheses mentioned earlier.

In a sample of six hallways at each school, both boys and girls were dressed in a more varied fashion in the fluid environment than in the constant school. This variety covered hair style, makeup, and costuming for girls; and type and color of fabric of shirts, pants, and shoes for boys. The fluid environment had more groupings of up to twelve persons than the constant school. Body and gestural movements were quite pronounced in the fluid school, with an accompanying noise level of almost "Beatle-like" proportions, and membership in hallway conversation groups varied from day to day, even though the students had consistent class schedules.

In the constant environment, dress was so similar as to appear almost uniform, with almost all boys in madras shirts, levis and penny loafers; girls with short-cropped hair, sweaters and skirts, often the same brands, bought from the same stores. As the students travelled from class to class, they were almost a caricature of an adult, with minimum body motion and few displays of affect. The size range of groupings was two to four, with the median at two persons per group. Sex groupings appeared equally split between boy-boy, girl-girl, and boy-girl, with very few shifts from day to day or even from week to week.

Supplementary comments and interview data suggested another aspect of hallway communication processes. At the fluid school, there appeared to be two styles of communication within groups: intense, aggressive gesturing and vocalization *or* no apparent communication at all. At the constant school, there was one style of low level commentary, almost as if attention were focused on a passing parade rather than upon the immediate group member.

Behavior in the respective principal's offices reflected similar trends.

In the fluid environment, there was a range of 30 to 110 entrances per three-minute period by teachers and students during the standard observation time. Many of these entrances, however, did not directly involve the principal, but instead his vice-principal, four secretaries, or student assistants who were dealing with entering students and faculty. In the constant environment, there was a range of 1 to 15 entrances per three-minute period. During the time of observation, only three of these entrances involved students who actually met with the principal. The remainder were teachers or administrative staff who had 20- to 35-minute discussions with the principal.

Observations of the cafeterias were limited by the fact that each school had split lunch periods, arbitrarily arranged. It was also difficult for the observers to obtain the same degree of agreement as in other settings; at times the mingling, scattering, and merging of students seemed to defy tabulation. The data that are available are consistent with the findings on behavior in the hallways and principal's offices. In the fluid environment, group membership varied more over time. The noise level was much higher in the fluid school, with communication focused between group members, in spite of the continued presence of student and faculty monitors. In the constant environment, there was more discussion among persons in small subgroups, and less table-hopping and less between-table communication.

Data from interviews with students in the two schools regarding their responses to new students underscored the impressions of distinctive functions. Characteristically, both boys and girls in the constant environment were unresponsive to newcomers. The boys indicated that the modus operandi toward the newcomer was a silent treatment, with the group waiting for the new person to declare himself. If the new student's behavior coincided with the norms of the school, then he was given some encouragement. If the student wore the wrong shoes, had the incorrect hairstyle, or acted conspicuously, he was hazed. Hazing consisted of after-school fights for boys or ostracizing behavior and focused gossiping for girls. Evidence from questionnaire data suggests that one of the best means for reducing trauma for the new student in the constant school was a visible competence or skill that was in short supply, together with a willingness to become absorbed and dominated by the society.

In the fluid setting, on the other hand, there was an informal welcoming committee operating whose membership varied. An incoming student would be met, his interests and needs identified, and information given to him as to what school life was like, including comments on which teachers to avoid and where to smoke. What the welcoming committee asked in return was for the newcomer to be pleasant and to try out the various suggestions. The committee welcomed exploratory behavior and even evolved a tutorial arrangement for the student who was shy, reticent, or seemed unwilling to begin his entry work. In summary, initiation and socialization processes were quite different in the two schools.

In the constant school, opportunities for leadership development were quite specific to well defined status positions. In the fluid environment, there was a wide variety of channels open for exploration. Interviews with the students indicated that at the constant school, students were troubled about "where they were in the school," while at the fluid school, students were troubled if "they personally were not going anywhere." In some respects, the constant school fits Redfield's definition of a folk society (Redfield, 1956). Analogously, the fluid school could approximate a developing society.

Finally, there are some data on the social-environmental correlates of coping preferences as measured by the scale discussed earlier. For example, male high school students who were assessed as high explorers were more likely to be nominated as deviant by the faculty of the constant school than were students with comparable preferences for high exploration attending the fluid school (J. G. Kelly, 1966b). In current work in four schools in southeastern Michigan, we are attempting to validate the relevance of these varied coping preferences in contrasting environments by examining in more detail whether students who are high and low in their preferences for exploration do in fact experience varied adaptive histories and assume different roles and status positions in different social environments.

Special Issues

The above schemata of the two types of environments are presented in order to describe what I believe are the essential contrasting functions of the two schools. Other relevant and simultaneous processes also contribute to the environmental effects. The task for theory construction is to differentiate these other correlated variables in order to specify how they differ from and interact with population exchange in their effects. There are a number of examples of such processes. First, the populations of the two schools, although equivalent in size and other details, differed in the average level of father's education. The average level of father's education was completion of high school for the constant school and only some high school attendance for the fathers of students at the fluid school.

This represents a possible confounding, in that youths from families of a slightly lower social status might tend to be more active, more expressive and exhibit a wider array of coping techniques.

A second correlated factor was the contrasting behavior of the two principals. A principal who is suppressive and unavailable to students, such as the reputed style of the principal of the constant environment, is likely to dampen the expression of spontaneous behavior and prefer the regimented, codified society that was characteristic of life at his constant school. A principal who is open to criticism, is morale-building and who has developed an administrative style where he can delegate authority and maintain feedback from his faculty and students, as the principal at the fluid school was reputed, can enhance a personal development orientation.

A third factor that might have contributed to the contrasting effects was the physical structure of the two schools. In the fluid environment, for example, the hallways were 40 ft. wide with 36-ft. ceilings, while the hallways at the constant school were 24 ft. wide with 18-ft. ceilings. Such dimensions might have facilitated gregariousness and elastic groupings at the fluid school and constricted the groupings at the constant school.

I have also learned from this preliminary work that observations of the two environments require different, even contrasting, approaches. In the fluid environment, observations were more easily accomplished. The observer's presence was not apparently noticed, nor did it appear to affect the overt behavior of the students in any particular direction. In the constant school, the observer's presence definitely seemed to elicit even more cautiousness and socially acceptable behaviors. The great need is for reliably similar, but varied, modes of observation for the two environments. For example, local students who function as hallway guards in the fluid school might replace college student observers. In the constant environment, the additional use of other methods, such as video-tape recordings and the use of longer periods of sampling will be required, particularly for the few private settings where maximal variability is expected. It will also be necessary to include members of the student body as research staff to help to identify covert, subtle expressions of gesture or dress that go unnoticed by the outside observer.

A major task in observing the fluid environment is to know enough about the total school system so that more precise statements can be made about its variable nature per se. Any unique episode occurring immediately prior to observation time has immediate and pronounced effects upon the small group structure in the hallways. Naturalistic observations can, of course, help to clarify the effect of such episodes upon the social life and ecology of the school.

Future Work

As this work continues, further attention will be given to the contrasting forms of adaptive behavior that emerge. The emergence of maladaptive behavior in a fluid environment is predicted to be related to expressions of isolation and identity diffusion. Maladaptive behavior emerging in a constant environment is expected to be more related to acts that go against the normative structures.

Furthermore, I hope that it will be possible to specify the relative benefits and costs of membership in these two societies. If this aim can be achieved, a framework for preventive services can be stated that takes into account the stage of the life cycle of an individual's primary environment, as well as his own personal development.

As work proceeds, two pairs of high schools that vary in their rate of population exchange, but which are equivalent in their demographic properties, will be studied intensively. The design will involve a cohort of ninth grade students, stratified according to their coping patterns, who will be followed from entry through completion of their high school careers. Samples of students with different histories of geographical mobility will be included in order to assess responses of varied environments to newcomers and the effective and ineffective coping styles of new students.

The objective of this research program is not only to contribute basic knowledge about relationships between social structures and individual effectiveness, but to establish an ecological basis for planning preventive services. One axiom of the ecologist is that any intervention in one part of the organization will affect the total organization. An ecological orientation is particularly important for most community mental health services, because not only are preventive services usually imposed or added on to ongoing organizations, but by the very nature of preventive work, complex agencies and organizations are usually participants or recipients.

Geertz (1963) reports an example, attributed to the ecologist Clarke (1954), that illustrates a complex ecological chain. Clarke tells of ranchers

who, disturbed by losses of young sheep to coyotes, slaughtered, through collective effort, nearly all coyotes in the immediate area. Following the removal of coyotes, the rabbits, field mice, and other small rodents, upon whom the coyotes had previously preyed, multipled rapidly and made serious inroads on the grass of the pastures. When this was realized, the sheep men ceased to kill coyotes and instituted an elaborate program for the poisoning of rodents. The coyotes filtered in from the surrounding areas, but finding their natural rodent food now scarce, were forced to turn with even greater intensity to the young sheep as their only available source of food. (Geertz, 1963, pp. 4–5)

While I do not wish to equate mental health professionals with these ranchers, I have observed mental health programs that do not even consider possible adverse effects of their interventions upon either the structures of community resources or the way these resources function. A more conventional style is to concentrate on the quick but permanent removal of a symptom, with meager assessment of organizational side effects. The ethic of the ecologist in community work is to make a careful assessment of the host organization in order to anticipate the effects of the intervention, not only upon the desired outcome, but upon other functions of the organization as well. My aim has been to document empirical relationships among, and interdependence of, personal behavior styles, adaptive roles, and organizational form, so that interventions can not only be designed for optimum benefit, but so that interveners can also predict other possible costs of interventions, both for the functions of the organizations and the adaptive behavior of their members.

Referring to constant and fluid environments as examples, I would predict that the concerns that are reported as mental health problems in a constant environment will be quite different from the reported concerns of the fluid environment. In the constant environment, with its value for norm-oriented absorption of members, consultees will probably ask for help for those persons who criticize, who question normative structures, or who "agitate for change." The hopes of the consultee will be either to fit persons in or to exclude them. Consultees from the fluid environment, which is oriented toward developing and actualizing its members, will tend to see anybody who prefers direction and structure as a person in crisis and will want advice from the consultant on how to motivate him, get him moving, and to make use of resources. The work described in this paper is one example of the type of analysis, based in part upon naturalistic observations, that I hope can suggest changes in defective organizational functions to consultants and interveners. The findings from the naturalistic observations provide preliminary support for defining the correlates of continually changing and unchanging social environments.

REFERENCES

Barker, R. G. Ecology and motivation. In M. R. Jones (Ed.), *Nebraska symposium on motivation: 1960*. Lincoln, Neb.: University of Nebraska Press, 1960. Pp. 1–49.

Barker, R. G. Ecological units. In R. G. Barker & P. V. Gump, *Big school, small school*. Stanford, Calif.: Stanford University Press, 1964. Pp. 11–28.

Barker, R. G. Explorations in ecological psychology. *American Psychologist,* 1965, **20,** 1–14.

Barker, R. G., & Gump, P. V. *Big school, small school.* Stanford, Calif.: Stanford University Press, 1964.

Carpenter, C. R. *Naturalistic behavior of nonhuman primates.* University Park, Pa.: Pennsylvania State University Press, 1964.

Clarke, G. *Elements of ecology.* New York: Wiley, 1954.

Coleman, J. *The adolescent society.* New York: Free Press, 1961.

DeVore, I., & Hall, K. R. L. Baboon ecology. In I. DeVore (Ed.), *Primate behavior.* New York: Holt, Rinehart and Winston, 1965. Pp. 20–52.

Geertz, C. *Agricultural involution: The process of ecological change in Indonesia.* Berkeley: University of California Press, 1963.

Goldschmidt, W. *Comparative functionalism.* Berkeley: University of California Press, 1966.

Jay, P. Field studies. In A. M. Schrier, H. F. Harlow, & F. Stollnitz (Eds.), *Behavior of nonhuman primates.* Vol. 2. New York: Academic Press, 1965. Pp. 525–591.

Kelly, G. A. *The psychology of personal constructs.* New York: Norton, 1955.

Kelly, J. G. The mental health agent in the urban community. In L. J. Duhl (Ed.), *Urban America and the planning of mental health services.* (Symposium No. 10) New York: Group for the Advancement of Psychiatry, 1964. Pp. 474–494.

Kelly, J. G. Ecological constraints on mental health services. *American Psychologist,* 1966, **21,** 535–539. (a)

Kelly, J. G. Social adaptation to varied environments. Paper read at American Psychological Association, New York, September, 1966. (b)

Lefcourt, H. M. Internal versus external control of reinforcement: A review. *Psychological Bulletin,* 1966, **65,** 206–220.

Lorenz, K. Z. *King Solomon's ring.* New York: Crowell, Collier and Macmillan, 1952.

Redfield, R. *Peasant society and culture.* Chicago: University of Chicago Press, 1956.

Rosenberg, M. *Society and the adolescent self-image.* Princeton: Princeton University Press, 1965.

Rotter, J. B., Seeman, M., & Liverant, S. Internal versus external control of reinforcements: A major variable in behavior theory. In N. F. Washburne (Ed.), *Decision, values, and groups.* Vol. 2. London: Pergamon, 1962. Pp. 473–516.

Rotter, J. B. Generalized expectancies for internal versus external control of reinforcement. *Psychological Monographs,* 1966, **80,** No. 1, Whole No. 609.

Schaller, G. B. Appendix: Field procedures. In I. DeVore (Ed.), *Primate behavior.* New York: Holt, Rinehart and Winston, 1965. Pp. 623–629.

Srole, L. Social integration and certain corollaries: An exploratory study. *American Sociological Review,* 1956, **21,** 709–716.

Washburn, S. L., & Hamburg, D. A. The study of primate behavior. In I. Devore (Ed.), *Primate behavior*. New York: Holt, Rinehart and Winston, 1965. Pp. 1–13.

Willems, E. P. Sense of obligation to high school activities as related to school size and marginality of student. *Child Development*, 1967, **38**, 1247–1260.

9

Intra-Setting Analysis: The Third Grade Classroom as a Special but Instructive Case

PAUL V. GUMP

TWO ASSUMPTIONS provide the foundation for the research reported in this essay. The first assumption—a substantive and theoretical one—is that our understanding of teacher effectiveness will be enhanced by paying attention to the ecology of learning, which means viewing the teacher as a manager of the learning activities, format, medium, and props of the classroom system. This assumption de-emphasizes the teacher's intimate personal qualities and focuses instead upon the ways in which the teacher generates a learning environment, and the assumption leads directly to the research questions to be pursued here: What are these classroom systems, these learning environments, like? What are their parts? How do the parts relate to each other? How do they relate to the behavior of occupants?

It might be possible to conduct tight experiments on the nature of classroom environments, but the second major assumption, a methodological one, is that the observation of intact classroom settings where they occur and in their complex, investigator-free arrays is the optimal investigative path. In other words, to develop a description and taxonomy of the parts and subparts of classroom systems, we must look at them in the place they occur, free of our isolation or manipulation of conditions.

These assumptions and the research to be reported fit into a broader context of research on behavior settings and ecological psychology, and I now turn to a presentation of that context.

The Ecology of Behavior

Ecological psychologists are perhaps best known for their study of individual behavior in natural habitats. An early publication, *One Boy's*

200

Day, described the behavior of a seven-year-old as he lived in a small Midwestern town (Barker & Wright, 1951). This document and others published by ecological psychologists (Barker *et al.*, 1961; Barker, 1963) are often taken to represent the core problems and findings of the field. But, the root problem in ecological psychology is conceptualization of the environment. The study of the subject's behavior in his natural habitat is *not* the same as the study of natural habitats, and as ecological psychology has developed, this fact has become increasingly obvious. Barker has traced the manner in which analyses of carefully recorded subject behavior suggest the necessity for conceptions of the environment (1965). As usually obtained, the specimen record of a person's behavior will yield information on those aspects of the environment with which he made some sort of transaction. In effect, one learns of the portion of the subject's environment that creates visible signals in his overt behavior. Other aspects of the subject's environmental context are not present in the specimen record of his behavior. For example, a study of the behavior objects with which a child dealt during a day does not give the list of all behavior objects in the child's environment, but only those that appeared in his stream of behavior (Barker & Gump, 1964). This issue— the extent to which the broader ecological environment, the environment extending beyond one person's behavior within it, can be assessed from a specimen record of his behavior—is one to which we will return. For now, it is sufficient to assert that the study of individual behavior in natural habitats may not be the study of habitats and may not be a direct attack on the root problem of ecological psychology.

A second issue in the study of environments is one of inclusion. What *kind* of phenomena beyond the skin of the subject should be included? Although it seems logical that the physical, nonsocial environment is worthy of study, the physical environment alone cannot be taken as a comprehensive representation of the context in which behavior occurs. The fact that the behavior of persons forms the environment for persons is so compelling that restriction of environment to nonbehavioral aspects of the context seems to avoid the problem of the person-relevant environment. The position taken here is that persons are usually in behavior-rich environments; that to conceive of the environment as without behavior is to omit the most coercive aspects of most human environments. To illustrate: While watching an athletic contest, we are told that Butch Armstrong has been sent *into* the game. The announcement implies that Butch has entered an environment made up of action structure as well as physical milieu.

To complicate the picture even more, once he is in the game as a linebacker, Butch is not only in the game environment, but he contributes to its maintenance. He helps to generate that to which he responds. The third issue, this circularity and simultaneity of relationship between person and environment, is difficult for some to accept. The stimulus-response model and other conceptual patterns in psychology have conditioned us to demand clean separation between the person and the environment. But the hard facts of experience show that persons create, to some degree, the contexts in which they behave and that there *is* a circularity between the person and his environmental context. Measurements may be taken of the context, independent measurements may be derived for subject behavior, and the relation between these two may be studied. No difficulty arises unless one is determined to assess the exact proportion of subject behavior due to person variables and the proportion attributable to variables in the setting without the subject. The problem is that some aspects of the person may contribute to both measurements. And, with supplementary measurements of the subject behavior and of setting qualities, even the assessment of person versus setting is possible (Raush *et al.*, 1959, 1960).

THE BEHAVIOR SETTING: AN ENVIRONMENTAL UNIT

The environmental unit employed in this discussion includes behavior, even the behavior of subjects. This unit is the *behavior setting*, an ecological entity defined by Barker and Wright as ". . . a standing pattern of behavior and a part of the milieu which are synomorphic and in which the milieu is circumjacent to the behavior" (1955, p. 45). The standing patterns of behavior are behaviors of persons en masse and tend to be extra-individual in the sense that the behaviors continue even if there is turnover in persons. For example, there is a pattern of teaching that occurs in the classroom whether the teacher is young or old, male or female, nice or not so nice. Pitching in ball games has certain regularities regardless of who is on the mound. More broadly, the behavior pattern of playing baseball—which includes pitching—functions in spite of many changes in players. Second, the synomorphy of behavior and milieu refers to the fit between the shape of behavior and the structure of the physical and temporal surroundings. Blackboards, podiums, pointers, and other object and site factors *fit* the occupation of teaching; they are synomorphic to it. Finally, the milieu that fits the behavior pattern also surrounds it; the classroom surrounds teaching and learning activity.

A full-fledged explication and defense of the conceptual structure for the behavior setting, the unit of choice, is beyond the scope of this essay. Fuller explanations can be found in the work of Barker (in press), Barker and Wright (1955), and Barker and Gump (1964). I should note that the behavior setting is not meant to be a constructed abstraction, but is a part of the real world; it has clear time and place loci. Further, the unit is a naturally occurring one that places people in the position of *components* contributing behavior to setting maintenance and in the position of *individuals* whose life spaces are partly formed by the settings' attributes. Finally, the behavior setting conception treats the environment as a constellation, a system of eco-behavioral units and not as a series of discrete, impinging stimuli.

A behavior setting can and often does contain subunits of quite dissimilar qualities. In a football game, the amount of competitive body contact is high only for those on the field and not for those watching from the sidelines. The field and sideline subunits belong within the same over-all unit because they are interdependent. For example, the coach sends orders and players from the sidelines and players and information come from the field to the sidelines. And yet, despite their interdependence, the subparts have distinct qualities. Intra-setting delineations are known to ecological psychologists and are considered in describing and unitizing environmental phenomena. However, direct research into intra-setting subunits has not been undertaken. The present paper addresses itself to conceptualization and investigation of intra-setting subunits, that is, their delineation, description, and relations to the behavior of participants in the settings.

INTRA-SETTING INVESTIGATION AND THE CLASSROOM

I selected third-grade classrooms as targets of study. One advantage of studying classrooms is the clarity of their spatial and temporal boundaries. The edge structure of the milieu and that of the behaviors that provide the classroom setting's action are relatively isomorphic. Although much can be made of the relevance of events outside the classroom to those within the classroom, the traditional elementary school class has a high degree of discreteness from, even protection against, happenings beyond its temporal and spatial boundaries. A complex set of physical arrangements and activity patterns are set up as if to say to pupils: "You are now in class; things and activities here are not to be confused with things and activities from other times and places."

Not only are boundaries clear, but the physical size and internal structure of the classroom assists intra-setting research. Most of what happens within the classroom boundaries is observable. Actors in the setting tend to remain in a circumscribed area where their activity can be seen and heard by an observer. Furthermore, the observable action reveals the information in which the investigator is likely to be interested. For example, teacher messages and pupil responses are observable and recordable without probing. Not all behavior settings are so easily observed. For example, bureaucratic units put essential information on memos, correspondence, and telephone calls. In offices, the direction and content of behavior setting activity is not so accessible to direct yet unobtrusive observation.

A third advantage of classroom research relates to the sharpness of the classroom's internal differentiation. Teachers are in the business of creating and maintaining environmental sections for different pupil populations and curricular purposes. Since walls are not available to mark off internal units, the teacher must use other methods to clarify and establish environmental subunits. That which the teacher makes clear for students, she also makes clear for researchers.

From the perspective of research methodology, the most significant aspects of the traditional elementary school classroom are the *ubiquity* and the *power* of the teacher. Events in a classroom involve the behaviors of twenty to thirty children and a teacher and involve numerous materials, tools, and facilities; the number of possible observational and recording targets is overwhelming. How can events in a classroom be systematically and comprehensively recorded? Various recording devices (TV and/or wireless microphones) can be used to freeze the data for later review, but this simply puts off the problem of where to look for the organization and the internal structure in the welter of information. The ubiquity and power of the teacher make it possible to use a record of her behavior as a major source from which to derive a fairly comprehensive picture of classroom happenings.

As I have already asserted, records of individual behavior were usually not adequate sources for description of environmental contexts and thus the claim that records of teacher behavior are useful sources for such description requires some explanation. First, while a record of behavior can be studied for information it gives about the behaver, it also may be used to create a picture of the environmental context with which the behaver is directly involved. In the investigation to be reported, when interest was centered on the classroom environment, records of teacher behavior were used for the second purpose. Secondly, the degree to which a record of one person's activity contains information about all aspects of the setting is dependent upon his position in the setting. The more a position is a point of intersection for lines of setting action, the more the various parts of a setting appear in the behavioral record of the person occupying that position. The ubiquity of the teacher position means that she becomes involved with almost all significant subparts of the classroom setting. She signals most beginnings, intermissions, and ends, and she defines the content and form of pupil action for various classroom sub-settings. She will say, for example, "All children except the Bluebirds are to begin on their arithmetic assignment; I want each to do his own work." For most of the highly interactive portions of the classroom environment, the teacher is likely to be the continuing action center. As a recitation leader, the teacher probes students for responses, weaves together these responses by connective discourse, and insures the forward movement of the activity. When one records the teacher's actions and input to her, one is likely to have recorded the essence of the recitation activity.

Regarding the contention that major aspects of the classroom ecology can be inferred from records of teacher behavior, it might be claimed that although the teacher emits environmental signals, definitions, and contents, these do not necessarily result in strong environmental subsystems. It is in relation to this possible claim that the *power* of the teacher is crucial. Relative to elementary school children, the power of their teacher is so high that the subenvironments she signals or initiates do come into being; those that she attempts to bring to an end, do end. If the record of teacher behavior reveals that at 9:29 A.M. she called a group of pupils back to a reading circle for a word drill, one may assume that the group went to the reading circle. At 9:31 the record will justify this assumption because the teacher will be recorded as already posing drill questions and obtaining answers. The power of the teacher to create and dismantle environmental subsections is so great and so assumed by teachers, that when any exception occurs, evidences of the exception are most clear in the record. If the word-drill group should not assemble promptly, if this piece of the environment should not get under way, the behavioral record of the teacher will reveal the fact, which is to say, teacher insistences and pressures will tell us that the proposed environmental phase is not yet operative.

Strictly speaking, the record desired is not a record of teacher behavior, but of environmental operations. From the teacher record, one can draw an organized, sequential picture of these operations. Only the special attributes of the teacher's position in the classroom make this possible. Positions in other settings, even responsible positions, may not be so helpful. For example, one could not learn all aspects of a cafeteria by observing the dietitian; too many major areas are beyond her sphere of direct activity.

SEGMENTS AS UNITS OF THE INTRA-SETTING STRUCTURE

Even a casual observer of a traditional classroom is aware that its many objects, persons, and behaviors are not randomly distributed, but form constellations, or patterns. On a particular morning, the observer may note eight children and a teacher seated in a semicircle in a corner of the room discussing a story from a reader. Members of this group are socially interactive. In the major area of the room, sixteen children study a chapter in a social studies book. Members of this collection work independently of the teacher and of one another. After twenty minutes, the teacher may direct the reading circle group to join the rest of the students in the main part of the room. After they are settled, the teacher, now with the total class, may begin a preview of the social studies work for the next week.

During the time span just described, three major environmental subsections were in existence. Two operated simultaneously. The differentiation also had a temporal aspect, that is, the total class preview followed seatwork and reading circle. Such sections of the classroom have been labeled *segments*. The use of segments has made it possible to describe classrooms in a manner that respects their structure and internal differentiation. Although segments show great variety, there are certain descriptive dimensions that are relevant to all. Every segment has a *concern*: its business or "what it is about." Concerns may relate to various academic fields (arithmetic, reading, science), to artistic matters (art, music), or to classroom activity maintenance (milk-money collection or dismissal regimes). Besides its own concern, every segment has an *activity pattern* that may be described in terms of (a) the nature of teacher participation in the activity, (b) the grouping of pupils, (c) the prescribed action relationships between pupils, (d) the kind of actions taken by pupils, and (e) the way in which pupil action is paced.

Finally, linked with the above behavioral aspects are *site* and *object* contributions to the segment's existence. The site of the reading circle was an out-of-the-way corner of the room; significant objects included chairs and reading texts.

The general nature of segments is usually apparent to a knowledgeable observer; he can see their operations and note their spatial and temporal boundaries. Segments are not *life spaces* in the Lewinian sense; they are units of the preperceptual world of classroom occupants.

Report of Research

A detailed account of the classroom research that developed the segment concept and data regarding its usefulness is given elsewhere (Gump, 1967). For present purposes, I shall limit myself to illustrative material that supports the following assertions:

(1) A comprehensive account of a day's classroom activity can be developed. This primary record, or *chronicle*, is relatively free of theoretically derived selections and abstractions.

(2) Study of a chronicle yields the structure, the segment composition, of the classroom day.

(3) Differences between segments are meaningfully related to the behavior of their inhabitants. In other words, pupils behave differently in different segments.

(4) Points within the segment structure, such as the beginnings of segments or the transitions between segments, are meaningfully related to behavior of pupils and teachers.

(5) Dealing with these contexts as units—rather than immediately dismantling them into stimuli, messages, and other molecular bits—can yield valuable understandings. The contexts make sense of the molecular bits.

DATA COLLECTION

Six third-grade classrooms served as targets for the research. Classes were selected from among nineteen surveyed in exploratory work. The selected classes ranged along the dimensions of pupils' academic aptitudes, novelty of teachers' presentations, and efficiency of teachers' managerial efforts. In the investigator's opinion, all classes were traditional as opposed to progressive or experimental.

Although description of intra-setting units was the basic research task, measures of individual student behavior were also desirable. Accordingly, samples of pupil behavior were collected by time-lapse photography. Every twenty seconds, pictures were taken by a camera equipped with a wide-angle lens. The resulting pictures were examined in terms of each pupil's posture, expression, and orientation toward significant objects and persons; the involvement, or noninvolvement, of each pupil in the ongoing and official segment activity could be judged by such examination. The percentage of pupils involved in the various parts of the classroom day provided a very useful statistic for the study.

The most essential task of data collection involved making an account of classroom happenings in a fashion that would enable later identification and description of intra-setting units, or segments. Such accounts were made by observers who dictated reports of classroom events as they occurred. Stenomask and Dictet devices were employed in a manner described by Schoggen (1964). The dictations formed the classroom *chronicles*, and two full-day chronicles were assembled for each of the six classrooms.

The major target of observation was the teacher, whose behavior usually pointed out the major subunits operating in the classroom. However, a record of these subunits, not of simple teacher behavior, was required. When the teacher was the action center of a particular activity, for example, a recitation, the account of her behavior yielded an account of the segment. When she was not the action center, for instance, seatwork, observers dictated enough beyond-the-teacher information so that an analyst ·could later determine the site, population, duration, concern, and general activity pattern of the segment. Other sources of information regarding the nature of the classroom activities included supplementary materials such as seating charts, copies of worksheets, reading materials, blackboard assignments and displays, and pupil products (tests, homework papers, drawings). These supplementary materials became a part of the chronicles' appendices. The chronicle of one classroom day usually required about one hundred pages of typescript.

After a chronicle was developed, it could be studied with a view to delineation of its parts or its segments. On the left-hand margin of the typescript, an analyst superimposed labels that identified or titled the segments and lines that enclosed their contents.[1] An illustration of a chronicle record, dealing with events in Mrs. Apple's classroom, is offered below.

After some preliminary segments, Mrs. Apple begins to structure the school day by going over the morning work schedule. She will spend most of the morning working with reading groups. When students are not part of a reading group, they are expected to study reading worksheets at their seats. Having answered several questions, Mrs. Apple continues:

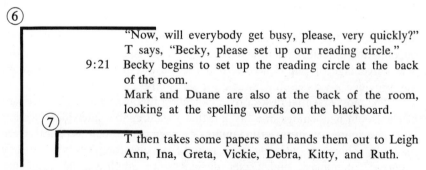

6)

"Now, will everybody get busy, please, very quickly?"
T says, "Becky, please set up our reading circle."
9:21 Becky begins to set up the reading circle at the back of the room.
Mark and Duane are also at the back of the room, looking at the spelling words on the blackboard.

7)

T then takes some papers and hands them out to Leigh Ann, Ina, Greta, Vickie, Debra, Kitty, and Ruth.

---

[1] The question arises as to whether segments can be identified reliably. Three independent analysts working from chronicles produced similar segment boundaries and titles (Gump, 1967).

⑥ ⑦

Seatwork (Study Group)

Worksheet Directions (Green Reader Group)

9:23   T says, "Children in the Green Reader Group, I want your attention. Pages 53 and 54." (See Supplementary Material: Workbook.)

T urges, "Ina, quickly."

T is in the middle of the room now. She walks back to Kitty and says, "Honey, we will not use that," and makes another comment.

O cannot hear the comment.

T backs up to the front of the room.

T, rather perturbed, again urges, "Quickly, Ina."

Then T goes over to Ina and helps her tear out two pages from her workbook.

Ina finally gets them torn out.

T says, "All right, good!"

T says, "Now I want to talk to all of the Green Reader people."

(Pupils in this group sit along the right side of the room; they are: Ruth, Ina, Leigh Ann, Debra, Vickie, Pamela, and Billy.)

T asks Billy to read the directions from page 53.

Billy reads these directions.

Billy finishes.

T says, "Now these are the questions about our story. Now, these are true and false and that's not too hard."

T cautions, "Now let's not work until we're finished with our directions."

T continues, "Now read the directions for the next section, Debra."

Debra reads.

9:25   T says, "All right now, we've talked about hard and soft sounds. Again I will go over the word, 'sit.' The sound is hard or soft?"

So the students in this reading group say, "Soft." . . .

[The explanation of worksheets continues four minutes.]

T says, "Who can put this word in a sentence?"

Billy raises his hand.

T asks Billy.

Billy uses the word in a sentence.

T says, "Good."

T then says, "Are there anymore questions?"

T continues, "All right, go to work on these pages and they'll be due this morning."

The students begin to work.

⑥ ⑧ ⑨c

Seatwork (Study Group)

Lessons (Red Reader Group)

Word Usage Drill (Red Reader Group)

9:29   T comes over to her desk and says, "Children in the Red Reader Group, why don't you just go back for a little bit without your books and we'll practice our game."
The students begin to gather at the back of the room in the reading circle.

9:30   T requests: "Move your chairs a little bit so that you can see the board."
T says, "Who would like to be the leader? Becky?" Becky comes up to the blackboard and points to a word on the blackboard with a pointer.
Some of the students answer but none of them have done it correctly yet.

9:31   So T goes to the blackboard and goes over it by syllables.
The students answer as a unit—they answer all together.
T then says, "Can you use this in a sentence for me, Danny?" . . .
[The game of pronouncing and using words in sentences continues sixteen minutes.]
Duane has trouble with the word "ashamed" so T goes over to the word and points out the number of syllables and goes over the word with him, syllable by syllable. Duane gets it correctly, then T continues.
T then asks Mark to go over several of the words.

T then asks them to return to their seats.
T adds, "Get your books."

9:47   T then says to the *seatwork* students, "Children, we will not do art activities that cause noise for the reading circle; that will have to be in the afternoon."
She adds, "See, it is not listed on our board, is it?"
T continues, "Unless you have a project right at your desk or over at the shelf, let's not be back here disturbing our readers, please."

9:48   Most of the students in the Red Reader Group come back to the reading circle with their books.

⑩c

T says, "Now let's turn to our story for today, please."
T says, "What things did you learn about the baby foxes as far as their habits and customs and appearance,

⑥ ⑧ ⑩c

Seatwork (Study Group)

Lessons (Red Reader Group)

Story Discussion (Red Reader Group)

things that you hadn't known before? What information did you learn about the animals in this story, Les?"
Les answers.
T says, "All right, good. Now we've heard lots about little bear cubs who often play around, but the young foxes did the same things in this story."
T says, "Did they remind you of some boys and girls we know once in a while?"
They nod their heads and say, "Uh huh."
T says, "What were they supposed to be doing?"
Randy has his hand raised and T calls on him.
Randy answers. . . .
[The story discussion proceeds for eleven minutes.]
T says, "Now do you think that there is anything in that sentence that also tells about their habits? Where do they live?"
Susan, Becky, and Mark raise their hands excitedly.
T calls on Susan, who answers.
T says, "All right."

T goes on, "Now is there anyone who would like to see if they can find three or four more things that they can tell; interesting things to tell us about foxes? Would you like to look up a report about this animal and tell us tomorrow, things that we didn't find out in our story?"
Randy says that he would like to do it.
Les says that he would like to help him.
T goes to the blackboard and writes down the names of Randy and Les under a report.
T says, "Now, we will come back to our reading circle right after gym. Our time is almost up, so we will not get our sheets checked."
T adds, "Would you please go to your seats quietly and get on your gym shoes?"

10:01 They return to their seats and get their gym shoes out.

T goes over to the cupboard at the back of the room and gets her gym shoes.

T says, "Row 2, get your gym shoes out."
T goes to the front of the room.
While T is up at her desk putting on her shoes, Ina

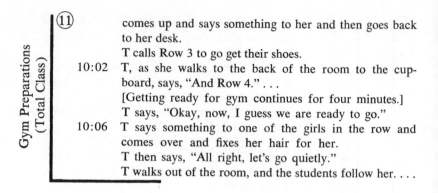

	comes up and says something to her and then goes back to her desk.
Gym Preparations (Total Class)	T calls Row 3 to go get their shoes.
	10:02 T, as she walks to the back of the room to the cupboard, says, "And Row 4." ...
	[Getting ready for gym continues for four minutes.]
	T says, "Okay, now, I guess we are ready to go."
	10:06 T says something to one of the girls in the row and comes over and fixes her hair for her.
	T then says, "All right, let's go quietly."
	T walks out of the room, and the students follow her. ...

The structure of the classroom events just described can be represented graphically, and a diagram or map of this same period appears in Figure 9-1.

The segment marked ⑥ Seatwork began the excerpted material, but within minutes the teacher began another segment, ⑦ Worksheet Directions, which operated simultaneously with the Seatwork segment. The organization here involved two parallel segments, one with active teacher leadership and the other without teacher contributions. There were some clear differences between the segments. Seatwork prescribed individual and private effort, whereas Worksheet Directions, as actually created by the teacher, became a cooperative recitation. Seatwork called for reading and writing activity; Worksheet Directions for reading, listening, speaking. Once Seatwork was underway, pupils paced themselves; in Worksheet Directions, questions and comments from the teacher and answers from peers paced the attentions and activities of the pupils. In terms of the research categories, Seatwork was *self-paced* and Worksheet Directions was *externally paced*. Finally, each segment had its own behavior objects and location. Thus, two discrete action arenas, two environmental segments, were in operation.

Worksheet Directions ended at 9:29 and its students entered the ongoing Seatwork activity. The teacher began a reading circle in the back of the room. Again parallel segments operated: ⑥ Seatwork and ⑧ Lessons (Red Reader Group). During operation of Lessons, two discrete segments were established: (a) an exercise in diction, ⑨c Word Usage Drill, and (b) a recitation around the assigned reading, ⑩c Story Discussion. Since these stretches of activity were within the general span of the segment Lessons (Red Reader Group), they were *contained* "c" seg-

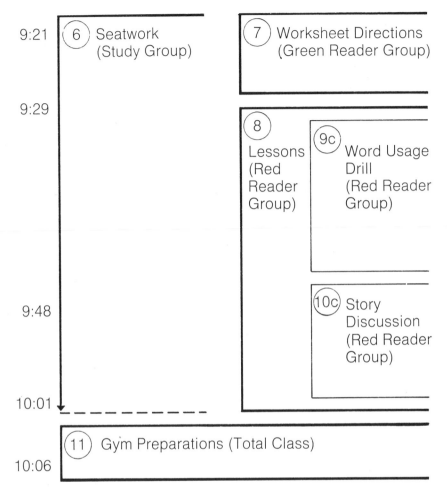

9.1.   *Segment map of events in Mrs. Apple's classroom from 9:21 to 10:06 a.m.*

ments. The reader will note Mrs. Apple's use of the brief period between the end of the Word Usage Drill and the beginning of the Story Discussion to admonish the children in the Seatwork segment (first sentence at 9:47).

The last change in segments that is displayed occurred at 10:01. Seatwork was interrupted, Lessons was closed, and all pupils prepared for gym. The last segment, ⑪ Gym Preparations, was not just a brief transition between activities, but had the structural quality and the persistence typical of segments, that is, *concern* and *activity pattern.* Development of dismissals into substantial routines was common practice in these third grades. In only one class would the teacher permit the pupils simply to leave the room when the bell rang.

Several issues regarding the intra-setting nature of classrooms are spatially represented in Figure 9–1. The maximum number of simultaneous or parallel segments in this figure is two; the number never exceeded two in any of the six classrooms studied. Yet, a third grade summer remedial class, observed during pilot work, often sustained three, and sometimes four, parallel segments. We have no systematic information regarding conditions encouraging parallel segments and effects created by their presence, but these might be interesting questions for future research.

Another issue suggested by the diagrammatic quality of Figure 9–1 is that of *transitions.* The reader will note that ends and beginnings appear in the figure. The closing of one activity and the initiation of another is an event requiring energy and redirection on the part of both teacher and pupils. The changes occurring in their behavior at these transition points have been studied and illustrative data will be presented later.

Once segment structure was described, it was possible to relate aspects of this structure to qualities of pupil and teacher behavior. Results of these comparisons are our next concern.

SEGMENT QUALITIES AND PUPIL BEHAVIOR

A very practical dimension of pupils' behavior is the extent to which they are involved in the official activity of the segment. As noted above, each pupil's involvement could be estimated from the pictures taken by time-lapse photography. Over time, the percent of pupils involved in the activity of segments rose and fell. When a line representing involvement rates was coordinated to a temporal series of segments, the line dropped for some segments and rose for others. Inspection of such lines suggested that segments in which pacing of pupil action came from the outside (for example, recitation and tests) showed greater involvement than segments in which pupil initiative provided the immediate push to activity (study sessions). Inspection also suggested that small group segments produced a higher percent of pupil involvement than total class segments.

To test the suggestions derived from this inspection of fluctuation in involvement, pupil involvement rates in the following segment types were compared: (a) Externally-Paced Small Group, that is, Reading Circle, (b) Externally-Paced Total Group, or, Class Recitations and Class Tests, (c) Self-Paced Groups, or, Seatwork with and without Teacher supervision.

Data analyses made possible comparisons employing each pupil as his own control. Results clearly substantiated the suggestions derived from data inspection: Externally-Paced Small Group segments produced involvement rates averaging 92 percent; Externally-Paced Total Class segments averaged 81 percent; and the Self-Paced Group segments 73 percent. All differences among the three types had associated probabilities of .025 or less.

Statistical results do not explain why involvement rates differed in the various segments, but the following explanations seem reasonable. Under conditions of low to moderate motivation, degree of involvement in an activity is somewhat dependent upon the presence or absence of external stimulators. Self-Paced Activity such as Seatwork has no continuing external stimulators; it may be assumed that motivation in Seatwork is typically low to moderate. Therefore, involvement in Seatwork, relative to recitations and tests is low. That better involvement occurs in small groups as opposed to total classes may be related to the fact that, given the same action structure, opportunity for individual participation is intrinsically greater in the small groups.

SEGMENT PHASE AND PUPIL BEHAVIOR

Inspection of the classroom data also suggested that pupils might react to the *phase* of the segment as well as to its general quality. Specifically, segments that depend upon self-pacing might show low pupil involvement in the early phases of getting started. Such low involvement might also occur at getting restarted or resuming, as in returning to self-paced work after recess or lunch. Accordingly, the involvement scores of pupils in the first three-and-one-half minutes (Start phase) of self-paced segments were compared to scores of these same pupils for the remaining portion of the segment (Remainder phase).[2]

Furthermore, the Start phase and Remainder phase scores of these same pupils were compared in externally-paced segments. As noted above, self-paced segments generally yielded less involvement than externally-paced ones. If pacing effects and getting started effects accumulate, one should expect the lowest involvement to occur in the Start phases of self-paced segments and the highest in the Remainder phases of externally-paced segments. Such an expectation is tested by the data presented in Table 9–1.

[2] Teachers, apparently aware of the starting difficulties in self-paced segments, often preceded them with a "priming segment." During these periods, pupils worked through a few problems or questions with teacher and group support. Starts of self-paced segments that had this kind of priming were not included in the analysis.

TABLE 9–1 *Mean percent of pupil involvement in start (or resume) phases and in remainder phases of self-paced and externally-paced segments*

	Start (or Resume) phases	Remainder phases
Self-paced segments	64	74
Externally-paced segments	76	81

Statistical tests applied to the data in Table 9–1 show that involvement in Start (or Resume) phases was significantly less than in Remainder phases. Furthermore, the expected accumulation of effects is confirmed by the lowest involvement score in the Self-Paced Start cell of the table and the highest involvement in Externally-Paced Remainder cell. The Self-Paced Start cell is significantly lower than all other cells (all p's < .01); the Externally-Paced Remainder cell is significantly higher than all other cells (all p's < .05).

SEGMENT STRUCTURE AND TEACHER BEHAVIOR

Since teachers were the major observational targets for the chronicles, it is possible to consider teacher behavior in relation to segment structure. Although teachers select and establish segments, they are also subject to their influence just as surely as are pupils. Teachers are influenced by their own creations.

The unit of teacher behavior employed here was the *act*. A teacher act is the shortest meaningful bit of behavior directed toward students. Acts changed when messages and/or targets shifted and were roughly analogous to moves in a game. For example, the following span of teacher maneuvering contains four acts:

(1) "All right children, let's see how sharp we are today.
(2) Open your books to page 19.
(3) Who remembers what it was that Jane was trying to do?
(4) (*Pause*) George?"

The first act calls for an alert stance; the second directs attention to a particular section of reading; the third is a recitation question; and the fourth is a delayed target selection. Teachers averaged 1300 acts during one classroom day. As might be expected, frequency of acts depended upon the kind of segment. Recitation segments demanded six acts per minute; music segments elicited three acts per minute; and supervised study elicited two.

The *kind* of teacher acts also changed as segment structure changed. One cluster of teacher acts identified were those that could be described under the general heading: Dealing with Deviating Behavior. Such acts pressed for more energetic or more careful pupil behavior, countered proposed behavior, or rejected behavior already emitted. These acts were managerial as opposed to pedagogical and they dealt with those pupil behaviors presumed to be at variance with good setting operation. In data explorations, sequences of coded teacher acts were viewed in relation to aspects of segment structure. Dealing with Deviating Behavior acts seemed to increase at certain points; concentrations of these pressing and countering actions appeared at or near breaks between segments, suggesting that transitions might provoke such teacher acts.

Before presenting more formal data on Dealing with Deviating Behavior and transitions, a brief explanation and illustration of the transition aspect of segment structure seems appropriate.

The *transition* is the activity that closes down one segment and sets up another. Transitions with a prolonged and established regime, such as the dimissals from class referred to above, can become segments in themselves. The transitions considered here are those briefer periods bridging within-classroom segments.

There are parts of the segment devoted to getting underway and to closing down and there is another larger portion devoted to neither. It is convenient to have a label for this part also, and it has been called the *base* of the segment. The part of the segment free of transition activity and usually directly aimed at the business or concern of the segment is the base. Usually, the great majority of activity in a segment occurs during its base period. The relationship between segment, base, and transition is illustrated in Figure 9–2.

The percent of Dealing with Deviating Behavior acts occurring in the base portion of segments was compared to the percent in transitions. For each of six teachers, on each of two days of observation, such acts increased during transitions; there were no exceptions in the twelve comparisons. Teachers differed in the amount of Dealing with Deviancy activity employed, but they did not differ in the need to increase this activity during transitions. Emphasis on Dealing with Deviating Behavior during transitions might be explained as follows: A segment is a behavior-milieu pattern that guides the behavior of its inhabitants. This pattern must be dissolved if the inhabitants are to enter a new behavior-milieu pattern. However, the new pattern does not exist instantaneously; it must become

Segment Structure	Base and Transition	Example of Teacher Acts
Milk and Story Time	BASE	"Class, how do you think the story will end?" "Well, we'll see tomorrow." "Do you like these kinds of tales?" "Let's get our desks cleaned up." "John, you collect the empties." (milk cartons) Teacher quietly shakes her head "no" to Billy. He has come up to her with some proposal. "Betty, put our chairs back under our desks."
	TRANSITION	"No, Mary, you don't need your pencil sharpened now."
Music		"Class, will you take out your song books?" "Mary, you make first choice today." "All right—'Old Dog Tray,' page 14." "Let's sing right out, children." Teacher gives chord on piano.
	BASE	Teacher plays and class sings verse 1. Teacher plays and class sings verse 2. "That was O.K. but I didn't hear the boys too well." "Let's have boys only sing the next verse." Teacher sings and plays verse 3, and so on.

FIGURE 9.2. *Illustration of relationship between base and transition within the segment structure (fictitious but representative case).*

established. In the transition from the old segment to the new, pupils may be without strong behavior guides. During this transitional time, pupil behavior becomes more individual and some of the individualism involves behavior divergent from that desired by the teacher. She responds by increasing pressure, countering, and rejecting moves, in other words, she increases her Dealing with Deviating Behavior acts.

Contextual Structure and Making Sense of Inhabitant Behavior

In its beginning, this research effort was faced with myriad observational and recording targets. The question was whether any order could be ascertained in the profuse array of the classroom. The order desired was one that delineated structure rather than destroyed it; one that highlighted the implicit organization of events rather than merely assigned isolated events to abstract categories. Further, the order desired was one that would yield molar rather than molecular units.

The issue of units was central in the research. What constitutes a unit in experiments is more readily (and more arbitrarily) decided. Frequently, the experimenter introduces a homogeneous and timed input and then observes the subject's response. Often, the subject's response is cut short by a succeeding input. The experimenter, by a series of thrusts and chops, insures "chunks" of data for his analysis. Unitization in non-experimental or "transducer" studies (Barker, 1965) is not such a simple matter. If structure is to be respected, the phenomena themselves must suggest their own chunks or units.

In the course of these classroom investigations, the natural order of implicit units was not too difficult to determine. In the elementary school classroom, teacher behavior, pupil movement, behavior objects, and site changes all helped to make these units, or segments, clear. The third grade day offered ecological segments of such strength and clarity that research could approach the problem of the relation of internal structure to inhabitant behavior rather directly and quickly.

The establishment of a segment structure facilitated a manipulation of the data that suggested hypotheses (as opposed to simply testing them). This structure was employed as a context against which to cast more molecular teacher and pupil behaviors. Such behaviors took on a significance that would have been lost if segments had been dismantled or ignored. The proportion of teacher acts that deal with deviancy becomes a more sensible statistic as one sees how this proportion changes from the base phases to transition phases of the segments. Pupil involvement in ongoing activity becomes a comprehensible dependent variable when its increases and decreases are linked to the segments' pacing provisions and to the beginning versus the remaining spans of segments.

This excursion into analyses of intra-setting units was made especially feasible by qualities of traditional elementary classrooms. Here, the teacher's position in the setting was particularly favorable for developing the method. By implication, we can conclude that the units are not universal; not all settings can be so analyzed. However, the classroom experience does indicate that complex behavior settings and the behaviors of their inhabitants are better understood when interior segments are identified and described.

REFERENCES

Barker, R. G. (Ed.) *The stream of behavior.* New York: Appleton-Century-Crofts, 1963.

Barker, R. G. Explorations in ecological psychology. *American Psychologist,* 1965, **20,** 1–14.

Barker, R. G. *Ecological psychology: Concepts and methods for studying the environment of human behavior.* Stanford, Calif.: Stanford University Press, in press.

Barker, R. G., & Gump, P. V. *Big school, small school.* Stanford, Calif.: Stanford University Press, 1964.

Barker, R. G., & Wright, H. F. *One boy's day.* New York: Harper & Row, 1951.

Barker, R. G., & Wright, H. F. *Midwest and its children.* New York: Harper & Row, 1955.

Barker, R. G., Wright, H. F., Barker, L. S., & Schoggen, M. *Specimen records of American and English children.* Lawrence, Kans.: University of Kansas Press, 1961.

Gump, P. V. *The classroom behavior setting: Its nature and relation to student behavior.* Final report to U. S. Office of Education, Project No. 5-0334, Contract No. OE-4-10-107, 1967.

Raush, H. L., Dittmann, A. T., & Taylor, T. J. Person, setting and change in social interaction. *Human Relations,* 1959, **12,** 361–378.

Raush, H. L., Dittmann, A. T., & Taylor, T. J. Person, setting and change in social interaction: II. A normal control study. *Human Relations,* 1960, **13,** 305–332.

Schoggen, P. Mechanical aids for making specimen records of behavior. *Child Development,* 1964, **35,** 985–988.

10

Behavior of Captive White-Footed Mice

J. LEE KAVANAU

WHITE-FOOTED MICE[1], genus *Peromyscus*, are one of the most widespread, geographically variable groups of North American rodents (Hall & Kelson, 1959). Over 55 species are recognized (Hall & Kelson, 1959; Walker, 1964), more than in any other North American mammalian genus. Species occur from extreme northern Colombia northward to Alaska and Labrador. The animals are found in almost every habitat within their range and often are the most abundant mammals. Some species are found in low arid deserts, others in high tropical cloud forests, and a few even inhabit barren arctic and alpine tundras.

Distinguishing characters of most species are long and bicolored tails, large ears and eyes, and conspicuously darker and more richly colored fur on the upper parts of the body. When excited, many species thump rapidly with the forefoot, producing a drumming sound. White-footed mice are active at night throughout the year. "Subzero temperatures do not keep these graceful little creatures at home, and the snow-covered ground is covered with their dainty tracks during the coldest periods of midwinter" (Hamilton, 1939). They spend the day in concealed nests of dry, unsoiled vegetation lined with plant down or shredded materials.

White-footed mice occasionally live in true pairs—a relatively rare occurrence among small mammals (Blair, 1958; Dice, 1932; Howard, 1949). Their home ranges usually encompass only 0.1 to 0.6 acre (Walker, 1964) and may overlap broadly between individuals differing in sex, age, and species (Blair, 1942). There is evidence of pronounced homing ability (Murie & Murie, 1931; Murie, 1963). Most individuals

---

[1] Following Hall & Kelson (1959) the plural common name "white-footed mice" is employed for the genus *Peromyscus*. The singular common name "white-footed mouse" is in common use for the species *Peromyscus leucopus*.

probably live less than one year in the wild, while captive animals attain three to five years. The diet is varied, including berries, fruits, greens, snails, beetles, crickets, and carrion. Large quantities of nuts, seeds, and pits are harvested for winter use. In turn, the mice are one of the main prey groups of many valuable game and fur-bearing animals.

The wide occurrence and extraordinary geographical variability of these mice make them particularly valuable for distributional, ecological, and evolutionary studies. Many species are ideal for laboratory studies. Captive animals generally are docile, clean, odorless, and easily fed and cared for. They have a high rate of reproduction, often breeding throughout the year under suitable conditions.

For the past six years I have been investigating the behavior of two species of this interesting genus that are readily available locally, primarily from the point of view of the behavior's significance for survival, adaptation, and evolution. One of these species, *Peromyscus maniculatus* (the deer mouse), is the most widespread, varied, and adaptable species of the genus. Recognition of over 60 subspecies (Hall & Kelson, 1959) testifies to its great plasticity. The other, *P. crinitus* (the canyon mouse), is confined to rocky habitats, but ranges from hot deserts to cool heights over 10,000 feet above sea level.

By means of automatic, long-term surveillance of gross overt activities, I am studying: (a) how behavior is distorted when animals are displaced from the stimulus and structure-rich natural habitat to the relatively barren, highly restrictive laboratory enclosure; (b) effects of compelling and attempting to compel animals to endure artificial nutritional, stimulus, and activity regimes; (c) effects of allowing animals to control certain components of the environment; (d) learning and memory capacity; (e) social interactions; (f) running in activity wheels; (g) effects of simulating twilight transitions and nocturnal illumination; and (h) individual behavior differences. The experimental approaches and some of the findings of these studies are presented here, beginning with a general overview and leading into more detailed considerations.

Control of Environment

Two important, related factors that greatly influence the behavior of captive animals are *control of environment* and *compulsory regime* or compulsion (Kavanau, 1963a, 1966). Animals in the wild exercise a relatively high degree of control over the environment, for example, by selection of nest site, territory, food, time and degree of activity, social contacts, and by manipulation of many objects. But the activities of captive animals and their opportunities to interact with and modify the environment are restricted severely, with the consequence that their behavior becomes markedly distorted.[2] A large amount of activity becomes channeled into controlling the environment, that is, into manipulating, and altering relationships with, any susceptible environmental features. The most rewarding of several alternative outlets for activity (that is, the one engaged in most) presumably is the one that substitutes best for (or possibly even would be preferred to) the spectrum of activities in the wild.[3] However, when outlets are highly restricted, as is usual in most laboratory regimes, virtually any opportunity to modify environmental variables is exercised repeatedly, in little apparent relation to the appropriateness of the act as a substitute activity.

The caged animals in my vivarium are given a 0.5-liter cardboard carton with a hole in its top and 50 grams of sand and a cotton wad inside. In addition to providing a dark, secluded nest, the carton furnishes a new channel for interaction with the environment. Thus, although some animals nest in the cartons without ever gnawing on them, others typically gnaw them into shreds and construct a nest. Nest construction apparently is only a secondary basis for this behavior, however. The modification of the environment accomplished by the gnawing seems to be the primary basis, for the animals continue to gnaw into shreds each new nest carton in turn, until the cage is full of shredded material.

A second example of control of environment is provided by the activities of several mice in an enclosure containing a plexiglas-wood nest and a wad of cotton. At the rear of the nest is a small crack through which the cotton can be grasped from outside the nest. Animals of both sexes spend hours reeling the cotton wad out through this crack, compacting the fluffy, strung-out mass with their forelegs and teeth, stuffing the wad back into the entrance to the nest, and then repeating the entire sequence hundreds of times, day after day.

These simple examples illustrate the fact that confined animals are likely to modify or manipulate repeatedly, or alter frequently their rela-

---

[2] An important factor contributing to this behavioral distortion is the fact that the captive animal is freed from the need to escape enemies and search for food, activities which occupy a large fraction of a mouse's time in the wild. The severe limitations imposed upon captive animals and the consequent distortions of their behavior are well known to workers in zoological gardens. This topic is discussed in detail by Hediger (1964).

[3] In the category of "rewarding acts" I include any acts (except those of avoidance) that captive animals engage in repeatedly without extrinsic reward (such as food, water, social contacts, a nest). For practical purposes the use of the word "rewarding" in the text sometimes is redundant.

tionship with, any susceptible features of the environment. The repeated acts might take the form merely of running in a wheel, jumping on and off a platform, patrolling an enclosure, traversing mazes, gnawing materials, or of turning on and off or otherwise modifying sound, illumination, a motor-driven activity wheel, intracranial stimulation, or other variables.

Compulsory Regime

An animal in the wild seldom is forced to endure conditions which it cannot escape or reduce in severity by appropriate behavior. There are at least two bases for this generally low level of compulsion. First, a relatively high level of control over the environment often permits the animal to escape noxious conditions and threats. Second, animals generally occupy niches in which unexpected events that have a critical significance for survival occur relatively infrequently. Much evidence suggests the existence of a conservative tendency of animals to avoid situations which arise unnaturally or "unexpectedly." One might justifiably assert the existence of a tendency to seek stability of many variables of the *milieu exterieur*, that is, to seek a state of affairs in which conditions are highly predictable. But when an animal is displaced from the wild to the laboratory, it is compelled to exist in an environment which, though relatively fixed, is completely foreign and, from the animal's viewpoint, unpredictable. Accordingly, captive small mammals, whether wild-caught or born in captivity, have a markedly conservative tendency to counteract or avoid unexpected and nonvolitional deviations from the status quo.

The failure to take into account the intrinsic tendencies of captive animals to modify environmental variables (almost independently of the nature of the variable) and to avoid or counteract unexpected and non-volitional changes may be responsible for many conflicting findings (Kavanau, 1963a). For example, taking these factors into account helps to explain why rats rapidly learn a means of escape from electrical hypothalamic stimulation but do not "learn" a simple means of avoiding the same stimulus (Roberts, 1958a). Apparently, hypothalamic stimulation is rewarding to the rats when its occurrence is expected (shortly after the warning stimulus), but provokes aversion when it occurs unexpectedly, just as a piece of meat induces anger when thrown at a sleeping tiger, whether the tiger is hungry or not.

Still better examples are provided by the so-called paradoxical rewarding and aversive effects of self-administered and nonself-administered electrical stimulation (Brown & Cohen, 1959; Miller, 1957; Roberts,

1958b). When hypothalamic stimulation is applied by the experimenter, cats escape it by running a T maze, but they themselves press levers that cause exactly the same stimulation to be applied. Rats repeatedly press a lever initiating hypothalamic stimulation and then rotate a wheel terminating it. In these cases, one probably can regard the sensations produced by the stimuli as secondary and interpret the responses solely in relation to control of environment and response to compulsion. Thus, levers leading to the stimulation are pressed because it is rewarding to exercise control over the stimulus. Wheels are rotated turning off the stimulus for the same reason. Repeated turning on and off, like repeated cycling of cotton into and out of the nest, represents continued manipulation of the environment. On the other hand, cats run a T maze and escape the stimulus because it occurs unexpectedly.[4]

In principle, animals' repeatedly initiating and terminating a stimulus is analogous to children's repeatedly turning toys on and off. Similarly, terminating nonvolitional brain stimulation, but initiating the same stimulation volitionally, can be interpreted in the same way we view the act of a kitten or puppy refusing repeatedly to stay in a nest box when placed there but subsequently entering the box volitionally. Neither of these common examples is considered to be paradoxical.

Rationale of Animal Selection

For many physiological studies it is desirable to work with highly inbred animals. By this means, individual differences in behavior, from the subcellular to the organismal level, are held to a minimum. One specific genetic pattern is selected from many possible ones. When highly inbred strains are used for behavior studies, the individual responses are likely to be much more uniform than those of wild animals, but the behavior may have only limited significance for the species as a whole, and could even be quite misleading. When traits characteristic of wild individuals have been selected against, as is usual with domestic strains, the behavior is likely to have minimal ecological and evolutionary significance.

Experiments in my laboratory generally are carried out with wild-caught and first-generation captive-born animals. These animals usually are not selected for homogeneity, either of capture site, length of captivity, age, weight, sex, heredity, or experience. Since broad scope is given to the influence of individual and sex differences, the behavior of such

---

[4] Of course, turning off an unexpected stimulus also is an act of controlling the environment.

heterogeneous stock tends to span a wide range of the response spectrum of the species. It thus provides a sound basis for interpretation and generalization.

Variations in the responses of individual wild-caught mice and their near descendents often are very great. In fact, notable individual differences might be said to be the rule rather than the exception. The existence of this great individual variability points to a high evolutionary plasticity of the species, that is, to great genetic variety and a rich repertory of responses upon which selective pressures can act (see also Hardy, 1965; Thoday, 1962).

Detection, Recording, and Data Reduction

The automatic, nonobtrusive detection and recording of overt activities of captive animals in my laboratory depend heavily on small, sensitive electromechanical and electromagnetic components, such as linear and rotary microswitches and solenoids, rotatable shutters, clutches, generators, and pressure transducers. Ferro-magnetic, conductance, capacitance, and reflective infrared sensors are employed for noncontact proximity sensing, while infrared and ultrasonic beams are used for line-of-sight sensing (Kavanau, 1961, 1962a, 1962b, 1963a, 1963b, 1963c, 1966, Kavanau & Norris, 1961). Computer-type panels and standard hardware are used for programming and systems controls. The programming system also functions as a real-time computer from which, by appropriate connections to digital printing timers and counters, all desired information is obtained (Kavanau, 1963b, 1966). Single and multipoint analogue and event strip-chart recorders complete the recording ensemble.

Enclosures

The *running-wheel enclosure* (Figure 10–1) is used primarily to obtain detailed activity profiles and to study learning. It consists of an activity wheel 30 centimeters in diameter mounted between transparent side-panes with attached nests, platforms, facilities for food and water, and programming, sensing, and control elements (Kavanau, 1962b, 1963a, 1963b, 1966). Wire grids beneath the wheel are shorted briefly by urine and droppings. A simplified enclosure of the same basic design (Figure 10–2) is used to study control of environment and effects of compulsion (Kavanau, 1962b, 1963a, 1966, and below).

FIGURE 10.1.   *Highly instrumented running-wheel enclosure used in some of the studies described in text.*

Social interactions are studied in the *social enclosure* (Kavanau, 1961, 1963c). Individuals are identified at key locations by proximity sensing of small metal collars. The running-wheel and social enclosures lie at one extreme of design; only a relatively small amount of space is available but this space is highly instrumented and several outlets for manipulating the environment are provided. Studies in these enclosures have shown that white-footed mice readily master complex relationships and characteristically exercise a high level of control over susceptible environmental variables.

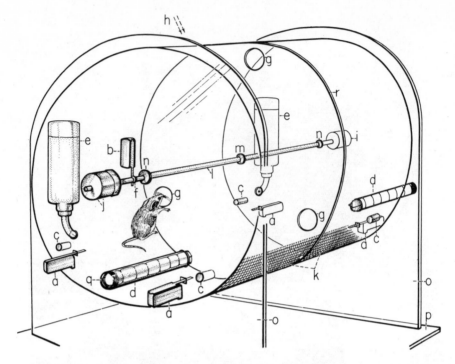

FIGURE 10.2. *Running-wheel enclosure for studies of control of illuminance and effects of compulsion: a, control microswitches; d food guns; e, water bottles; g, passageways in center pane; h, position of light source; i, tachometer generator; o, side panes; r, center pane; the motor is not shown.*

In a third type of enclosure, the *extensive enclosure*, space itself, that is, the size of the inhabited region, is the chief environmental variable controlled by the animal (Brant & Kavanau, 1964, 1965). Extensive

FIGURE 10.3 (*opposite*). *Event record for deer Mouse 1 during a night of the 15 percent ethanol regime, illustrating reactions to deprivation of wheel-running (beginning at the point marked "clutch failure"): open blocks, repetitive discharges; solid blocks, one continuous discharge; single lines, single discharges or a short repetitive burst. At the right are identified the channels indicating times of: eliminations; obtaining food pellets (after pressing the levers of switches 1 and 2 in sequence); unlocking the water shutter (switch 3); opening the water shutter; unlocking the wheel (switch 4); wheel rotations; interrupting the beams of electric eyes; presence on platforms; presence in the right nest; opening the nest shutters; and unlocking the right nest shutter from inside (switch 7). The left nest was closed off. The time scale reads from right to left.*

EXCRETION
FOOD PELLET
WATER SHUTTER
SWITCH 1
SWITCH 2
SWITCH 3
SWITCH 4
WHEEL ROTATION
WHEEL I-R EYE
AXLE I-R EYE
UPPER PLATFORM
SWITCH 5
SWITCH 6
LEFT PLATFORM
LEFT SHUTTER
LEFT NEST
RIGHT PLATFORM
RIGHT SHUTTER
RIGHT NEST
SWITCH 7

CLUTCH FAILURE

OPERATION RESTORED

10:30   11:00   11:30 PM   12:00   12:30   1 AM.

enclosures contain hundreds of meters of linear runways and vertical, burrow-simulating mazes with hundreds of blind alleys.

Activity Profiles

White-footed mice learn complex experimental regimes with such facility that their learning capacity may have to be probed at the high levels employed with nonhuman primates. The program of the following study probably is the most complex experimental regime mastered by a nonprimate. To obtain a 97-milligram food pellet, the mice had to press two levers (of switches 1 and 2, Figure 10–3) in correct sequence within five seconds. To obtain water, a third lever (of switch 3, Figure 10–3) had to be pressed, unlocking a shutter which had to be brushed aside within three seconds. To leave the nest, a fourth lever (switch 7) had to be pressed, unlocking the nest shutter for three seconds, permitting the animal to brush it aside and go out. To run the activity wheel, a fifth lever (switch 4) had to be pressed, which unlocked the wheel for five minutes. This regime was learned readily with the aid of programmed auditory cues (Kavanau, 1963b). A 20-channel event record for a male deer mouse on this regime in the running-wheel enclosure is given in Figure 10–3; two one-week activity profiles are given by the sets of bars labeled "before" and "after" in Figures 10–4 through 10–6.

In brief synopsis, on an average day of the first one-week regime, the animal spent the daylight period resting in the nest, except for three brief excursions to the wheel during which it eliminated and often ate and drank (Figures 10–4 and 10–5). During the nesting period it shifted its position 191 times. The nest was vacated 34 minutes after the bright (4 ft.-candles, 42.5 lumens per square meter) day lights gave way to dim (0.0008 ft.-candle) night lights (downward pointing arrows in Figures 10–4, 10–5, and 10–7). Departure was preceded by a "restless" period of 13 minutes during which body position was shifted 26 times. The animal spent the night running 33,000 revolutions in the wheel (83 percent of the time), eating, drinking, exploring the enclosure, and so forth. It

FIGURE 10.4. *Activity profiles for deer Mouse 1 for one prior week on water (first set of bars labeled "Before"), three days on 25 per cent ethanol (open blocks), and one subsequent week on water (second set of bars labeled "After"). The quantities plotted represent the totals for each hour of the day for a one-week period. The night period (dim light) begins at 5 p.m. (downward-pointing arrows) and ends at 5 a.m. (upward-pointing arrows).*

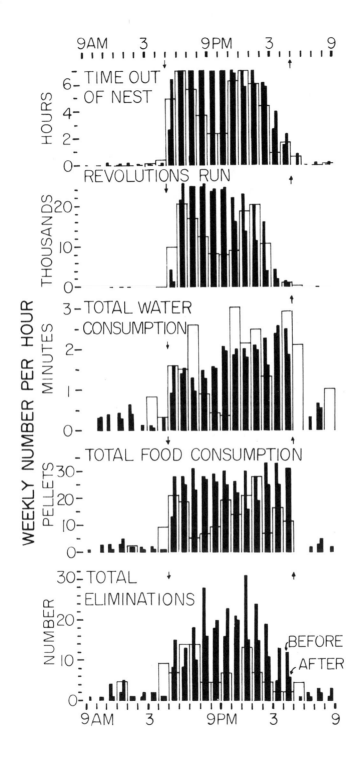

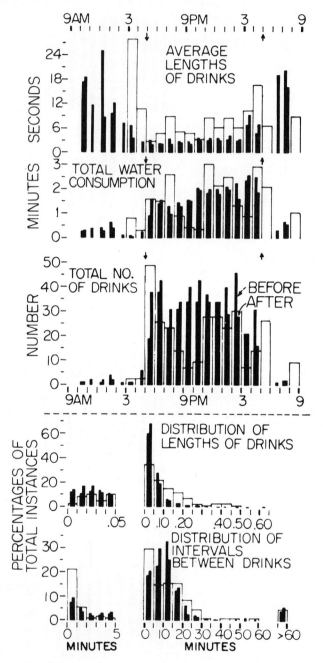

FIGURE 10.5.   *Drinking profiles and distributions for the regimes of Figure 10.4.*

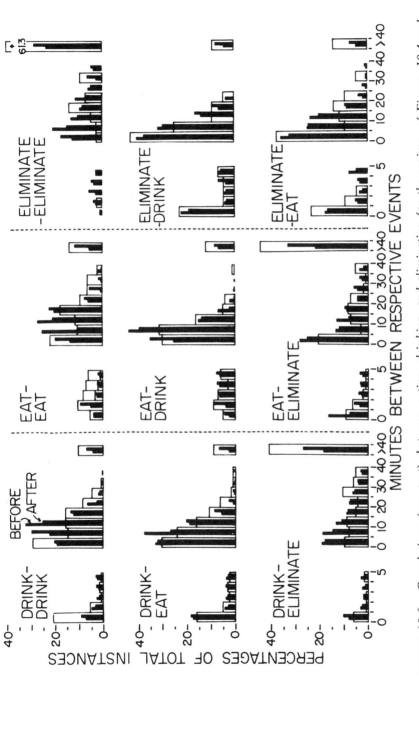

FIGURE 10.6. Correlations (see text) between eating, drinking, and eliminating for the regimes of Figures 10.4 and 10.5.

visited the nest briefly seven times. The nest was reoccupied two to four hours before the lights were brightened (upward pointing arrows). However, the mouse left it again several times before "dawn" and ate, drank and eliminated (Figures 10–4 and 10–5). The animal ate 51 food pellets, took 57 drinks, averaging 3.6 seconds per drink, and eliminated 33 times per 24-hr. period.

Correlations between eating, drinking, and eliminating are given by the first bars in each pair in Figure 10–6. Each plot gives the distribution of time intervals (in percentage of the total number) between the beginning of an event and the next occurrence of the same or a different event. Eating and drinking tended to precede or follow elimination by less than one minute. Except for periods between daytime excursions, only infrequently did a period of greater than 15 minutes intervene between eating and the next drink; 69 percent of all instances occurred within 10 minutes.

Of course, the performance values and correlations obtained under these highly artificial conditions of environment, activity, diet, and ad libitum food and water do not necessarily give information regarding the feeding, drinking, and excretory behavior of the animal in the wild. To obtain such information, animals would have to be studied in their natural habitat or under conditions closely approximating it. However, these activity profiles and correlations are useful both for studying individual and species differences and for pinpointing performances under precisely specified conditions. These performances provide controls for studies of the effects of diet, drugs, diseased states, surgical intervention, and environmental changes. By way of illustration, some effects of modifying the liquid intake are given (Figures 10–4, 10–5, and 10–6). Following the regime described above, 15 percent ethanol was substituted for one week and 25 percent ethanol for an additional three days before water was restored. The second bar in each pair (Figures 10–4 to 10–6) represents the same regime as the first bar, but for the week after the regime of 25 percent ethanol (after three intervening days of adaptation). The open bars are for the three days on 25 percent ethanol (expressed as seven days to allow direct comparisons).

Behavior patterns changed markedly on 15 percent ethanol and more so on 25 percent ethanol. After return to water, the patterns, (except for sleeping in the wheel) gradually returned to normal (Figures 10–4 to 10–6). In general, ethanol produced an increasing lethargy and "attachment" to the nest. On 25 percent ethanol, the animal spent 23 percent less time out of the nest at night than when on the water regime and made brief visits to the nest 120 percent more frequently. About one-half hr. per night was spent resting in the wheel, a habit which developed on 15 percent ethanol. Running declined 33 percent, recorded eliminations

45 percent, and food consumption 37 percent. Total liquid consumption increased 40 percent but water consumption was up only 5.5 percent. Although the number of drinks declined 21 percent, their average length doubled. Eating and eliminating less and taking fewer drinks resulted in a lengthening of most correlation intervals (Figure 10–6). The unlengthened correlations are noteworthy; drinks were clustered together much more frequently within one minute, and the habits of frequently eating food pellets within five minutes of each other, and drinking and eating within five minutes after eliminating were maintained. The zero-to-three-minute eliminate-eat correlation increased markedly, mostly at the expense of the three-to-five-minute one.

Much time was spent in the nest between 7 P.M. and midnight (Figure 10–4), a habit which is reflected in the profiles for other activities (Figures 10–4 and 10–5). Part of the decrease in recorded eliminations resulted because the animal began to foul the nest, in sharp contrast to its normal habits.

Social Interactions

Effects of social interactions are illustrated by studies of two mature female deer mice in the social enclosure (Kavanau, 1961, 1963c). Each animal was studied alone for seven days, then both together for seven days, and then each separately again for a like period. Living alone, each had a distinctive behavior pattern; Mouse 2 spent most of the night running the wheel, whereas Mouse 8 was relatively inactive and spent most of the night in the nest. In consort, the animals' activities changed markedly, with the pattern of each changing in the direction of the other's. For example, Mouse 2 now spent 47 percent less time out of the nest at night, whereas Mouse 8 spent 19 percent more time out. The mice had a strong tendency to remain in each other's company. Mouse 8 followed Mouse 2 to and from the nest and through a passage between compartments on 52 percent of all possible occasions—31 percent of the time within one minute and 70 percent within five minutes. On 63 percent of the occasions when Mouse 8 left the company of Mouse 2 (without being followed) it returned within two minutes. When returned to a solitary existence, each animal resumed its previous pattern of behavior.

Another study involved six captive-born, 36-day-old deer mice littermates (two males and four females) in the social enclosure. Even though two nests were available, the animals spent 543 minutes per day together in one or the other nest. Since all six were out of the nests 70 minutes per day, all were either together in one nest or outside 43 percent of the

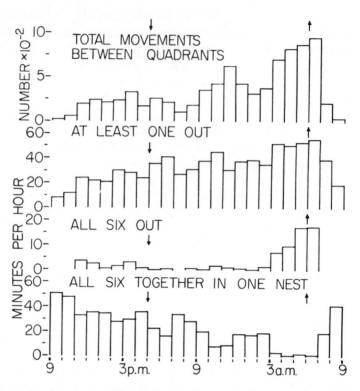

FIGURE 10.7. *Average daily nesting patterns and movements between quadrants for six immature deer mouse littermates for six days in the social enclosure (activity wheel locked).*

time. Contagious behavior was much in evidence; one animal leaving the nest often was followed by others, until all were out. Thirty percent of the ambulatory movements occurred during the day, mostly in the first daylight hour (Figure 10–7). This polyphasic activity was at least partly attributable to immaturity (Fujimoto, 1961); the animals did not fight, and there was no evidence of dominance relationships, which might cause different animals to be active at different times (Calhoun, 1956).

Studies in Extensive Enclosures

The most complex extensive enclosure contains 427 meters of linear runways. The shortest one-way path through its vertical maze system is

96 meters long, has 1205 90° turns, 48 meters of vertical passageways, and opens into 445 blind alleys, the latter occupying 53 percent of the total space. White-footed mice explore and learn to traverse this complex maze system in as few as two or three days without extrinsic reward or prior deprivation (Brant & Kavanau, 1965). Even though this maze is vastly more complex than the ones employed in studies with domestic rodents, there is no reason to believe that the limits of the learning capacity of white-footed mice have been approached.

Maze learning much resembles the learning of serialized activities by human beings, as when one learns a piano piece from memory. In the case of the mice, however, the mazes must be learned both forward and backward, since there is but one point of access and exit. Animals that pause to groom or sleep often appear to be lost upon resuming movement. They then make slow progress and many mistakes before resuming rapid passage along the direct route, much as the beginning pianist playing from memory has difficulty resuming after an interruption.

Once learned, mazes can be negotiated with remarkable speed and agility. Animals usually explore one maze completely and re-traverse it several times before beginning to explore another. Sometimes they fail to return to explored regions, just as portions of the habitat are abandoned in the wild. Return trips usually are much faster than outward ones, for there is a much greater tendency to re-explore the maze on outward trips.[5] Active animals tend to avoid a dark maze, suggesting that dim light is preferred to darkness (see also below).

Patterns of spontaneous movement in extensive enclosures are similar to known patterns in the wild (Brant & Kavanau, 1964, 1965). Because the movement patterns are established and followed without extrinsic reward, these activities appear to be the expression of inherited tendencies to explore and to develop wide-ranging locomotor activity. This interpretation is in conflict with the generally accepted postulate that hunger and thirst play leading roles in motivating wide-ranging locomotor movements. Accordingly, studies of learning in simple mazes with deprived domestic animals and extrinsic rewards may have but limited significance for understanding the behavior of wild and relatively unconfined animals.

---

[5] Since there is no extrinsic reward at the farthest point in the maze (that is, at its end), this point will be the goal of animals on outward trips only relatively infrequently. Consequently, considerable exploration of the maze may occur before the farthest point happens to be attained. On the other hand, on return trips, the nest, food, water, or the running wheel frequently will be the goal, accounting for the minimal amount of exploring en route back.

Post-Reward Lever Pressing

The fact that experimental animals frequently continue to make instrumental responses after delivery or onset of rewards is well known, but has been little understood. Several factors undoubtedly are involved, of which neither control of environment nor the adaptive value of the behavior has been given adequate attention. It is unrealistic to expect animals to cease pressing levers immediately after onset or delivery of a reward, for "rewards" in the wild often are proportional to the degree of repetition of responses. Wild animals seldom encounter successive situations identical in all discernible ways, in which the same response that leads to a reward at one instant does not do so a moment later.

The significance of post-reward lever pressing is elucidated by studies in which: (a) different rewards are obtained by pressing different levers; (b) levers have more than one function; (c) sequential lever pressing brings about stepwise changes; and (d) lever functions are altered in different phases. Some of these studies and their bearing on this problem are treated below. In general, my findings are consistent with anthropomorphic interpretations. Excluding accidental and immediate supernumerary presses occurring in cases of sequential stepwise control, the animals appear to be seeking: (a) immediate further reward or alteration of the environment; (b) prolongation or accumulation of reward; or (c) some other previously programmed or unknown reward. Post-reward lever pressing rarely occurs when a second press withdraws the reward (Kavanau, 1963a).

"Incorrect" Responses

"Incorrect" responses are closely related to post-reward lever pressing. Investigators sometimes are puzzled by the fact that once an animal has learned a discrimination well, it nonetheless still makes some "incorrect" responses. Actually, these responses are incorrect only from the narrow point of view of the investigator's unnatural and rigidly prescribed program, not from that of the animal. The basis for these responses is that the animal has a certain degree of variability built into many of its behavior patterns. This variability is adaptive to the conditions encountered in the wild, where many relationships are not prescribed rigidly.

The marked variability of certain responses of white-footed mice is illustrated by food pellet procural on the regimes of Figures 10–4 through 10–6. Deer Mouse 1 did not always approach the levers directly and press them in correct sequence, despite long practice (Kavanau, 1963b). Often it investigated the food tray first. On a typical night on the water regime it obtained 50 pellets using the correct sequence but failed 23 times using incorrect lever-pressing patterns. This, behavior is adaptive to variable conditions. Thus, when there is a pellet in the tray, lever pressing is skipped; when the sequence is changed, or a single or double pressing of either lever suffices, the change is discovered quickly. The habit of deviating fairly frequently from stereotyped "correct" responses, together with a high level of spontaneous activity, underlie the remarkable facility with which white-footed mice can be taught to cope with complex contingencies.

Lever pressing becomes highly selective on complex regimes. A striking illustration is the reaction of deer Mouse 1 when its pressing of the switch-4 lever failed to unlock the wheel (Kavanau, 1963b). The animal customarily unlocked the wheel every five to six minutes at night and ran until the wheel relocked five minutes later. When the wheel failed to unlock ("clutch failure," Figure 10–3), the behavior of the "frustrated" animal changed markedly. It became intensely active, eliminating often and visiting all parts of the enclosure frequently, including areas otherwise visited infrequently (Figure 10–3). The animal pressed the switch-4 lever 110 times in the next 90 minutes in unsuccessful attempts to unlock the wheel, and pressed all other levers that were functional in the program 131 times. But even during this period of excitement it was highly selective, for it largely ignored switches 5 and 6 (only five presses) which never had been functional and normally were pressed only rarely. As soon as the clutch was repaired (Figure 10–3, 12:45 A.M.) the normal routine was resumed.

Wheel-Running

When fully adapted to the running-wheel enclosure on a bright-dim light regime, white-footed mice typically spend most of the dim phase (up to 89 percent of the time) running the wheels. Similar, but less striking, behavior is well known for small mammals on bright-dark regimes (bright light, then darkness, then bright light, and so forth). It is important to elucidate the causal factors underlying wheel-running, for in small enclosures this activity is, perhaps, the best substitute for the spectrum of activities in the wild, and wheel-running is used extensively as a quantitative measure of activity and rhythmicity.

Running a wheel provides a means of sustained vigorous exercise otherwise difficult to achieve for closely confined animals. Since vigorous activity keeps muscles in optimum condition, this aspect of wheel-running can be regarded as adaptive. However, the opportunity for vigorous exercise can explain the appeal only partly, for in enclosures which provide ample space for sustained vigorous running and jumping, mice frequently spend much time running a wheel (Brant & Kavanau, 1964, 1965). Furthermore, rodents that have escaped or been released enter and run accessible activity wheels (see Kavanau, 1967). Accordingly, other rewarding features of the act must be sought. One such feature is the manipulation of the wheel (such as in accelerating and decelerating). Another is the acrobatics performed in large wheels, such as jumping onto and over the axle and across it along a diameter, as well as darting back and forth through passageways in the center pane (Figures 10–1 and 10–2).

Another clue was provided by some preliminary studies (Kavanau & Brant, 1965) in which canyon mice obtained experience running several different coaxially mounted "wheels." In a free-choice situation, animals experienced with and proficient in running all the wheels tended to prefer a square "wheel" to a round one. Starting, stopping, and running in the square wheel require jumping at the corners at rates up to 15 times per second. Accordingly, this preference suggested that exercise in which quick reflex actions and split-second timing and coordination of movements play a large role is preferred to exercise in which vigorous muscular activity is the primary requirement.

To test this hypothesis, additional studies employing a round wheel with hurdles have been carried out (Kavanau, 1967). I reasoned that if split-second timing and coordination and quick reflex actions are important, a round wheel with hurdles probably would be even more suitable than a square wheel, for an animal actually must jump upward to clear the hurdles, whereas an animal running in the proper rhythm in a square wheel merely has to jump across to the approaching sides as the corners pass beneath.

The four wheels used were two round wheels 15 and 25 centimeters in diameter, a round wheel 25 centimeters in diameter with four 1.9-centimeter-high hurdles, and an 18-centimeter square wheel. Three captive-born female littermates and three wild-caught male deer mice were studied individually. As in the preliminary study, all four wheels were available to the inexperienced animals in Phase 1, until a constant pattern of running was established and maintained for two to four days. The preferred wheel then was locked and the experiment continued with the partially experienced animals until a new constant pattern was established and maintained (Phase 2). The favored wheel of the remaining three then was locked (Phase 3) and, afterward, the favored wheel of the remaining two (Phase

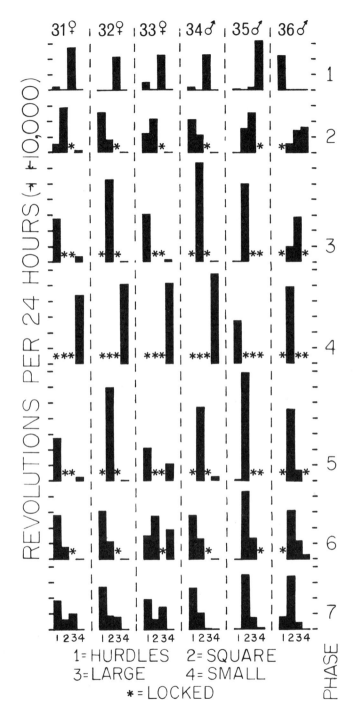

FIGURE 10.8. *Wheel-running preferences of six deer mice during Phases 1 through 7.*

4). After the animals had learned to run the last wheel, the wheels were unlocked in the reverse order (Phases 5 and 6) until all four wheels were available to the fully experienced animals (Phase 7). The running patterns in each phase are plotted in Figure 10–8.

In Phase 1, four animals (including the three littermates) preferred the large round wheel, one the small round wheel, and one the hurdles. The small round wheel was the last choice of the same four animals in Phase 4, whereas the hurdle wheel and the square wheel were the last choices of the other two, respectively. However, the fully experienced animals with the full range of choice in Phase 7 showed a large preference for either the hurdles or the square wheel. The same group of four animals preferred the hurdle wheel, the other two the square wheel (Figure 10–8). Thus, the wheel preferred by fully experienced animals turned out to be only the second choice (twice), third choice (thrice), or the last choice (once) of the inexperienced animals of Phase 1—never the first choice.

These results confirm the thesis that one of the rewarding aspects of wheel-running for wild rodents is its requirement for split-second timing and coordination of movements and quick reflex actions. The results also point up a significant fact for the design of laboratory studies, namely that results obtained in free-choice experiments with inexperienced animals may be completely misleading, even after long experimental periods. This comes about because, as mentioned above, some behavior of animals tends to be quite conservative. In this case, the first one or two wheels run may monopolize subsequent running (Kavanau, 1967).

The same conservatism is seen in selection between sources of food and water. For example, in the enclosure of Figure 10–2, paired food guns (*d*) and water bottles (*e*) are available. Although some variability is exhibited (as with other categories of behavior), typically only one food source is used. The other often is left untouched until the first is exhausted. If the first source is replenished periodically, the second may remain untouched. Conservatism also applies to the use of water sources, but is more dependent upon enclosure design. To a degree, such conservatism has survival value; animals that tend to confine their movements to well-worn beaten tracks within the home range (recall conservatism in wheel-running) and to eat and drink only at familiar sites (when alternate sources are available) are the ones most likely to survive.

Another approach to the significance of wheel-running utilizes motor-driven wheels. White-footed mice engage repeatedly in motor-driven running (MDR) if they themselves start the rotation of the wheel (Kavanau, 1963a). Accordingly, one can make direct comparisons of the reward value of running in free and motor-driven wheels. Two wild-caught male canyon mice (Nos. 20 and 25) were studied on a regime in which pressing either of two levers unlocked the wheel for two minutes, making free running possible, and pressing either of two other levers started rotation of the wheel for two minutes at 33 revolutions per minute. On this program, sessions of running the free wheel occurred over three times as frequently as those of MDR (Kavanau, 1963a). These findings reinforce views on the importance of vigorous exercise, manipulation, timing, and so forth, in wheel-running, because running the free wheel allows much manipulation and acrobatics, and can occur at high speeds, whereas manipulation is more limited in MDR and the speed must be kept comparatively low (for purposes of safety).

In another experiment with the same animals, pressing any lever started rotation (at 25 r.p.m.) of the stationery locked wheel but stopped rotation and locked the wheel if it already was rotating (Kavanau, 1963a). On this program (see also the treatment below) the animals ran less than 40 percent as much as they did with free wheels, a result which substantiates the existence of a preference for free running.

Activity and Orientation Responses to Light

A significant feature of the sustained wheel-running of white-footed mice is that most individuals run almost entirely (up to 99.99 percent) in one direction (Kavanau, 1962c, 1962d, 1963a, 1963b). The position of the dim light source is the chief factor determining running direction, although other features of the enclosure also can play a role. If the light source is mounted in alignment with the wheel (Figure 10–2h), most animals consistently run either toward or away from it. On the other hand, in darkness—on the commonly employed bright-dark regime—running direction tends to be haphazard.

Artificial twilight transitions about one hour long have been simulated by two methods: (a) in the varying-color-temperature method, the potential applied to a cluster of four miniature lamps is varied continuously between one and 6.5 volts; (b) in the constant-color-temperature method, 92 bulbs of 15 different intensities are turned on or off progressively in a sequence of 52 steps (Kavanau, 1962c, 1962d). Both types of light transition elicit several additional photo-responses. Whereas animals that begin to run in light of constant intensity—whether bright, dim, or dark—often warm up to top speed gradually over a period of one to three hours, animals that begin during a dusk usually run in a brief burst at high speed during the first 5 to 15 minutes (Figure 10–9; Figure 10–10, small arrow).

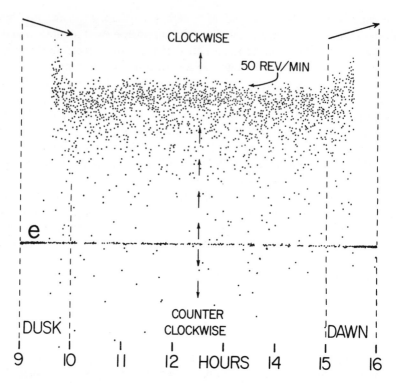

FIGURE 10.9. *Speedomax G running record for deer Mouse 2 during a night on a 16-hour periodicity employing twilight transitions of varying color temperature. Each dot gives the instantaneous speed (linear scale) and direction of running at four-second intervals. The dim-light source was in the clockwise direction in all phases. This running record (and that of Figure 10.16) was drawn from a more complex multicolor record for more than one variable, whereas the record of Figure 10.10 was photographed directly from the original unicolor record for running only.*

An analogous brief burst of running at high speed also occurs if the animal is running sustainedly at the time of the dawn transition, just before running ceases (Figure 10–9), whereas no characteristic pattern emerges when the phase of sustained running ceases before dawn (Figure 10–10) or under other constant conditions of illumination. The onset and cutoff intensities for twilight running usually range from one to 50 times that of the full moon (FM = 0.012 to 0.023 ft.-candle).

The middle to late phase of dusk has a great activity-stimulating effect upon white-footed mice, whereas the middle to late phase of dawn has a strong inhibitory effect. One of the most striking ways to show these strong influences is to present a series of alternate dusk and dawn transitions in immediate succession through the normal activity period. Of two male canyon mice tested on this regime, one responded to almost every transition (Kavanau, paper in preparation). It began running in a high-speed burst, as usual, in the first dusk, and ceased in a high-speed burst and retired to its nest during the first dawn. The same responses occurred during the second dusk and dawn. The animal "overslept" the middle phase of the third dusk but began running in the late phase (warming up rather than beginning at high speed). It ceased in a high-speed burst and retired to its nest a third time during the third dawn. The fourth dusk also was "overslept," the animal once again warming up rather than beginning to run at high speed. Sustained running ceased, as usual, before the final dawn, which began at its usual time, two hours after the end of the fourth dusk. Both animals always ceased running "promptly" in response to dawn. Failure to respond promptly at midphase of every dusk apparently is a consequence of the strong activity-inhibiting effect of the immediately preceding dawn.

These twilight responses show clearly that if approximately natural stimuli are presented to captive animals, even on a thoroughly unnatural time schedule, the animals can be "forced" to respond in an approximately natural way, almost at the will of the investigator.

Many animals are known to show peaks of activity during dusk and dawn in the wild (see, for example, Brown, 1956; Pearson, 1960; Tinbergen, 1953); some animals are active only during twilight periods. The facts that artificial dusk stimulates activity of nocturnal mice and artificial dawn inhibits it, and that peaks in the speed of wheel-running occur during these transitions suggest strongly that peaks of activity during twilight in the wild are responses to illuminance changes. Since both wild-caught and captive-born animals respond in this way to artificial twilights, the responses are determined genetically and are indicative of a high degree of adaptedness to the natural regime of illuminance and, of course, for a nocturnal existence.

A significant feature of twilight running is that a given animal consistently runs with the same orientation to the setting and rising "sun" as to the "moon." In early studies there was only a single fixed light source. Thus, in running in one direction all night (Figure 10–9), the mice might have been orienting relative to any one of the three dim-light phases (setting "sun," rising "sun," or "moon") and ignoring the other two, or they simply could have been orienting relative to any dim light. The use of independent light sources mounted opposite one another reveals a strong orienting effect of any dim light on the running direction of the mice.

Most animals run almost exclusively toward or away from constant dim light and the artificial twilight sun at low intensities, regardless of the direction in which the lights are presented. When the "moon" and the twilight "sun" are present concurrently, the animals orient with respect to the "sun" (that is, to the source of changing intensity). If the "moon" is omitted or cut off temporarily, running remains predominantly unidirectional, with the direction determined by the position of the last light source seen. These findings suggest that white-footed mice use the twilight sun and moon (and possibly other celestial light sources and prominent geographical features) as navigational references.

The consistency of the orientation to dim light is shown strikingly by the running record of Figure 10–10 for a male canyon mouse. The animal was on an imposed 24-hour light cycle (14 hours of bright light), with the "sun" setting and rising in the same direction.[6] The "moon" appeared opposite the "sun" at the end of dusk (8 P.M.) and its longitude was shifted 180° every hour during the night. The animal consistently (98.7 percent) ran toward the source of dim light, changing direction every time the source changed.

The observed effects of artificial twilight transitions on speed of wheel-running and of total darkness and dim light on directionality suggest that both of these properties of the performance depend very much on the level of illuminance. To study this dependence more closely, three different levels of dim light lasting one-half hour each have been presented in sequence to white-footed mice during their normal activity period (Kavanau, paper in preparation). The results show clearly that at least five different parameters of the wheel-running performance are proportional to the illuminance level of dim light: maximum speed, average speed, amount of time spent running, average running-session length, and consistency of directional orientation. It seems likely that such dependencies on the level of artificial illuminance reflect related dependencies of activities in the wild on natural illuminance levels, and that they are the basis for effects of artificial and natural twilights.

If deer mice are given complete control over the intensity of ambient illuminance (Kavanau, 1966, and below), they select dim light during active periods and very dim light during inactive periods (see Figures 10–14 and 10–15). This finding emphasizes the unsuitability of the unnatural, abrupt bright-dark laboratory regimes that are employed customarily with nocturnal animals. In the wild, nocturnal mice generally are in very dim light or darkness during the day, not bright light. During the

---

[6] Note that on this light cycle canyon mice cease sustained running 30 to 120 minutes before the beginning of "dawn" and run only sporadically without consistent orientation thereafter (Figure 10–10).

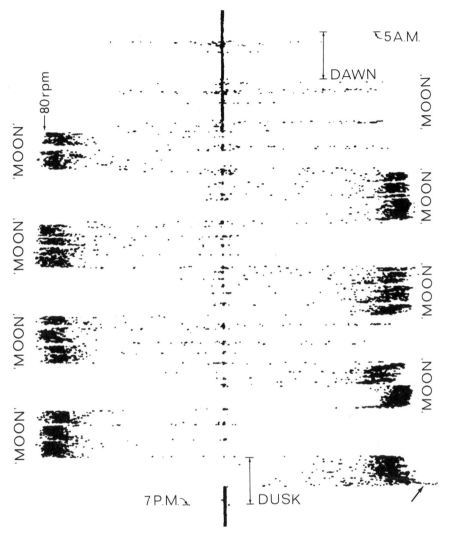

FIGURE 10.10. *Photograph of a Speedomax G running record (points at four-second intervals) for a captive-born canyon mouse (No. 337) on a night during which the direction of the 'moon' was changed every hour. The unlabeled arrow at the lower right indicates the early burst of high-speed running (very brief for this animal) during the variable-color-temperature dusk; dots to the right of the centerline represent running in one direction, to the left, in the other; the positions of the 'moon,' dawn, and dusk markers indicate the directions of the artificial moon and twilight sun with respect to the direction of running.*

night they generally are in dim light, not darkness. Laboratory bright light is appropriate during the day only if a dark nesting area is provided. The unnatural bright-dark regime of the laboratory succeeds because active nocturnal animals avoid bright light much more than darkness. In fact, on abrupt dark-dim regimes, mice are active in the dim light, not darkness. In other words, the preference of the active animal for dim light (over darkness) exceeds that of the inactive animal.

In the experiment just referred to, six deer mice and two canyon mice (four males and four females, all wild-caught) were exposed to a 24-hr. dark-dim (14:10) regime for seven days, beginning with a dim phase at normal nighttime. Four deer mice and one canyon mouse ran vigorously during the dim phase (Figure 10–11, top); the other three animals scarcely ran at all and virtually ignored the light regime.[7] To show that the five animals actually were following the light regime, rather than simply maintaining an endogenous 24-hr. rhythm in synchrony with it, a 23.5-hr. light cycle was instituted for nine subsequent days. All five animals entrained to the shortened rhythmicity (Figure 10–11, beginning second from top).

Compulsion and Nest Occupancy

When mice in experimental enclosures are disturbed during the day, they often leave the nest. Sometimes they re-enter almost immediately; at other times they wait until the disturbance is over. But, if they are placed back in the nest by hand, they leave it again immediately (as do kittens and puppies). They persist in leaving, no matter how many times they are put back. In this relatively clear-cut case, an act or situation which is rewarding when carried out volitionally is avoided when initiated by force— the animal responds by doing the opposite.

Compulsion and Wheel-Running

An equivalent response is elicited when one attempts to force mice to run a motor-driven wheel. If the experimenter starts the wheel rotating, and the mice are able to stop it by pressing levers, they do so within

[7] Of the other three animals, one followed an endogenous 24.5-hr. rhythmicity and one a 24-hr. rhythmicity in phase with its prior activity cycle. The second canyon mouse was erratic at first but eventually (last nine days) followed a 24-hr. rhythmicity with activity from 10 P.M. to 7 A.M.

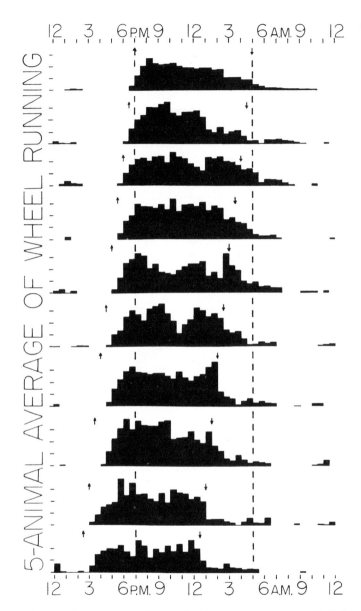

FIGURE 10.11. *Average, equally weighted, running patterns (half-hour grid) for four deer mice and one canyon mouse during a dark-dim (0.0008 foot-candle) light regime for seven days (averaged at top) on a 24-hour rhythmicity and nine subsequent days on a 23½-hour rhythmicity.*

seconds (Kavanau, 1962b, 1963a). No matter at what time, at what rate or direction of rotation, or how experienced the animals are at MDR (motor-driven running), they turn off the rotating wheel promptly. MDR is rewarding only when it is initiated volitionally.

A striking example of avoidance of nonvolitional MDR is the behavior of deer mice in two isolated running-wheel enclosures when the wheel in each enclosure is programmed to start rotating when the rotation of the other wheel is stopped (by pressing any of the four levers). Confronted with this program, a pair of mice engages for hours in a tenacious alternating lever pressing "tug-of-war." Each animal repeatedly—usually within seconds—turns its motor off, and thereby turns on the other's (Figure 10–12, a_1, and a_2).

When an animal starts and runs a motor-driven wheel volitionally, there is also a strong tendency to restart the wheel promptly after it is stopped by the experimenter. Thus, canyon mice repeatedly turn the wheels back on within seconds after they go off automatically after 15- or 30-second sessions (Figure 10–12, b and c). These results make a strong

FIGURE 10.12.   *(a₁ and a₂) Alternate lever pressing sequences of two deer mice in isolated running-wheel enclosures; each line along a₁ marks the time of pressing of a lever by one animal which stops the rotation of its wheel and starts the rotation of the other's; each line along a₂ marks the time of pressing of a lever in response by the other animal which stops its wheel and restarts that of the first animal. The relatively long periods when the wheel of the second animal was rotating do not necessarily represent time when the second mouse was running the wheel. Usually, at these times the mouse was seeking other means of avoiding running, such as balancing on the axle or trying to find purchase on the tip of a food gun. (b) Each line marks the time of pressing of a lever by canyon Mouse 25, starting 15 seconds of rotation of its wheel on its first night of experience with volitional motor-driven running (MDR). (c) Same as b but for canyon Mouse 20, for 30 seconds on its second night of experience.*

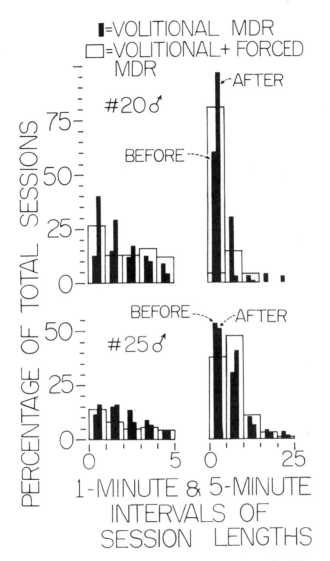

FIGURE 10.13. *Distributions of session lengths of volitional MDR on two programs for canyon Mice 20 and 25. The first set of bars is for volitional MDR before, and the second set for volitional MDR after the program of volitional plus forced MDR. The volitional MDR on the latter program is shown by the open blocks. The periodic forced MDR on this program was negligible and is not depicted.*

case for avoidance of actions or events instituted nonvolitionally, regardless of whether the animal is being forced to initiate or cease an activity. However, the case to this point is not conclusive. One could argue that the animals are not responding conservatively but merely are exercising control over the wheel, that is, that since they find it rewarding to be able to start and stop the rotation of the wheel, they do so at every opportunity.

The first thesis—of response to compulsion—is supported by experiments in which animals both start and stop the rotation of the wheel volitionally. Under these conditions they start or stop the wheels only 20 to 50 times per night. But when they are able only to start or stop the wheel, after it is either stopped or started automatically, they do so hundreds of times. More support comes from experiments in which the motor was started periodically during a regime in which canyon Mice 20 and 25 were engaged in volitional MDR, that is, they were both starting and stopping the wheels (Kavanau, 1963a). First, there were eight days of volitional MDR (Figure 10–13, bars labeled "before"). The volitional MDR was continued for the next 12 days but, in addition, the motor also was turned on automatically every 60, 30, and 15 minutes during consecutive four-day periods. The responses were clear cut. Both animals turned off the motor within seconds of the 672 automatic starts.

Session-length distributions for the concurrent volitional MDR are given by the open blocks in Figure 10–13. The amount of volitional MDR of Mouse 25 did not change but the average session-length increased somewhat. However, the superimposed forced schedule markedly reduced Mouse 20's volitional MDR, which practically ceased after the sixth day. In the last six days, Mouse 20 turned off the motor 478 times and turned it on only 12 times. Considering that the same levers turned the motor on and off, this behavior was remarkably selective and goal directed.

These results show that the response to nonvolitional MDR is primarily one of avoidance or conservatism rather than a manifestation of control of environment—otherwise, the mice would not stop the wheel promptly after each automatic start. Thus, the responses after the motor started automatically (at least during active periods) would be expected to be the same as those following volitional starts if the mice were exercising nothing more than environmental control in both cases. The results also show that attempts to compel animals to engage in an otherwise rewarding activity may make even the volitional performance nonrewarding. When the animals were returned to a purely volitional regime (Figure 10–13, second set of bars labeled "after"), Mouse 20 showed a dramatic resumption of MDR. Both animals now found it more rewarding to start and stop the wheels, for the daily number of sessions (but not revolutions) increased markedly over that for any of the previous 20 days (Kavanau, 1963a).

The very different responses of Mice 20 and 25 in these studies should serve to alert us against the hazards of the prevailing tendency to carry out behavior studies with relatively large groups of domestic animals selected for genetic and experiential homogeneity. Skinner (1956) has emphasized the importance of intensively concentrated experiments on single animals, as opposed to what he terms the "mechanized statistics" of experimentation with groups (see also Sidman, 1962). I would like to emphasize as well the need for more studies of randomly chosen wild animals over long periods of time. Findings on MDR based upon the behavior of an inbred strain responding as did Mouse 20 would support a theory incompatible with an equally compelling theory based upon the uniform behavior of an inbred strain responding in Mouse 25's fashion. By giving rein to the marked individual differences existing in populations of wild animals, one obtains the added perspective needed to interpret many aspects of behavior.

Compulsion and Control of Ambient Illuminance

In studies of control of ambient illuminance, the interaction of at least three factors influences responses: (a) the conservative tendency to counteract promptly any nonvolitional change in level of illuminance (response to compulsion); (b) the tendency to alter the level of illuminance frequently (control of environment); and (c) the tendency to spend more time at certain illuminance levels than others (selectivity). Each factor may vary with the phase of the activity cycle, the type of previous experience, the degree of adaptation to the regime, and the type of regime (Kavanau, 1966). Accordingly, interpretation of responses is far more difficult than for nest occupancy and wheel-running studies. However, the experiments give greater insight into the interaction of behavioral variables, have greater ecological significance, and allow greater scope for the expression of individual and species differences. For these reasons, the following findings are treated in considerable detail.

Complete Control. The studies of control of illuminance proceeded through nine phases spanning 15 to 20 weeks. Space permits treating only the first two and last phases. In the last phase, four fully adapted wild-caught deer mice (two males, two females) were studied individually for two to four weeks in the isolated running-wheel enclosures of Figure 10–2

(Kavanau, 1966). The animals had bidirectional instrumental control over the level of illuminance in 10 steps.[8] Each press of either of two levers (Figure 10–2*a*) on one side of the enclosure stepped the illuminance one level higher, on the other side, one level lower.

Although no external time cues were given, the mice maintained 23- to 25-hr. endogenous rhythms and established characteristic patterns of controlling the illuminance (Figures 10–14 and 10–15). Selected illuminances were roughly the same as those experienced at corresponding phases of activity in the wild, with a lower average level being maintained during rest and sleep than during activity (Figure 10–15). The animals exercised a high level of control over ambient illuminance during active

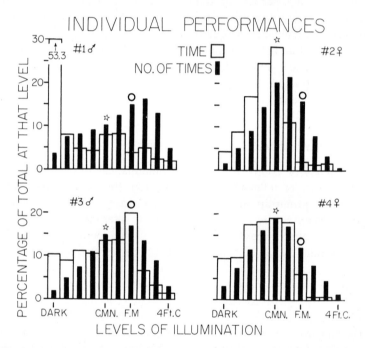

FIGURE 10.14. *Distributions of numbers of times visited (bars) and total time spent (blocks) at various illuminance levels (see footnotes 7 and 9) by four deer mice having bidirectional stepwise control (by pressing switch levers) of the level of ambient illuminance (see text); open circles, intensity of full moon; open stars, intensity on clear moonless night.*

[8] Levels of illuminance for all animals on complete control and for Mice 3 and 4 in Phases 1 and 2 were: darkness, 0.00008, 0.00011, 0.00029 (roughly one-half starlight), 0.0008 (roughly clear moonless night), 0.003, 0.018 (roughly full moon = FM), 0.094, 0.62, and 4.0 ft.-candles (Kavanau, 1966).

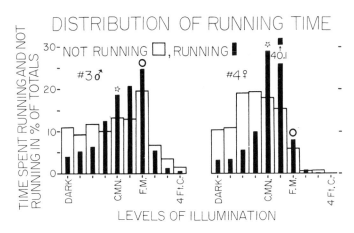

FIGURE 10.15. *The total time (open blocks of Figure 10.14) subdivided into distributions of the time spent running (bars) and not running (open blocks) at the various levels of illuminance (see footnote 7) for deer Mice 3 and 4 on the regime of Figure 10.14 (data not obtained for Mice 1 and 2).*

periods, frequently running back and forth, stepping the intensity of the lights up and down (Figure 10–16). Exposure to the brightest level (four ft.-candles) was infrequent and typically very brief. Periods in darkness also were infrequent but lasted longer and seldom occurred during activity. Mice 2 through 4 spent 77 percent of the time in the range of one-half starlight to full moon (FM = open circles in Figures 10–14, 10–15, 10–16, and 10–18), eight percent in darkness, and only 0.5 percent at four ft.-candles. However, Mouse 1 spent 53 percent of the time in darkness, for it usually turned the lights off at the beginning of inactive periods.

These results on complete control are the simplest to interpret, for the animals were fully adapted to controlling illuminance, and compulsion was absent (Kavanau, 1966). The findings provide controls and baselines for other phases of the study. First, they show which intensity ranges are preferred during different phases of activity; second, they show that fully adapted animals continue to alter the intensity of illuminance frequently, months after the novelty has worn off; and third, they give values for the frequency of these alterations[9] by fully adapted animals exhibiting a high degree of selectivity.

[9] Average numbers of level changes per day on complete control were: 172, 123, 101, 137 for deer Mice 1 through 4, respectively. For comparison, when Mice 3 and 4 were inexperienced and the levers were functionless, rates of lever pressing were only 9.0 and 9.4 per day (Kavanau, 1966).

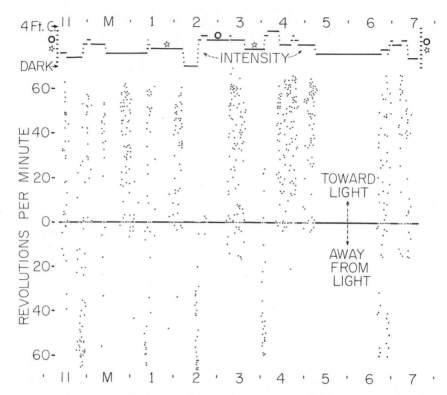

FIGURE 10.16. *Reconstruction of Speedomax G record of the speed and direction of wheel-running and the concurrent levels of illuminance for deer Mouse 4 during a typical period of activity on the regime of Figures 10.14 and 10.15 (complete control). Direction of running was predominantly toward the light and the animal made most alterations of the level of illuminance while it was running. The amount of running, compared to that in Figure 10.9 and 10.10, was more than is indicated by the record, for points were recorded only at eight-second intervals. The record of levels of illuminance, although overlapping the running record in the original (in ink of different color) has been condensed and displaced to the top of the figure.*

Phase 1. In Phase 1 of the same study, the lights were turned fully on every half hour for Mice 1 and 2 and every hour for Mice 3 and 4. Each press on any lever stepped the illuminance one level lower. The levels for Mice 3 and 4 were the 10 used on the regime of complete control (see footnote 8). For Mice 1 and 2 the levels were brighter,[10] with none between

[10] Levels of illuminance for Mice 1 and 2 in Phases 1 and 2 were: darkness, 0.0008, 0.0059, 0.025 (roughly FM), 0.094, 0.25, 0.62, 1.0, 2.2, and 4.0 ft.-candles.

those of darkness and a clear moonless night (open stars in Fig. 10–14 10–16 and 10–18). Program details were the same in Phase 2 except that the lights then were turned off periodically and could be stepped back on. The following results are for seven days of each phase (after two to four days of adaptation).

When the lights were turned on periodically, the animals responded (Table 10–1) by stepping their intensity down at least one level 67 percent of the occasions possible, and fully off after 56 percent of the responses (unless otherwise indicated, figures given in the text are equally-weighted averages for two or four animals; individual figures are given in the tables). The behavior of Mouse 2 was striking, for it stepped the lights fully off 279 times (of 336 possible). It also was in the process of stepping the lights fully off two other times, but was interrupted by their going on automatically.

A general impression of the individual performances, which differed greatly, can be gained from the upper graphs in each set in Figure 10–17. The elapsed time from the lights' going on to the first step down is plotted against the time taken to step from the second level to the last level

TABLE 10–1   *Figures for the performances of Mice 1 through 4 in the study of compulsion and control of illuminance*

	Possible times mice stepped at least one level (%)	Responses in which mice stepped all 9 levels (%)	Average no. of level changes per 24-hr. period	Minutes to first step off or on during active periods		Minutes taken to attain level 10 after first level change	
				< 9 steps	9 steps	During active periods	Beginning active periods
Phase 1							
Mouse 1	55	65	210	2.7	2.8	8.2	2.7
Mouse 2	84	99	360	†	2.2	1.1	1.3
Mouse 3	55	29	82	3.2	3.1	36	23
Mouse 4	74	36	119	2.0	0.91	24	18
Phase 2							
Mouse 1	58	41	174	2.6	2.3	12	4.4
Mouse 2	31	52	92	4.1	3.8	11	13
Mouse 3	49	59	83	3.5	3.1	24	17
Mouse 4	66	78	124	3.6	.2.4	13	11
Phase 1*							
Mouse 3	62	47	108	1.9	1.3	32	22
Mouse 4	87	38	138	1.8	1.2	19	13

* Second week of Phase 1.
† No occurrence.

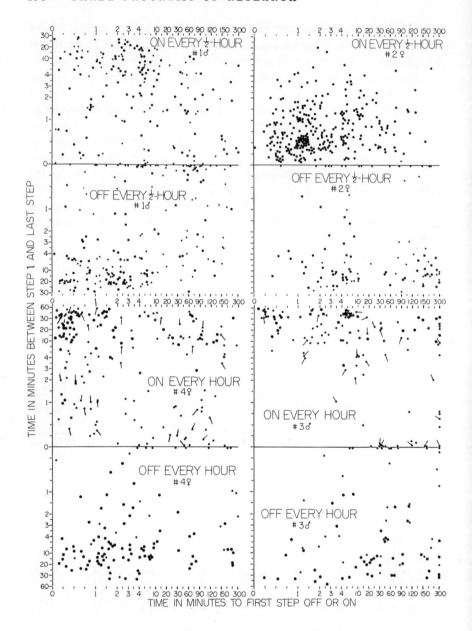

visited during each half-hour or hour period. Performances are far more selective than might appear at first sight, since both scales are partially logarithmic.

Responding occurred mostly during periods of running. The condition of the lights was not altered during long intervals of rest and sleep. Mouse 2 (and to some extent Mouse 4) was exceptional in that, contrary to its normal habits, it became active much of the time; its longest period of inactivity was only 3.5 hrs. All four animals maintained 23- to 25-hr. endogenous rhythms.

One cannot conclude that the mice were not aware of the condition of the lights while asleep, for inactive white-footed mice usually are very alert to their surroundings. In fact, when Mice 3 and 4 were awakened periodically by sound, they did not step the intensity down more frequently nor behave differently in other respects. This is shown in Figure 10–17, where the large solid stars and small stars with tails are for a three-day continuation of Phase 1 with sound presented hourly on the hour for one minute. Hence, inactive mice often may be aware of the bright light being turned on, but may be too drowsy or insufficiently motivated to respond.

One can divide the responses roughly into two groups—those that occur during active periods and those that occur at the beginning of active periods (and during inactive periods)—by taking responses that occur within 10 minutes of the lights' going on as opposed to those that occur after 10 minutes. By this criterion, the first press after "lights on" during active periods occurred after 2.4 minutes. The sooner the first step down occurred, the more likely it was that the animal would step the lights all the way off (Table 10–1). Thus, elapsed times to the first step generally were less for nine-step cases than for cases of fewer than nine steps.

FIGURE 10.17. *Partially logarithmic plots of elapsed time to taking the first step versus elapsed time from the first step to the last step achieved for deer Mice 1 through 4 during Phases 1 (lights on periodically) and 2 (lights off periodically) of the control of illuminance study. Large dots are for cases in which the lights were stepped fully off or fully on (nine steps); small dots are for fewer than nine steps; small dots lying very close to the abscissae generally are for only one or two steps. The large stars and small stars with tails have the same significance as the large and small dots, except that they are for the three-day extension of Phase 1 (for Mice 3 and 4) in which sound was presented hourly (see text). The ordinates of this figure are reflected about the abscissae to facilitate comparisons; if the patterns were mirror images, the role of selectivity could be presumed to be relatively small. The patterns of deer Mouse 1 are most like mirror images.*

This suggests that the motivation to respond was stronger, the sooner the first response occurred after the lights went on.[11]

The time taken to step the lights fully off after the first step (Table 10–1) was 34 percent less at the beginning of active periods than during active periods (excluding Mouse 2 whose time of only 1.1 minutes scarcely could be improved upon). Hence, once the resting animal was aroused to respond, it stepped the lights fully off much more quickly than it did when it was already active. It is significant that Mice 1 and 2 stepped the lights fully off much more rapidly and much more frequently than did Mice 3 and 4.

Lever pressing did not cease after the lights were fully off. On 59 percent of these occasions, the mice continued to press the levers in darkness ("false offs"). There were six presses per period off amounting to 11 presses per hour off, with the first "false off" occurring after four minutes (Table 10–2). The occurrence of these frequent (but not prompt) "false offs" suggests strongly that the mice were seeking further control over the intensity of illuminance—perhaps trying to regain dim levels.

The performance of Mouse 2 was most clear cut (Figures 10–17 to 10–19). Its rapid stepping of the lights fully off almost every time was not because of a preference for darkness, for with complete control it spent only 4.3 percent of the time in darkness (Figure 10–14). Moreover, the plots in Figure 10–18 (bars) show only weak selectivity from level to level. Either Mouse 2 was responding vigorously to compulsion or it was seeking control over the lights to the greatest degree. The latter explanation is unlikely, since Mouse 2's "false offs" were the least for the group (Table 10–2). Nor did Mouse 2 show the greatest tendency to control the lights during the regime of complete control (see footnote 9). Accordingly, it can be concluded that Mouse 2 responded vigorously to compulsion but exercised only moderate environmental control characterized by weak selectivity.

Mouse 1 showed greater selectivity (Figure 10–18, bars); in stepping the lights down, it tended to dwell ("average per change") longest at the lower illuminance levels, and often left the lights at dim levels. It is unlikely that the frequent "false offs" by Mouse 1 were due to a strong tendency to seek dim light and avoid darkness, for with complete control (Figure 10–14) this mouse spent 53 percent of the time in darkness. Hence, the most frequent, soonest, and highest rate and number of "false offs" by Mouse 1 (Table 10–2) probably should be interpreted mainly

---

[11] The data of Table 10–1 suggest that these differences can be attributed only partly to the fact that the sooner the first step was taken, the more time there was available (before the next automatic alteration) to step the full nine steps.

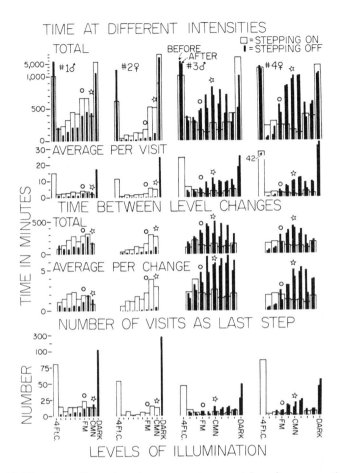

FIGURE 10.18. *Overall total and average times, total and average times between level changes (dwelling times), and number of visits as last step at the various levels of illuminance (see footnotes 7 and 9) during Phases 1 (bars) and 2 (open blocks) of the control of illuminance study for deer Mice 1 through 4. For animals 3 and 4 both the first and second weeks (bars labeled "Before" and "After") of Phase 1 are plotted. Ordinates of the top and bottom plots are partially logarithmic.*

as a seeking of further control of the lights. This interpretation is consistent with the fact that Mouse 1 altered the level of illuminance most frequently on the regime of complete control (see footnote 9).

Mice 3 and 4 were highly selective, as is shown clearly in Figure 10–18 (first set of bars). Much time was spent at intermediate dim levels.

TABLE 10–2 *Data on "false presses" (continuation of lever pressing after lights had been turned on or off) by Mice 1 through 4 in the study of compulsion and control of illuminance*

Phase or transition period	Percentage of occasions off or on that false presses occurred	False presses per period off or on (No.)	False presses per hr. off or on (No.)	Minutes to first false press after off or on
Phase 1				
Mouse 1	73	11	28	2.0
Mouse 2	33	5.0	4.1	5.4
Mouse 3	59	3.1	6.0	4.1
Mouse 4	69	4.6	6.0	4.5
Phase 1–2				
Mouse 1	100	44	86	0.42
Mouse 2	100	54	240	1.0
Mouse 3	93	14	34	3.1
Mouse 4	100	47	82	1.2
Phase 2				
Mouse 1	89	15	54	2.0
Mouse 2	93	24	120	1.2
Mouse 3	75	19	34	4.6
Mouse 4	99	58	75	2.7
Phase 2–1				
Mouse 3	81	19	91	2.3
Mouse 4	92	19	23	2.7
Phase 1*				
Mouse 3	72	6.7	11	4.0
Mouse 4	78	9.6	2.0	6.0

* Second week of Phase 1.

In fact, the illuminance distributions for these mice, even in this first phase, begin to resemble those exhibited months later on complete control (Figures 10–14 and 10–15). On 67 percent of responses, they left the lights at dim levels.

It cannot be argued that this frequent leaving of the lights at dim levels was because Mice 3 and 4 could not see at these low levels and "thought the lights were off." The results of other phases of the study (Kavanau, paper in preparation), in which some intensity levels were omitted, as well as the results on the phase of complete control, show that the mice select levels by means of the intensity or color temperature of the light, not by counting the number of steps.

Transition to Phase 2.   Dramatic reactions occurred during the two-day transition to Phase 2. Now that lever pressing stepped the lights on instead of off, the mice pressed more and more quickly as the lights brightened, and often in a fast staccato after the lights were fully on and further presses were without effect. "False ons" occurred on virtually every occasion the lights were fully on (Table 10–2). There were 40 presses per occasion on, amounting to 110 presses per hour, with the first "false on" occurring after 3.3 minutes. These figures are markedly different from those of Phase 1.

It appears that the strong tendencies to modify the level of illuminance repeatedly and to respond conservatively to nonvolitional alterations led the animals to step the lights fully on over and over again, even though this entailed passing beyond the preferred dim range to the level avoided most on complete control. It is difficult to avoid the anthropomorphic interpretation that the rapid and frequent "false ons" were attempts to turn the lights back off or to lower intensities, especially since such behavior at the "on" switches did not occur during the program of complete control, when "off" switches also were present.[12] Both the tendency to avoid bright light, and a vigorous reaction to the loss of the step-down control of intensity of Phase 1, underlie this response. Such loss is a form of compulsion, since the animals are forced to exchange the control of illuminance of Phase 1 for that of Phase 2.

The influence of withdrawal of environmental control also is shown by the following experiment. On return to a second week of Phase 1 (Figures 10–18 and 10–19) after Phase 2, similar vigorous prompt "false pressing" by Mice 3 and 4 occurred in the transition period (Table 10–2), even though the levers then were being pressed when the lights were fully off. Thus, responses to withdrawal of environmental control occur regardless of whether it is the ability to step the lights on or off that is withdrawn, and even when other environmental control is substituted. As noted above (see Figure 10–3), when control over the environment is withdrawn without substitute, the mouse reacts with astonishing vigor.

[12] Average numbers of "false ons" per occasion fully on during the regime of complete control were only 2.2, 1.2, 1.0, and 0.50 for animals 1 through 4, respectively. The lights were turned fully on 119, 11, 83, and 50 times, for an average visit length of 3.4, 1.1, 6.8, and 0.33 minutes. On this regime, "false ons" were almost all immediate supernumerary presses, whereas in the transition to Phase 2 and in Phase 2 "false ons" occurred mostly during repeated subsequent visits to the switches.

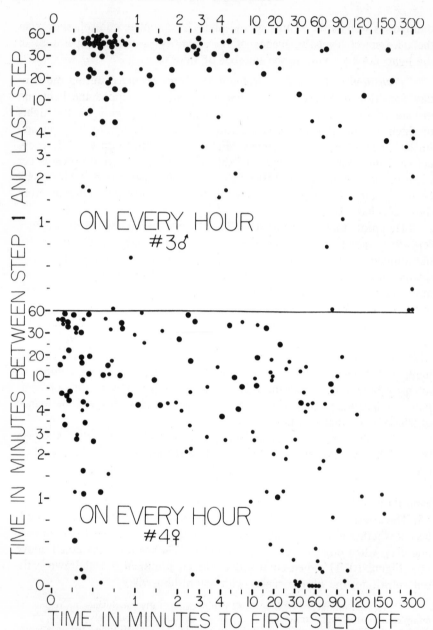

FIGURE 10.19. *Partially logarithmic plots of elapsed time to taking the first step versus elapsed time from the first step to the last step achieved (see Figure 10.17) for deer Mice 3 and 4 during the second week of Phase 1.*

Phase 2.   The mice responded to the lights going off periodically by stepping the intensity up at least one level on 51 percent of the occasions possible, and fully on after 58 percent of these responses (Figure 10–17, lower graphs in each set). While the percentage of nine-step responses (that is, to lights fully on) declined markedly for Mice 1 and 2, it increased markedly for Mice 3 and 4 (Table 10–1). Once again, the sooner the first step occurred, the more likely it was that the light intensity would be altered the full nine steps (see footnote 11). Compared to Phase 1, the times taken to go from the second level to the tenth (fully on) during active periods are markedly greater for Mice 1 and 2 but markedly less for Mice 3 and 4. "False on" performances were "toned down" considerably from the transition period, but they still greatly exceeded the negligible "false ons" on the program of complete control (see footnote 12).

Mouse 2 showed definite signs of selectivity for the lower illuminance levels (Figure 10–18, blocks versus bars). It waited much longer than in Phase 1 before the first step (Figure 10–17) and stepped nine levels (fully on) much less quickly and much less frequently. In brief, response to compulsion (that is, conservative responses to nonvolitional level changes) now played a much smaller role for Mouse 2 and selectivity a much greater role. Selectivity also played a greater role for Mouse 1 (Figure 10–18), but a glance at Figure 10–17 reveals that its performances in the two phases were not radically different.

Animals 3 and 4 responded fewer times than in Phase 1 but they stepped the full nine steps almost twice as often (Table 10–1), despite the fact that they avoided bright light much more than darkness on complete control (Figures 10–14 and 10–15). For both mice, the amount of selectivity, although considerable, declined markedly from Phase 1 (Figure 10–18, open blocks versus first set of bars). Both the average dwelling times and the last-step visits at intermediate levels declined extensively.

Phase 1 versus Phase 2.   Perhaps the best indicator of selectivity for levels of illuminance is the concomitant wheel-running (measured only for Mice 3 and 4). During Phase 1, Mice 3 and 4 averaged 16 revolutions in bright light before pressing a lever. But during Phase 2, in darkness, they averaged 93 revolutions before the first press. These data suggest that active animals avoid bright light much more than darkness, in agreement with the definitive results on complete control (Figures 10–14 and 10–15). Moreover, in bright light the animals altered the intensity much more frequently (11 and 17 percent of occasions) before beginning to run than they did in darkness (only 1.2 and 6.4 percent of occasions).

To attempt a definitive interpretation of these findings would be premature, since the results of Phases 3 through 8 are pertinent but cannot be treated here. However, the basis for the quantitatively different behavior of the two pairs of deer mice between the two phases may be sought among three factors. First, Mice 1 and 2 had long prior experience with other instrumental control (see above), whereas Mice 3 and 4 were inexperienced. Second, Mice 3 and 4 were subjected to much less compulsion and had twice as much time to step the lights off and on, since their lights were turned on and off hourly rather than half-hourly. Third, there were six dim levels of full moon intensity and less for them, but only three for Mice 1 and 2.

One of the reasons for repeating Phase 1 with Mice 3 and 4 was to test whether prior experience with instrumental control would affect their performances. Although the "false off" performances (Table 10–2) were somewhat more vigorous than during the first week of Phase 1, these do not supply a valid criterion for comparison, since they were strongly influenced by withdrawal of the environmental control of the preceding Phase 2. On the other hand, in the second week of Phase 1, increases occurred in all frequency-of-response categories and decreases in most response-time categories (Table 10–1; see also Figure 10–18, second set of bars versus first set; Figure 10–19 versus Figure 10–17). Accordingly, the long prior experience of Mice 1 and 2 with instrumental control probably was partly responsible for the quantitative performance differences between the two pairs of animals.

But the chief basis for the difference in results probably lies in the differences in the regimes themselves. If all else was equal, Mice 3 and 4 would be much more likely to reach the tenth level than would Mice 1 and 2, since they had twice as much time in which to do so. Although Mice 3 and 4 did, indeed, step the lights fully on a larger fraction of the times, they stepped them fully off a smaller fraction (Table 10–1). In fact, for Mice 3 and 4 these fractions almost doubled from Phase 1 to Phase 2, while at the same time declining 43 percent for Mice 1 and 2. This consideration leads us to look at the averages of the dwelling times (Figure 10–18, "average per change"), since in any given hour or half-hour period, the sum of the dwelling times at the second to ninth levels is the time taken to step from the second to the tenth level. One finds that the average dwelling times (averaged over each of the eight intermediate levels) decreased greatly in Phase 2 for Mice 3 and 4 (from 4.6 and 2.6 to 2.3 and 1.5 minutes) but increased greatly for Mice 1 and 2 (from 0.88 and 0.14 to 1.7 and 2.1 minutes). These changes, of course, mean that the probability that an animal would step fully on in Phase 2 was greatly increased for Mice 3 and 4 but greatly decreased for Mice 1 and 2.

But recounting these facts is simply another way of asserting the differences and changes in selectivity that were found.

The analysis, then, hinges upon the bases for the greater selectivity of Mice 3 and 4 in Phase 1 and for the marked decreases in their selectivity in Phase 2. As a working hypothesis, one can suggest that the chief basis for the first difference is that Mice 3 and 4 had six nonavoided dim levels (FM and below) to select among, whereas Mice 1 and 2 had only three. Thus, putting the matter simply, since Mice 3 and 4 had a much greater opportunity for selecting, they selected to a much greater degree.

The great drop in selectivity of Mice 3 and 4 in Phase 2 seems to have been largely a consequence of a much greater competition in Phase 2 between the tendencies to alter the level of illuminance repeatedly and to react to compulsion on the one hand, and selectivity on the other. The propensities to modify the environment repeatedly and react to compulsion probably are strongest at the moment lever pressing in response to the changed level of illuminance begins, and lessen progressively in a sequence of repeated presses. Accordingly, competition between these acts and level selecting would be greatest for Mice 3 and 4 in Phase 2, when the non-avoided dim levels were attained in the first few responses, and least in Phase 1, when they were attained in the last few. Although similar considerations would hold for Mice 1 and 2, their opportunity to select between levels of dim light was so much less that the effect of competition on the overall response pattern probably was much less.

Summary

Detailed studies of the behavior of captive white-footed mice have cast a number of old problems in new perspectives. Many responses of small captive mammals cannot be interpreted at face value because of the severe distortions of behavior that are caused by depriving the wild animal of natural outlets for activity. Confined animals (both wild-caught and their captive-born offspring) are likely to seize upon, and repeatedly exercise, virtually any opportunities to modify and alter their relationships to their surroundings. In addition, they have a strong conservative tendency to counteract nonvolitional, "unexpected," and unnatural deviations from the status quo. As a result, their responses do not bear an immutable relationship to the nature of the stimulus or other variables being modified; for example, stimuli and activities that are rewarding in certain circumstances are avoided in others. These aspects of behavior have been illustrated by studies of nest occupancy, running in motor-driven wheels, and control of level of ambient illuminance. The results of the studies of control of illuminance suggest the complex interplay of tendencies of captive animals to modify features of the environment, to avoid conditions imposed compulsorily, and to select preferred levels of illuminance.

The importance of split-second timing, coordination, and quick reflex actions in the running of activity wheels is indicated by the fact that experienced white-footed mice prefer to run in square "wheels" and wheels with hurdles, rather than to run in plain round wheels. The relatively conservative behavior of these mice in selecting between multiple sources of food and water and different types of activity wheels suggests the need for careful experimental design in free-choice studies with inexperienced animals. The tendency of trained animals to give some so-called "incorrect" responses, even after long experience, can be interpreted most reasonably in terms of the adaptive value of a certain degree of variability of behavior in the wild.

White-footed mice readily master complex regimes in which several different levers and shutters must be pressed or rotated in certain sequences, within seconds, for different rewards. They quickly learn to traverse mazes containing hundreds of blind alleys and do so frequently without extrinsic reward. Furthermore, it is unlikely that these remarkable learning performances even begin to approach the capacities of the animals.

When two female mice having markedly different solitary behavior patterns were placed in consort, the behavior of each changed, becoming more like that of the other, and the animals showed a strong tendency to remain in each other's company. The behavior of mice in enclosures of great extent casts doubt upon the postulate that hunger and thirst play leading roles in the motivation of wide-ranging locomotor movements. Accordingly, studies of deprived domestic animals carried out in simple mazes may have but limited significance for understanding the behavior of wild and relatively unconfined animals.

The existence of marked individual differences between white-footed mice selected at random from wild populations sounds the need for a cautious approach in the interpretation of results obtained with highly inbred domestic animals. The relatively uniform behavior of inbred strains represents only a fragment of the total response spectrum for the species and probably has minimal significance for adaptation and evolution in the wild.

When allowed to control the level of ambient illuminance by operating a series of switches, white-footed mice establish a roughly 24-hr. regime consistent with that experienced in the wild, namely dim light during periods of activity and very dim light during periods of inactivity. Total darkness is avoided by active animals. Consistent with these findings, when exposed to a dim-dark light cycle, the mice are active during the dim phase and sleep during the dark phase. Artificial twilight transitions of both constant and varying color temperature have several marked effects upon the activity of white-footed mice. The existence of strong orienting influences of dim light on the direction of wheel-running suggests that mice in the wild use the twilight sun and the moon (and possibly other celestial light sources) as navigational references.

REFERENCES

Blair, F. W. Size of home range and notes on the life history of the woodland deer-mouse and the eastern chipmunk in Northern Michigan. *Journal of Mammalogy*, 1942, **23**, 27–36.

Blair, F. W. Effects of X-irradiation on a natural population of the deer-mouse (*Peromyscus maniculatus*). *Ecology*, 1958, **39**, 113–118.

Brant, D. H., & Kavanau, J. L. 'Unrewarded' exploration and learning of complex mazes by wild and domestic mice. *Nature*, 1964, **204**, 267–269.

Brant, D. H., & Kavanau, J. L. Exploration and movement patterns of the canyon mouse *Peromyscus crinitus* in an extensive laboratory enclosure. *Ecology*, 1965, **46**, 452–461.

Brown, G. W., & Cohen, B. D. Avoidance and approach learning motivated by stimulation of identical hypothalamic loci. *American Journal of Psychology*, 1959, **197**, 153–161.

Brown, L. E. Field experiments on the activity of small mammals, *Apodemus*, *Clethrionomys* and *Microtus*. *Proceedings of the Zoological Society of London*, 1956, **126**, 549–564.

Calhoun, J. B. A comparative study of the social behavior of two inbred strains of house mice. *Ecological Monographs*, 1956, **26**, 81–103.

Dice, L. R. The prairie deer-mouse. *Cranbrook Institute of Science Bulletin*, 1932, **2**, 1–8.

Fujimoto, K. Diurnal activity of mice; effect of social relationship of mice on their diurnal activity. *Seiri Seitai (Japan)*, 1961, **5,** 97–103; *Technical Translations*, 1961, **5.**

Hall, E. R., & Kelson, K. R. *The mammals of North America*. New York: Ronald, 1959.

Hamilton, W. J. *American mammals*. New York: McGraw-Hill, 1939.

Hardy, Sir A. *The living stream*. London: Collins, 1965.

Hediger, H. *Wild animals in captivity*. New York: Dover, 1964.

Howard, W. E. Dispersal, amount of inbreeding, and longevity in a local population of prairie deer-mice on the George Reserve, Southern Michigan. *Contributions of Laboratory of Vertebrate Biology of University of Michigan*, 1949, **43**, 1–52.

Kavanau, J. L. Identification of small animals by proximity sensing. *Science*, 1961, **134**, 1694–1696.

Kavanau, J. L. Precise monitoring of drinking behavior in small mammals. *Journal of Mammalogy*, 1962, **43**, 345–351. (a)

Kavanau, J. L. Automatic multi-channel sensing and recording of animal behavior. *Ecology*, 1962, **43**, 161–166. (b)

Kavanau, J. L. Twilight transitions and biological rhythmicity. *Nature*, 1962, **194**, 1293–1295. (c)

Kavanau, J. L. Activity patterns on regimes employing artificial twilight transitions. *Experientia*, 1962, **18**, 382–384. (d)

Kavanau, J. L. Compulsory regime and control of environment in animal behavior I. Wheel-running. *Behaviour*, 1963, **20**, 251–281. (a)

Kavanau, J. L. Continuous automatic monitoring of the activities of small captive animals. *Ecology*, 1963, **44**, 95–110. (b)

Kavanau, J. L. The study of social interactions between small animals. *Animal Behaviour*, 1963, **11**, 263–273. (c)

Kavanau, J. L. Automatic monitoring of the activities of small mammals. In K. E. F. Watt (Ed.), *Systems analysis in ecology*. New York: Academic Press, 1966. Pp. 99–146.

Kavanau, J. L. Wheel-running preferences of mice. *Zietschrift für Tierpsychologie*, 1967, **24**, 858–866.

Kavanau, J. L., & Brant, D. H. Wheel-running preferences of *Peromyscus*. *Nature*, 1965, **208**, 597–598.

Kavanau, J. L., & Norris, K. S. Behavior studies by capacitance sensing. *Science*, 1961, **134**, 730–732.

Miller, N. E. Experiments in motivation. *Science*, 1957, **126**, 1271–1278.

Murie, M. Homing and orientation of deermice. *Journal of Mammalogy*, 1963, **44**, 338–349.

Murie, O. J., & Murie, A. Travels of *Peromyscus*. *Journal of Mammalogy*, 1931, **12**, 200–209.

Pearson, O. P. Habits of harvest mice revealed by automatic photographic recorders. *Journal of Mammalogy*, 1960, **41**, 58–74.

Roberts, W. W. Rapid escape learning without avoidance learning motivated by hypothalamic stimulation in rats. *Journal of Comparative and Physiological Psychology*, 1958, **51**, 391–399. (a)

Roberts, W. W. Both rewarding and punishing effects from stimulation of posterior hypothalamus of cat with same electrode at same intensity. *Journal of Comparative and Physiological Psychology*, 1958, **51**, 400–407. (b)

Sidman, M. A note on functional relations obtained from group data. *Psychological Bulletin*, 1952, **49**, 263–269.

Skinner, B. F. A case history in the scientific method. *American Psychologist*, 1956, **2**, 221–233.

Thoday, J. M. Causes and functions of genetic variety. *The Eugenics Review*, 1962, **54**, 195–200.

Tinbergen, N. *Social behavior in animals*. London: Methuen, 1953.

Walker, E. P. *Mammals of the world*. Vol. 2. Baltimore: Johns Hopkins, 1964.

Interpretations and Impressions

EDWIN P. WILLEMS *and* HAROLD L. RAUSH

WHILE A CONCISE SUMMARY is made difficult by the diversity in commitments, targets of research, and modes of argument that we wanted to preserve in this project, some persisting questions, apart from the internal merit of the individual essays, have nagged us into adding a final chapter. Having become victims of all the artifacts of personal involvement, we sense some issues which, through our selective eyes, need to be highlighted.

One thread running through the essays, indeed, the main stated purpose of the volume as a whole, has been to argue that naturalistic research uniquely performs certain functions. This chapter will not review in detail the assertions and arguments that have been marshalled in support of this major purpose. The burden of detailed argument is left to the contributors. Rather, we shall discuss several areas whose importance has struck us and several issues that are only hinted at in the collection. In other words, we are now jumping at the chance to discuss some interpretations and impressions.

Naturalistic Research: The Methodological Context

Before one can discuss the merits, strengths, and advantages of a particular viewpoint in detail, one must generate at least a working definition of what that viewpoint is. As points of departure for presenting their arguments and theses, a number of the contributors have offered such representations of naturalistic research. From these representations, there emerge two clear themes: (a) consistency of definition, and (b) a trend toward single methodological frameworks.

271

WHAT IS NATURALISTIC RESEARCH?

Barker speaks of the importance of studying behavior under "natural" conditions and says that natural conditions are "investigator-free," that is, wherein nature is the inducer and the investigator is only a transducer. In other words, naturalistic research is a mode in which the investigator functions in a distinctive way in the process of generating data.

To Willems, the laboratory experiment, as traditionally conceived, is a strategy by which an investigator produces phenomena and makes them occur at his behest, while naturalistic study is a strategy by which an investigator records, or commits to analyzable form, descriptions of phenomena that he does not bring about. Willems suggests that two continuous dimensions, descriptive of what the investigator does with reference to a behavioral target, provide a way to characterize research: (a) degree of manipulation of antecedent conditions and (b) degree of imposition of units. Naturalistic research tends toward the low end of both dimensions, although perhaps mainly the first.

Menzel deplores the tendency to assume a discontinuity between experimental and naturalistic research. For him, naturalistic research is generic, it is "any form of research that aims at discovery and verification through observation." On this view, what we usually call an experiment is a special case, a strategy in which, by bringing the independent variables under his direct control, the investigator simplifies and restricts the domain of observation. In naturalistic research, the investigator purposefully avoids pervasive control, but it is fruitless to search for clear boundaries between true experimentation and what we commonly call naturalistic observation. Menzel develops a second characterization of research based upon his *zooming* analogy. That is, while the goal of all behavioral research is to find precision and regularity, the laboratory worker tends to begin with a small field of view and *zoom out* to more molar units and larger contexts, and the field worker or naturalistic investigator tends to begin with a broad ecological view and *zoom in* to more molecular phenomena.

Raush also argues that, in practice, experimental and naturalistic strategies tend to coalesce and merge with respect to designs and methods of sampling. In what we typically call the experiment, the investigator controls and restricts the domain of inputs to the subject and the domain of behavioral outputs; in other words, he restricts the domains of both stimuli and responses. What we commonly call the naturalistic study tends to restrict neither. On this view, the investigator can be highly selective of what he studies and where he studies it and still be engaged in a naturalistic investigation. That is, Raush points out the important difference between *selection* and *interference*, between selecting conditions of study and disrupting events.

To Sechrest, naturalistic method is defined by the stimulus situation and not the response. A stimulus situation is naturalistic to the degree that it (a) does not require the cooperation of the subject, (b) does not permit the subject to be aware that he is being measured or treated in any special way, and (c) does not change the phenomena being measured. These criteria depict complete unobtrusiveness. Another way of phrasing Sechrest's view might be that in a fully naturalistic method, the phenomena are in no way influenced by the investigative use to which they will be put.

Finally, Gutmann speaks of the importance of naturalistic research in creating new domains of data. One interpretation of Gutmann's treatment is that, in contrast to the purposeful management of hypothesis-determined order in the typical experiment, the unique function of naturalistic study is to document and make focal and public the implicit order of events that have not been instigated by the observer.

Despite some variations in terminology and emphasis, these independent attempts to define naturalistic research converge. First, all six views suggest that naturalism is a matter of degree. Second, they all suggest that the degree to which a study is naturalistic is a function of what the investigator does. Third, all six views suggest that what the investigator does in relation to the stimuli, independent variables, or antecedent conditions of a subject's behavior is one crucial dimension. Fourth, two authors add a dimension describing the extent to which the investigator restricts the response range or domain of the subject's output. Fifth, more than the other contributors, Barker, Menzel, and Gutmann elaborate upon the ways in which naturalistic research provides the means for an investigator to approach behavioral phenomena as if for the first time, with minimal determination by prior theoretical categories. Finally, it is interesting to note that all of these authors agree that "naturalistic" is an adjective that modifies "research" or "method" and not "phenomena." That is to say, the authors do not seem to find it useful to speculate about how natural the *findings* of a study are, but they do find it worthwhile to differentiate the *activities of investigators*. Thus, while we may all have intuitive ideas as to what natural events are, the concept of "natural" here becomes translated into an arbitrary label attached to investigative activities that fall at one end of a complex spectrum.

THE TREND TOWARD A SINGLE FRAMEWORK

Many of the most widely used sources in the literature of methodology leave the reader with the impression that there are qualitative distinctions or discontinuities between various strategies of research. For example, they speak of laboratory experiment, field experiment, naturalistic observation, and ex post facto research as if they represent clearly demarcated arenas or modes. While such distinctions may be useful for pedagogical purposes, several of the present contributors, as noted above, suggest that these qualitative distinctions among research strategies can fruitfully give way to single frameworks based on continuous descriptive dimensions. Several authors propose such single, inclusive frameworks that focus on the subtly varying ways in which investigators place themselves and operate in the process of obtaining data. What are commonly called laboratory experiments, field experiments, naturalistic observation, and so on, are only variations on common, underlying dimensions, and may in fact be very difficult to differentiate in rigorous detail. Whether these frameworks are based primarily on the degree to which the investigator manipulates or restricts antecedent conditions of behavior or whether they include the orthogonal dimension of degree of imposition upon or restriction of the response range, the trend toward single frameworks and the arguments marshalled suggest that what an investigator does, what he sets out to find, what he finds, and what he says about his findings are more important than whether his study can be called an experiment or a naturalistic study.

Several contributors discuss the question of the merits of various modes of research and they agree that it is not only pointless, but probably impossible, to judge the merits of one mode as against another intrinsically, or in terms of the methods alone. They agree that the only fruitful way to approach the question of the relative merits or strengths is in terms of criteria that are external to the methods themselves—that is, in terms of "strength for what?" or "merit for what?"—and that these criteria depend upon investigators' purposes. Several of the contributors also warn us not to confuse the products and models of our favorite research strategy for all there is to know. That is, we often hear the abstract plea that to achieve the goal of understanding and explaining behavior, all the various kinds of methods and strategies of research must be mobilized. Probably, few persons would disagree with this call for multiple methods and interplay. In any case, not only do a number of the present contributors make this plea, but several suggest how it might be done.

It is commonly felt that different strategies are limited to certain functions. For example, we sometimes hear that the functions of naturalistic research are to suggest hypotheses, create domains of investigation, and provide field tests of models, while the special function of laboratory experimentation is to test theory-derived hypotheses. The laboratory mode is often assumed to be the cleaner, sharper pruning edge of science. Whether this is so is difficult to answer in the abstract, but we can derive two conclusions from the plentiful arguments and examples in this volume: (a) The judgment as to sharpness or definitiveness will depend upon investigators' purposes. (b) The various functions are not *necessarily* tied to either lab or field in an a priori way. It may seem radical in some circles to assume that research functions cannot necessarily be allocated to certain research modes. However, this assumption has been a viable and productive one in ethology.

Finally, most of the contributors affirm, in one way or another, a prescription that is stated most explicitly by Menzel: To answer your questions clearly, manipulate and control only as much as is necessary. Running through this simple prescription are two important assumptions, or values: (a) The long-range goal of behavioral research is to understand behavior as we know it in common, everyday experience, "in the wild," or "in nature." (b) The degree of manipulation or control, per se, is neither good nor bad; it is used and evaluated in terms of the investigative purposes it serves and the questions it helps to answer.

The Issue of Generalization

Closely related to the issues of which investigators' purposes are best served by various strategies and interplay of methods is the theme of generalization. In a sense, all the contributors address themselves to the issue of generalization, although some do it more explicitly and directly than others. Sells raises the question of valid simulation of everyday, contextual behavior, and wonders about factors that undermine valid simulation. Barker recommends that a new breed of investigators, with new tools, study phenomena whose direct relevance to everyday human affairs is optimized. Willems and Raush both suggest that one of the most important reasons for engaging in naturalistic research is its unique function in generalizing. Menzel argues the importance of testing behavioral models in the field, demonstrates how it might be done, and shows how such observations can feed back upon the models and concepts. Sechrest introduces us to the importance of nonreactive, cooperation-free, unobtrusive measures to completing the conceptual picture of attitudes. Kavanau shows a number of ways in which the relevance of laboratory behavior to behavior in the wild can be jeopardized. The reports by Kelly, Gutmann, and Gump, all seem to be predicated on the assumption that observations in which manipulative and theoretical restrictions are minimized yield the most generalizable picture of psychological phenomena as they occur in everyday life. In other words, one of the most pervasive themes of the collection is the belief, with supporting arguments, that naturalistic research performs the singularly important function of not only *assessing* generality, relevance, fidelity of simulation, ecological validity, representativeness, or "external validity" (Campbell & Stanley, 1963), but perhaps even *ensuring* generalizability. Another way of stating the belief is in the form of a prescription: If generalization about a phenomenon is one of an investigator's aims, then his program of research should include naturalistic strategies. The ethological movement has this prescription as one of its programmatic canons (see Hess, 1962, p. 160).

It would be presumptuous to suggest that this view of naturalistic research and generalization has sprung full-blown from the pages of this volume alone. In addition to ethologists and the present contributors, some influential writers on methodology (for example, Brunswik, 1955, 1956; Campbell & Stanley, 1963; Kerlinger, 1964; Scott & Wertheimer, 1962, pp. 95–96; Shontz, 1965; Underwood, 1957, p. 171) argue (a) that the investigator's manipulative control in the laboratory enables him to make precise statements, but (b) unless someone explicitly investigates the phenomenon outside the laboratory, the investigator has no basis for knowing whether his statements are important or trivial beyond the conditions of the laboratory. In other words, there is an implicit methodological tradition and some explicit arguments and demonstrations to support the widely held belief that naturalistic research is uniquely important in generalizing. Despite this wide agreement, there remains the crucial question of the grounds for the common belief.

The question of what makes this common belief tenable can be dealt with at two levels, the first of which is the level of methodological argument. To simply assert that generalizability is enhanced when the conditions of study are maximally similar to the conditions of application only answers the question in an intuitive way. Furthermore, a number of writers agree that the problem of criteria of valid generalization cannot be resolved in a neat and conclusive way at the level of strict logic (see Turner, 1967; Campbell & Stanley, 1963; Raush, Chapter 5 of this volume). Must we conclude, then, that whether naturalistic research is important in generalization is a matter for pure intuition to decide, subject to the individual tastes of investigators? We think not, and we think that part of the impasse here comes from the way in which the questions are usually asked: (a) What are the criteria of valid simulation? (b) How do we know when a set of findings is relevant to everyday life? (c) When is a finding applicable? (d) What are the criteria of accurate generalization to naturally occurring behavior? (e) How do we know when we have a finding that represents the real-life behavior of the organism? (f) How do we know when a model is not representative or generalizable? (g) By what criteria do we know when we have found what an everyday behavioral event is really like? Running through all of these forms of the question is an implicit search for strict, a priori, logical criteria.

The common belief outlined above makes a unidirectional assertion, namely, that *naturalistic* research enhances generalizability. If, for the moment, we assume this unidirectionality, we can pose a useful question: What are the specifiable aspects of the carefully manipulated laboratory experiment that jeopardize generalization to the phenomena of everyday life? In this form, the question suggests a list of threats to generalization, a list to which authors in this volume have contributed some significant items. Campbell and Stanley (1963) and Webb *et al.* (1966) have written extensively on threats to generalization, and the reader should refer to their discussions. Here, we shall discuss such threats that have become especially salient in the present volume.

Temporal Perspective—1.   The length of time covered by an experiment can limit generalizability. Work with animals (for example, Breland & Breland, 1961, 1966) and work with human beings (Pugh, 1966) suggests that arbitrarily demarcated spans of experimental time can sharply limit generalizability to behavioral sequences that emerge over extended periods outside the laboratory. Sells, Willems, and Kavanau discuss this issue in the present volume. However, Kavanau's report suggests a dilemma over time span in the laboratory. While a long experimental sequence may enhance understanding of behavior and reduce distortion by studying long-range behavioral emergents, Kavanau suggests that a long experimental sequence may at times also *reduce* generalizability and increase distortion by allowing the subject to become fully adapted to artificial conditions.

Temporal Perspective—2.   Especially with humans, there is a second aspect of temporal perspective that jeopardizes generalizability. This problem occurs when subjects perceive the short span of experimental involvement in a task, free of long-range consequences for them, as different from the real-life situation that clearly involves consequences beyond a few immediate next steps.

Tying and Untying of Variables.   This label covers a whole family of specific threats to generalization, and is perhaps what we usually mean when we speak of the "artificiality" of experiments. The category is mentioned separately here because it is discussed so often and because it is so well documented (Shontz, 1965; Breland & Breland, 1966, pp. 62–69; Brunswik, 1956; Hovland, 1959). Experimental connecting and disconnecting of variables in ways that subjects do not confront outside the laboratory is the issue here. Most of the authors in the present collection either hint at this threat or discuss it explicitly. A special instance is the threat to generalization that results from enforced exposure and constrained response with respect to experimental events. A close correlate is the restriction that is placed on behavioral alternatives in the typical experiment. Such constraint and restriction, of course, are often the great advantage and strength of laboratory experimentation, but enforced exposure can yield findings that do not match those obtained when organisms select stimuli and response sequences more freely.

Correlates of Subject Selection.   A host of possible threats to generalizability cluster around the correlates of subject selection, only two examples of which are the special syndrome of volunteering and arbitrary selection for homogeneity on some trait or set of traits.

Other Factors.   In Chapter 10 Kavanau suggests a number of specific aspects of the typical experiment that may jeopardize generalizability. Many of his suggestions are strongly seconded by Menzel (Chapter 4) and Breland and Breland (1966). Some of the factors that fall under environmental arrangements are (a) the arbitrary demarcation of "correct responses," as against the functional value of response variability for organisms outside the laboratory; (b) careful arrangement and regularizing of the environment, as against the complexity of the extra-laboratory world; (c) simplification of the laboratory environment; and (d) reduction in spatial extent in the laboratory. In the domain of selection of subjects and how behavior is viewed, he points to (a) selection for homogeneity, either purposefully or accidentally, so that the spectrum of responses is fragmented and attenuated; (b) attempts to control experimental error, which usually represents the kind of subject differences and variability that one finds in such extremes outside the laboratory; (c) frequent disregard for the development of adaptation to the laboratory regime; and (d) the conservatism of subjects, whereby early responses can influence subsequent developments and impose unexpected stereotypes upon later behavior. Finally, Kavanau, in agreement with Menzel and the Brelands, points out that findings from the regularized and simplified laboratory environment often lead investigators to disregard the remarkable mutability of stimulus-response relations and the mutability of what is a reinforcing event.

Thus, if we accept the common unidirectional belief that the empirical proof of generalization lies in naturalistic investigation and if we ask how generalizability is jeopardized in carefully manipulated experimentation, we can see some of the reasons why naturalistic research is so crucial to the process of generalizing.

It is worthwhile to note that those aspects of the laboratory mode that jeopardize generalizability are precisely the ones that gives it its power as an analytical strategy. That is, (a) arbitrary and experimenter-determined arrangements and manipulations of temporal duration, spatial extent, and variance; (b) arrangement, at the investigator's behest, of the connections and disconnections of variables; (c) enforced regimes and enforced exposure; (d) regularizing and demarcation of environments and response alternatives; and (e) simplification—all of which refer to strengths of the laboratory mode in fulfilling certain investigative purposes—also refer to the aspects that limit generalizability.

There is a second level at which we can deal with the common belief in the importance of naturalistic research to generalization, but, to explore this level, we must begin a step back by *not* assuming the unidirectionality of the belief. Let us suppose that an investigator, or two different investigators, conduct a laboratory experiment and a naturalistic study on the same phenomenon, and let us suppose that the studies yield different conclusions. In one sense, in this simplified paradigm case, all we have are descriptions of different conditions and conclusions that differ. Why choose to believe one set over the other? We must admit that both the common belief among methodologists and thrust of argument in this volume boil down to the assertion that to generalize, we should lend more credence to the one set of conclusions than to the other.

Why should one lend more credence to the conclusions of one type of study then the other? There are several approaches to answering this question. One answer might be that we can list the names and publications of influential methodologists who have said we should lend greater credence to the one set of conclusions. Basing an answer on this kind of vote is not very satisfying, partly because it is an appeal to authority and leaves unanswered the question of how to choose among authorities. A second answer might be that the set of descriptions and conclusions from the naturalistic study map reality or the real world better than the other. However, this answer should leave the questioner just as cold as the argument from who says so, because it begs the question of criteria for reality and absolute truth, a question that has plagued some of the best minds in the history of science and philosophy.

There is a third alternative that is based upon the language, terminology, descriptions, and parlance of everyday life. Everyday actions are predicted on these terminologies and descriptions. Since, in naturalistic research, the conditions of behavior, the units of behavior, and the descriptions and predicates of these conditions and units are more frequently based on everyday events and more frequently couched in the common, everyday parlance than are those of laboratory experimentation, these naturalistic descriptions have more direct everyday relevance. The more direct relevance here resides in the fact that the phenomena and descriptions of naturalistic research are more probably represented in a language on which persons can predicate their actions in the everyday world.

If this management of the problem of generalizing is tenable, then there are at least two implications. First, we cannot represent or promote the conclusions from naturalistic research on the grounds of better approximation to truth; we now represent their relevance in terms of being couched in the kind of common language that predicates everyday actions. Second, we can no longer promulgate the belief concerning naturalistic research and generalizing in its unidirectional form. That is, we must now assert the *bidirectional* belief that generalization from investigations of everyday events to laboratory is just as tenuous and problematic as generalization from laboratory to everyday events.

Unresolved Issues

If we accept these various arguments, can we assume that we are now home free and that business is finished? We have argued that one of the most important functions of naturalistic research is its function in generalization and that its importance here is based in the fact that the activity of naturalistic research takes place in everyday affairs and its resulting descriptions and conclusions arise from everyday events. We shall now argue that just because of this strength and the basis for it, we are left with some very problematic, complex, unresolved issues. One of these is a dilemma that is every bit as great as, if not greater than, the issue of reduced generalizability faced by the experimenter in the laboratory. This dilemma has its joint basis in a long-standing hope of naturalistic research and in an emerging technological development.

Traditionally, investigators in naturalistic research have hoped for, and pushed the development of, techniques of observation and measurement that are low in obtrusiveness, interference, or intrusion. Given their tradition and values, investigators in naturalistic research usually wish to use techniques in which sensitivity and unobtrusiveness are combined to the highest possible degree. Thus, we would expect them to exploit the great promise that lies in the current proliferation of finely sensitive, unobtrusive monitoring equipment. The dilemma here involves the temptation to press such equipment into service, on the one hand, and the lack of resolution of ethical issues for their use on the other. To complicate the picture, there are not only circumscribed, bedrock legal issues involved, but, perhaps just as important, there are personal, human questions concerning relations to subjects and care of data, and perhaps even important considerations of the public image of the behavioral disciplines.

These issues are especially acute for naturalistic research. The special situation or ecological niche represented by the laboratory experiment is constructed and arranged by the investigator, and it is constructed for the explicit, focal purpose of investigation. Investigation of its internal affairs is the laboratory's reason for existence and the subject comes into a situation created by the investigator. Thus, even though there may be some probability of harm to the subject or even though some investigative purposes and conditions may be masked from the subject, his role as experimental subject is usually clear to him and there is usually some semblance of consent or some contractual basis that governs his participation. In fact, it is when such aspects of the experiment are lacking that we begin to question the ethics of the experiment and the experimenter.

In contrast, the targets of naturalistic research are not arranged by the investigator. They are arranged by other persons, for purposes other than investigation. In these situations, the investigator is, in a very real sense, the intruder and interloper; he comes into a situation created by someone else. Under conditions of maximal unobtrusiveness, there is no built-in provision for consent and contractual arrangement by the subject. It is our feeling that the emergence of equipment that allows true unobtrusiveness and noninterfering observation makes the ethical issues of naturalistic research particularly knotty.

The array of specific ethical and legal questions involved is too extensive to treat here. For an analysis of some of the issues as they pertain to research on human beings, the reader should refer to the *American Psychologist* for May, 1967 (Vol. 22). Only to illustrate some of the questions that might come up, let us consider a hypothetical case (adapted from Herbert & Swayze, 1964, pp. 17–19). Suppose someone wishes to use some of the new electronic apparatus to record occurrences at selected locations among the opposing audiences at a junior high school basketball game. What ethical and legal questions might arise for investigators using such listening devices? When, how, and in what detail must subjects be told that they will be or have been observed? How much detail must be given them regarding uses and users of the transcripts? Must the right to privacy, to choose to be recorded or not, be respected in all circumstances and all cases? What guidelines govern who can use the transcripts and what kinds of doctoring or editing is to be done? Who should be asked for consent to record—adult supervisors, parents, the children themselves, school boards? For what investigative purposes must signed releases be obtained? If descriptions or transcripts have more than short-term value, if they are preserved in archives of data, new questions arise. What guidelines cover such long-term storage and use? What about later uses not originally intended? What about later doctoring and editing? Who can use the transcripts later, and for what purposes? What long-range security precautions need to be taken by the original investigator?

Clearly, there are legal precedents and social conventions that offer suggestions for many of these questions, but we should not assume that this one hypothetical example raises all of the important questions, either. The various courts are hammering out decisions concerning eavesdropping and invasion of privacy, but there are many questions that are not strictly legal questions that derive from very reasonable and important research questions and fall under the halo of scientific research. For example, even if a specific step is perfectly legal, there are questions of how to go about research so that social sensitivities are honored and so that the long-range image and interests of psychology are preserved.

One very important problem is who shall establish guidelines for persons working under the halo of science—scientists themselves or persons outside the disciplines who react in terms of what they judge to be lapses of ethics? In this volume, Barker offers one solution when he recommends the establishing of locally grounded, institutionalized organizations that have long-range time perspectives and solicit cooperation, trust, and even monitoring from the community. Such establishments, called field stations, represent a positive, programmatic solution to many issues, but they clearly do not suffice to cover all the contingencies and purposes of short-term, but still naturalistic, research. McGuire (1967) offers two warnings related to the question of ethics. He warns that scientists must censor their own work and generate ethical guidelines. However, he also warns against becoming immobilized because of ethical questions.

The contributors to this volume have mentioned a number of other unresolved issues in naturalistic research. Rather than to retrace the arguments and contexts for these issues, we shall simply list some of them here. (a) Sells and Barker both recommend extensive programs of research and raise the joint problems of financial support, manpower pools, and facilities to carry out the programs. (b) Sells, Barker, and Raush argue compellingly about the need for new and special techniques for the reduction, representation, and analysis of data from naturalistic research. These needs fall into two main areas: the multifaceted, interdependent, and complex nature of many of the phenomena and their sequential nature, the disruption of which often destroys the very things the investigator wants most to preserve. (c) Barker, and by implication, several other contributors, discuss the need for archives of data. Unsolved are the problems of optimal ways to establish and organize archives and agreement upon the criteria for admitting data to them. (d) Sells, Barker, Menzel, Raush, Sechrest, Gutmann, Kelly, and Gump, though from different viewpoints, all suggest that we have scarcely begun to exercise our ingenuity in generating ways for observing, describing, recording, and coding environmental and behavioral events in naturalistic research. All seem to agree that this state of affairs is partly a function of the complexity of the targets of research. (e) Menzel explicitly raises an issue that several other contributors hint at and which we hope is satisfactorily laid to rest by now. Menzel says that proponents of naturalistic research are often more literal minded than they need to be, or should be, and seem to assume that they are dealing with the reality and truth of behavior more directly than investigators in other modes. All scientific investigators, including those in naturalistic research, deal in models, in choices of what is important and what is not, and in doing something, at some particular place, to generate data. The assumption of closer contact with reality and truth only leads to fruitless controversy.

Two Impressions

It is perhaps inevitable that editors, dealing with a set of papers over an extended period of time, would become enamored of some impressions that they have gleaned. We have had many such impressions from this project, some of which have been blended into the introduction, commentary passages, and this chapter. There are two remaining impressions that we feel deserve separate mention, and we mention them here without extensive evaluation.

The first such impression relates to the nature of data. If we assume, with the contributors to this collection, that the laboratory experiment tends to fall at one end of a spectrum and the naturalistic study at the other end, it would appear that there is a strong correlation between these strategies and the molarity of the units of data with which they typically deal. It is our subjective impression that laboratory experiments typically deal with behavioral units that are more molecular than the units in naturalistic studies. Assuming this correlation, is it a necessary, built-in accompaniment of the methods? Is it a function of what investigators consider important? Does it reflect theoretical differences? Perhaps, as the units of behavior become more molecular (for instance, from behavioral approach down to dilation of pupils as indicators of attitudes), the requirement for special controls and apparatus goes up. If this is so, it would suggest that one can study behavioral units of a substantial size range experimentally, but one would be hard pressed to study extremely molecular units by naturalistic methods. This line of argument leads to the interesting conclusion that the range of things that can be studied by naturalistic research, especially highly unobtrusive research, is smaller than in experimental research. However, there is perhaps a shift in scale for the size of researchable units as between laboratory and field, with the scale for naturalistic research beginning at a higher minimum and reaching up into extended sequences that one can scarcely study in the laboratory.

The second impression relates to orientations toward data. Although there may well be important exceptions, there appears to be a modal difference inherent in carefully manipulated experimentation as against naturalistic research in how data are viewed, or in terms of the range of phenomena that are allowed to become data. We are referring here to the domain of events on which the investigator actually bases interpretations and conclusions and differences in what is allowed to become focal in that domain. We are not speaking of serendipity, or negative findings, or even unanticipated findings. That is, negative or unanticipated findings refer to unconfirmed hypotheses, and a serendipitous finding is one that leads the investigator in directions he had not planned. Negative, unanticipated, and serendipitous findings are common in the laboratory.

One of the strengths of experimentation in the laboratory is that the investigator can, in principle, define the set of *possible* outcomes, some of which will certainly be less likely to occur than others. It seems to be characteristic of the naturalistic mode that a comparable set is often not definable; that is, there are possible outcomes or findings that cannot even be conceived of on an a priori basis, perhaps because the occurrence of *a* set has not been arranged. In the present volume, Gutmann speaks of the naturalistic strategy as one through which the investigator's relation to habitual ecologies and viewpoints can be disrupted, thereby creating new domains of data. Menzel, in his discussion of how he discovered edging effects, shows how this can occur. Kelly, in describing his attempts to generate consistent observational techniques across schools, tells how his observers were forced to adopt differing techniques. This shift itself became data, a source of information, in that it suggested characteristic ways in which the two schools assimilated outsiders and newcomers. It might be tempting to assume that differences in investigators' personalities are operating in these varying orientations toward domains of data. However, we find it more satisfying to assume that the differences reside in the strategies and methods of investigation.

Concluding Comments

It is our hope that this collection has fulfilled the purposes stated in the introductory chapter. Some significant steps have been taken toward (a) demonstrating that naturalistic research is uniquely suited to certain investigative purposes; (b) building the methodological rationale for naturalistic research; and (c) undermining some unnecessarily negative sentiments toward naturalistic research. While little has been said about "how to do it" in naturalistic research, we hope that the arguments and discussions have been stated in terms that will be useful and that will generate more than sentimental allegiance.

If we assume that these goals have been accomplished, there is still a great deal to be done. One great need is to extend the amount of research that demonstrates empirically where and how the arguments of this volume apply. Empirical research on the range of application for naturalistic research must supplement and replace pure argument; there is a great need to devote ingenuity and effort to naturalistic research. Perhaps, some members of the existing manpower pool should extend their investigative repertoires to fill this need.

However, just as important as the immediate, empirical extension of naturalistic research by available investigators is the need to extend the base for long-range development, that is, the need to establish explicit training in naturalistic research in our graduate programs. In many cases, this will involve important shifts in atmosphere and philosophy to the point where naturalistic research is not only seen as possible, but as praiseworthy and as uniquely suited to certain purposes, and where these values are explicitly communicated to students, who provide the pool of potential manpower for research. One burden that we can derive from accepting the arguments in this volume is that not only must some old attitudes toward naturalistic research be shed, but the formal, academic rubrics for teaching naturalistic research must be created.

There is a subtle issue here that brings us back to the teachers, the members of the existing pool of manpower. Graduate training often places apprenticeship in research, the actual practice in research under senior investigators, at or near the top of the hierarchy of educational importance. If this is true, if such apprenticeship actually involves the conditions of learning to which we attach importance, then the activities in which students engage while in the apprenticeship should include naturalistic research. It follows that we need not only to *have* effective examples of naturalistic research to teach to students, but we also need to *be* effective examples by applying it to our research whenever appropriate.

REFERENCES

Breland, K., & Breland, M. The misbehavior of organisms. *American Psychologist*, 1961, **16**, 681–684.

Breland, K., & Breland, M. *Animal behavior.* New York: Macmillan, 1966.

Brunswik, E. Representative design and probabilistic theory in a functional psychology. *Psychological Review*, 1955, **62**, 193–217.

Brunswik, E. *Perception and the representative design of psychological experiments.* Berkeley, Calif.: University of California Press, 1956.

Campbell, D. T., & Stanley, J. C. *Experimental and quasi-experimental designs for research.* Chicago: Rand McNally, 1963.

Herbert, J., & Swayze, J. *Wireless observation.* New York: Bureau of Publications, Teachers College, Columbia University, 1964.

Hess, E. H. Ethology: An approach to the complete analysis of behavior. In R. Brown, E. Galanter, E. H. Hess, & G. Mandler, *New directions in psychology.* New York: Holt, Rinehart and Winston, 1962. Pp. 157–266.

Hovland, C. I. Reconciling conflicting results derived from experimental and survey studies of attitude change. *American Psychologist*, 1959, **14**, 8–17.

Kerlinger, F. N. *Foundations of behavioral research.* New York: Holt, Rinehart and Winston, 1964.

McGuire, W. J. Some impending reorientations in social psychology: Some thoughts provoked by Kenneth Ring. *Journal of Experimental Social Psychology*, 1967, **3**, 124–139.

Pugh, D. S. Modern organization theory: A psychological and sociological study. *Psychological Bulletin*, 1966, **66**, 235–251.

Scott, W. A., & Wertheimer, M. *Introduction to psychological research.* New York: Wiley, 1962.

Shontz, F. C. *Research methods in personality.* New York: Appleton-Century-Crofts, 1965.

Turner, M. B. *Philosophy and the science of behavior.* New York: Appleton-Century-Crofts, 1967.

Underwood, B. J. *Psychological research.* New York: Appleton-Century-Crofts, 1957.

Webb, E. J., Campbell, D. T., Schwartz, R. D., & Sechrest, L. *Unobtrusive measures.* Chicago: Rand McNally, 1966.

Name Index

Abrahams, D., 60, 70
Allport, F. H., 52, 67, 82, 93, 101, 119
Allport, G. W., 33, 41
Altman, P. L., 24, 28
Altmann, S., 78, 89, 109, 119, 120, 130, 145
Anderson, L. F., 155, 156, 159, 160
Appley, M. H., 18, 28
Aronson, V., 60, 70
Ashby, W. R., 18, 28
Ashton, M., 35, 41
Astin, A. W., 27, 28
Atkinson, J. W., 26, 28
Attneave, F., 137, 145

Bachrach, A. J., 7, 9
Bakan, D., 23, 28, 134, 142, 145
Baker, R. A., 45, 67
Barker, L. S., 36, 38, 42, 43, 52, 67, 220
Barker, R. G., 5, 9, 13, 20, 25, 26, 28, 31, 35, 36, 38, 42, 43, 46, 49, 52, 67, 126, 128, 131, 135, 137, 145, 180, 183, 185, 189, 197, 198, 201, 202, 203, 219, 220, 272, 273, 275, 282
Bauer, R. A., 64, 68
Bechtel, R. B., 48, 68
Beecher, H. K., 62, 64, 68
Bendig, A. W., 137, 145
Berg, I. A., 23, 28
Berscheid, E., 60, 70
Blair, F. W., 221, 268
Blake, R., 49, 69, 154, 160
Bordin, E. S., 125, 145
Borgatta, E. F., 27, 29
Boring, E. G., 2, 9, 85, 119
Brady, K., 49, 69
Brant, D. H., 228, 236, 237, 239, 268, 269
Bratfisch, O., 157, 159
Breed, W., 156, 159
Breland, K., 21, 28, 53, 64, 66, 68, 75, 77, 180, 182, 277, 278, 286
Breland, M., 21, 28, 53, 64, 66, 68, 75, 77, 180, 182, 277, 278, 286
Brown, G. W., **224, 268**
Brown, L. E., 245, 268
Brunswik, E., 32, 42, 51, 55, 68, 83, 90, 119, 128, 145, 276, 278, 286
Bryan, J. H., 49, 68
Bugental, J. F. T., 125, 145
Burns, N. M., 24, 28
Butterfield, H., 2, 9

Cairns, R. B., 115, 119
Calhoun, J. B., 235, 268
Campbell, D. T., 7, 9, 46, 50, 59, 68, 70, 77, 135, 145, 147, 149, 151, 153, 156, 159, 161, 276, 277, 286
Campbell, W. J., 60, 68
Carpenter, C. R., 89, 119, 184, 198
Cartwright, D., 5, 9
Casey, A., 51, 68
Chambers, R. M., 24, 28
Chein, I., 134, 145
Church, J., 149, 159
Clarke, G., 196, 198
Cleveland, S. E., 160
Cofer, C. H., 18, 28
Cohen, B. D., 224, 268
Coleman, J., 184, 198
Cook, S., 151
Crespi, L. P., 151, 159
Cronbach, L. J., 76, 77

Darwin, C., 83, 112, 124
Davenport, R. K., 84, 92, 98, 115, 119
Davis, M., 156, 159
Davis, T. R. A., 17, 28
DeCharms, R., 59, 68
Delprato, D. J., 29
Dembo, T., 20, 49, 52, 67
Dempsey, P., 155, 156, 159
DeVore, I., 78, 89, 120, 132, 145, 146, 183, 198
Dice, L. R., 221, 268
Dickman, H. R., 26, 28
Dittmann, A. T., 43, 133, 135, 136, 137, 145, 146, 220
Dittmer, D. S., 24, 28
Dobzhansky, T., 17, 28
Doob, A. N., 148, 154, 159
Draper, W. A., 105, 120
Dyck, A. J., 53, 68

Einstein, A., 140
Ekman, P., 152
Epstein, S., 5, 10
Epstein, W., 51, 68
Eriksen, C. W., 76, 77
Erikson, E., 140
Etkin, W., 24, 28
Eysenck, H. J., 59, 68

Farbman, I., 135, 137, 146
Fawl, C. L., 20, 28, 52, 68

Subject Index